Essays and Studies 2004

Series Editor: Peter Kitson
Associate Editor: Helen Lucas

The English Association

The objects of the English Association are to promote the knowledge and appreciation of the English language and its literature, and to foster good practice in its teaching and learning at all levels.

The association pursues these aims by creating opportunities of co-operation among all those interested in English; by furthering the recognition of English as essential in education; by discussing methods of English teaching; by holding lectures, conferences, and other meetings; by publishing journals, books, and leaflets; and by forming local branches.

Publications

The Year's Work in English Studies. An annual bibliography. Published by Oxford University Press.

The Year's Work in Critical and Cultural Theory. An annual bibliography. Published by Oxford University Press.

Essays and Studies. An annual volume of essays by various scholars assembled by the collector covering usually a wide range of subjects and authors from the medieval to the modern. Published by D. S. Brewer.

English. A journal of the Association, *English* is published three times a year by the Association.

The Use of English. A journal of the Association, *The Use of English* is published three times a year by the Association.

Newsletter. A *Newsletter* is published three times a year giving information about forthcoming publications, conferences, and other matters of interest.

Benefits of Membership

Institutional Membership

Full members receive copies of *The Year's Work in English Studies, Essays and Studies, English* (3 issues) and three *Newsletters*.

Ordinary Membership covers *English* (3 issues) and three *Newsletters*.

Schools Membership includes copies of each issue of *English* and *The Use of English*, one copy of *Essays and Studies*, three *Newsletters*, and preferential booking and rates for various conferences held by the Association.

Individual Membership

Individuals take out Basic Membership, which entitles them to buy all regular publications of the English Association at a discounted price, and attend Association gatherings.

For further details write to The Secretary, The English Association, The University of Leicester, University Road, Leicester, LE1 7RH.

Essays and Studies 2004

Contemporary British Women Writers

Edited by
Emma Parker

for the English Association

D. S. BREWER

ESSAYS AND STUDIES 2004
IS VOLUME FIFTY-SEVEN IN THE NEW SERIES
OF ESSAYS AND STUDIES COLLECTED ON BEHALF OF
THE ENGLISH ASSOCIATION
ISSN 0071–1357

First published 2004
D. S. Brewer, Cambridge

D. S. Brewer is an imprint of Boydell & Brewer Ltd
PO Box 9, Woodbridge, Suffolk IP12 3DF, UK
and of Boydell & Brewer Inc.
PO Box 41026, Rochester, NY 14604–4126, USA
website: www.boydellandbrewer.com

ISBN 1 84384 011 1

A catalogue record for this title is available
from the British Library

The Library of Congress has cataloged this serial publication:
Catalog card number 36–8431

This book is printed on acid-free paper

Typeset by Mizpah Publishing Services, Chennai
Printed in Great Britain by
The Cromwell Press, Trowbridge, Wiltshire

Contents

Notes on Contributors

David Ellis is a Lecturer in English at the University of Derby. He has published on black British writing and post-war popular culture, and is currently editing a volume of essays on riots in London.

Clare Hanson is Professor of English at Loughborough University. She has published widely on nineteenth- and twentieth-century women's writing and on the short story. Her publications include *Virginia Woolf* (1994), *Hysterical Fictions: The Woman's Novel in the Twentieth Century* (2000) and *A Cultural History of Pregnancy. Pregnancy, Medicine and Culture in Britain 1750–2000* (2004).

Maroula Joannou is Senior Lecturer in English and Women's Studies at Anglia Polytechnic University's Cambridge campus. She is the author of *'Ladies, Please Don't Smash These Windows': Women's Writing, Feminism and Social Change 1918–1938* (1995) and *Contemporary Women's Writing: From The Golden Notebook to The Color Purple* (2000). She is the editor of *Women Writers of the 1930s: Gender, Politics and History* (1998), co-editor of *The Women's Suffrage Movement: New Feminist Perspectives* (1997) and of *Heart of the Heartless World: Essays in Cultural Resistance in Memory of Margot Heinemann* (1995). She has also co-edited a new critical edition of Ellen Wilkinson's novel, *Clash*.

Paulina Palmer is Senior Lecturer in the English department at the University of Warwick where she teaches undergraduate and graduate courses in women's fiction and feminist theory. She also contributes to the teaching of the MA degree in Interdisciplinary Women's Studies. Her publications include *Contemporary Women's Fiction: Narrative Practice and Feminist Theory* (1989), *Contemporary Lesbian Writing: Dreams, Desire, Difference* (1993) and *Lesbian Gothic: Trangressive Fictions* (1999).

Emma Parker is a Lecturer in English at the University of Leicester, where she is Convenor of the MA in Modern Literature. She has published essays on Margaret Atwood, Angela Carter, Toni Morrison, Michèle Roberts and Jeanette Winterson, and contributed to *The Cambridge Guide to Women's Writing in English* (1999). She is also author of *Kate Atkinson's Behind the Scenes at the Museum: A Reader's Guide* (2002).

Felicity Rosslyn is a Reader in English at the University of Leicester. She has published widely on eighteenth-century literature, the literatures of central and eastern Europe, and tragic drama. She is the author of *Alexander Pope: A Literary Life* (1990) and *Tragic Plots: A New Reading from Aeschylus to Lorca* (2000), and is editor of *The Cambridge Quarterly*.

Christiane Schlote lectures in the department of English and American Studies at the Humboldt University, Berlin. Her main research interests and publications are in the fields of Postcolonial Studies, contemporary British and American drama, Latino and Asian American Studies, transnational migration literatures, and Cultural and Urban Studies. She is the author of *Bridging Cultures: Latino- und asiatisch-amerikanisches Theater in New York City* (1997) and co-editor of *New Beginnings in 20th Century Theatre and Drama* (2003). She is presently working on a book on South Asian women writers and artists in Britain and the United States.

John Sears is Senior Lecturer in English Literature at Manchester Metropolitan University (MMU Cheshire). He is author of *Angela Carter's Monstrous Women* (1992), and has recently written on Neil Bartlett, on doubling in Schwarzenegger's films, on Eugene Atget (in Dutch), as well as on Guy Debord and Situationism. He is Associate Book Reviews Editor for the internet magazine *PopMatters*, and is a regular reviewer for print and internet journals of contemporary poetry, fiction and theory.

Eluned Summers-Bremner is Lecturer in Women's Studies at the University of Auckland, New Zealand, where she teaches on gender and sexuality in the arts and media. Her research interests are in the interface between psychoanalysis, cultural memory, literature and performance. She has published articles in such journals as *New Formations*, *Hypatia* and *Feminist Studies*, and is currently at work on two book-length projects, one on the function of memory in the imagination of home and exile, and the other on the contemporary function of the fantasy of childhood in photographic, literary and televisual texts.

Imelda Whelehan is Professor of English and Women's Studies at De Montfort University, Leicester. She is the author of *Modern Feminist Thought* (1995), *Overloaded* (2000), *Helen Fielding's Bridget Jones's Diary: A Reader's Guide* (2001), the co-author of *Fifty Key Concepts in Gender Studies* (2004) and co-editor of *Adaptations: From Text to Screen, Screen to Text*, and the Pluto Film/Fiction annual journal. Her forthcoming work includes *From Sex and the Single Girl to Sex and the City* and a revised and expanded editon of *Modern Feminist Thought*.

Gina Wisker is Professor of Learning, Teaching & Women's Writing, and Coordinator of Women's Studies and Director of Learning and Teaching at Anglia Polytechnic University where she also teaches literature. Her publications include *Postcolonial and African American Women's Writing: A Critical Introduction* (2000), *Margaret Atwood's Alias Grace: A Reader's Guide* (2002), and has written a number of beginner's guides to literature: *Virginia Woolf* (2001), *Sylvia Plath* (2001), *Toni Morrison* (2002) and *Angela Carter* (2003). She is editor of *Black Women's Writing* (1992), *It's My Party: Reading Twentieth Century Women's Writing* (1994) and co-editor of *Fatal Attractions* (1998).

Introduction
'The Proper Stuff of Fiction': Defending the Domestic, Reappraising the Parochial

EMMA PARKER

In *A Room of One's Own* (1929), Virginia Woolf asserts the value of women's writing – commonly dismissed as domestic and parochial – by questioning patriarchal ideas about what constitutes a suitable subject for a work of literature, or what she elsewhere terms 'the proper stuff of fiction' ('Modern Fiction' 106). Woolf resists the belittlement of woman-centred fiction and defends its 'difference of view' ('Women Novelists' 204). She points out that as men and women have different experiences of the world, it is unsurprising that these differences are reflected in their fiction. While men's interests and concerns are seen as universal, women's are seen as specific to them alone. Accordingly, 'masculine' subjects are seen as serious and important and 'feminine' subjects are dismissed as frivolous or insignificant: 'This is an important book, the critic assumes, because it deals with war. This is an insignificant book because it deals with the feelings of women in a drawing room. A scene on a battlefield is more important than a scene in a shop' (*Room* 67). Woolf reveals that the devaluation of female experience in literature stems from a devaluation of women. Therefore, to accuse women's writing of being 'slight' because it focuses on small, domestic or personal aspects of life, is to slight not only women writers but all women. Resisting this position, Woolf challenges the prevailing hierarchy of value by refuting the notion that football is more important than fashion.

Despite a huge proliferation of women writers in the post-war period and several decades of feminist criticism, the views that Woolf was challenging nearly eighty years ago remain pervasive today and 'feminine' is still a pejorative term when used in relation to fiction. Lesley Chamberlain complains that the 'problem' with women's writing is that its characters are tedious and limited. Women's fiction, she argues, consists of 'middle-brow women's talk: all gossip and lament; centred on the sacrosanct body'. Chamberlain laments the narrowness of fiction by women: 'Women need to write about women whose horizons and experiences are wide'.[1] In his introduction to Granta's second *Best of Young British Novelists* (1993), Bill Buford likewise asserts that 'Women novelists, with the exception of Jeanette Winterson, are writing too cautiously, too unambitiously' (15). While Chamberlain's comment demonstrates that women's writing is still subject to disparagement in general terms, Buford's remark reflects the way in which complaints about the weakness of women's writing has come to be focused specifically on the work of *British* women writers. Nowhere is this clearer than in the recurrent furore that erupted over the Orange Prize for Fiction throughout the 1990s.

Since its inception in 1996, the Orange Prize has repeatedly been seen to focus on a gulf between the quality of work produced by British and American women writers. Judging the first competition, Susan Hill claimed that, 'the sharper writing is coming from America. There is something vigorous and energetic about the Americans which we didn't find in this country'.[2] Val Hennessy likewise asserted that 'American women writers seem to be more energetic and exciting. They seem to be able to lift themselves out of their own domestic routine in their books. They go away from all that, move out of their own spheres and go further abroad for their experiences'.[3] Hill and Hennessy attacked British novels for their 'dreary, domestic self-obsessions' and described the books they read by British women as 'drivel', 'abysmal' and 'terrible'. Hill stated, 'so many books were about domestic obsessions, marriages and . . . boring lives. They were parochial, small-minded and inward-looking in approach. Too many writers were obsessed with trivia and their own psyches. They were all writing about themselves'. Hennessy likewise condemned 'women writers who could not see beyond their own lives'.[4] The following year, Lisa Jardine expressed similar views, arguing that British women write 'narrow-minded' books that are 'smug and parochial'. She asserted that 'English writers should look further afield, look at worldwide issues for their subjects.' In contrast, she praised American novelists whom, she said, 'address wider and bigger contemporary issues. Americans are much more ambitious in their scope. They really take the world by the throat and shake it.'[5]

[1] Leslie Chamberlain, 'Just like a woman', *Prospect*, 20, (June 1997): pp.12–13.
[2] See Nigel Reynolds, 'All-women book prize shortlist attacked', *Daily Telegraph*, 15 April 1996.
[3] Ibid.
[4] Ibid.
[5] See Nigel Reynolds, 'Book prize judge attacks "smug" English novelists', *Daily Telegraph*, 7 May 1997.

Commenting on the fact that only one out of the six writers on the 1999 shortlist was British (Julia Blackburn), Chair of Judges Lola Young dismissed British women's fiction as 'piddling' and 'parochial'. According to Young, 'The British books tended to fall into two categories. There were ones by thirtysomethings, quite insular and parochial. Some were entertaining in their attitudes to sex, but you got no sense of the bigger picture. The more traditional novels were good on a certain level, but they tended towards the domestic in a piddling sort of way, which is very British.' Young explained that work by North American writers, praised for its epic scale, was simply more exciting. While British women's fiction was 'insular' and 'parochial', North American women have, she argued, the ability to take 'small intimate stories and set them against this vast physical and cultural landscape which is very appealing'.[6] Countering the spirit of the Orange Prize, as well as sentiments espoused by the Orange corporate slogan, such remarks suggested that the future of British women's fiction was far from bright.

Remarks made by Orange Prize judges sparked a stormy debate about the character and quality of British women's writing. Although not speaking specifically of women's writing, Robert McCrum, literary editor for *The Observer*, insisted that, 'Just because our writers are not compelled (in part by the demands of the marketplace) to compose on a symphonic scale does not mean either that they are tone-deaf or that a string quartet cannot be as significant as a composition for full orchestra.'[7] Similarly, David Lodge dismissed the notion that insular, parochial or domestic fiction cannot be 'great' literature.[8]

As critics waded in, the wounded responded with defiance. Amanda Craig defended her choice of subject matter, and remonstrated, 'given we do not have the scholarships, writers' faculties, university posts and high advances our American sisters enjoy – let alone their 'vast physical and cultural landscape' – it does seem a little harsh to criticise those of us whose creative work is fitted around dirty nappies, domestic chores, broken sleep, the school run, earning money doing something else, and usually composed on the kitchen table, for failing to ignore these facts in our fiction'.[9] Having had her prose implicitly slated,

[6] See Fiachra Gibbons, ' "Piddling" British fiction loses out to Americans', *The Guardian*, 10 May 1999.
[7] Robert McCrum, 'McCrum on New Fiction', *The Observer*, 25 May 1997.
[8] David Lodge, 'British writers bite back', *The Guardian*, 11 May 1999.
[9] Amanda Craig, 'A Vicious Circle', Letters to the Editor, *The Guardian*, 11 May 1999.

Maggie Gee chose to respond in verse and produced a light-hearted if pointed poem:[10]

> Prof Lola Young
> We are mildly stung.
> We thought we were middling;
> Alas, we are 'piddling'.
> (That's the whole lot of us –
> Lola's got shot of us.)
> She and her buddies
> In cultural studies
> Have glanced at our stuff
> And declared it all guff.
> The Yanks, au contraire,
> Have Big Themes, and they care.
> There are no surprises:
> The Yanks get the prizes.
> Our thanks, dear Prof Young,
> For putting us right;
> This side of the Atlantic
> Women are shite.
> And congrats, Orange Prize,
> On this feminist coup –
> Now, thanks to you . . .
> Stop Press: we've just heard
> She did not say 'That Word'.
> The whole thing's a twist
> By a male journalist –
> They enjoy nothing more
> Than women at war.
> So now we're all off
> For a drink with the prof:
> If I buy her a beer
> Can I win it next year?

As Gee's poem indicates, Young denied calling British women's writing 'piddling' and distanced herself from the comments attributed to her by arguing she had been misrepresented by journalists who prefer to focus on friction rather than fiction. Nicci Gerrard's view that the media

---

[10] Maggie Gee, 'Ode to Prof Lola Young of the Orange Prize judges, after reports she informed the world that British women writers are "piddling"', Letters to the Editor, *The Guardian*, 13 May 1999.

manufactured a row about the poor state of British fiction by women writers is supported by the way in which successes such as Kate Atkinson's *Behind the Scenes at the Museum* (1996), Whitbread Book of the Year, and Meera Syal's *Anita and Me* (1996), winner of the Betty Trask Award, were overlooked in debates about the state of British women's fiction.[11] It is also amply demonstrated by the headlines of Nigel Reynolds's annual reports on the Orange Prize in the *Daily Telegraph*, which repeatedly stressed an assault on British women's writing: 'Book prize judge attacks "smug" English novelists' (1997), 'Americans pip Brits for Orange prize again' (1998), 'Book prize judge attacks British women writers' (1999). Controversy over the Orange Prize may be generated by sensation-seeking journalists, but it also serves those who oppose a women-only prize.[12] As the rumpus generated by accusations of plagiarism levelled at Orange Prize winner Linda Grant's *When I Lived in Modern Times* (2002) illustrated yet again, bad publicity works not only to embarrass and discredit the Orange Prize, but also to hijack it by distracting attention from its primary purpose: to celebrate writing by women.

The adverse publicity the Orange Prize attracts makes it easy to overlook the fact that the recent disparagement of British fiction is not confined to women writers. Several literary commentators bemoaned the impoverished state of British fiction throughout the 1990s, and continue to do so into the twenty-first century. Richard Gott, *The Guardian's* literary editor, has published numerous baleful features documenting the 'decline of British fiction'.[13] In 1992 Gott boldly declared that the best lay west of Britain: 'The English novel is in a poor and feeble condition . . . Our cultural critics have been forced to gaze westward – to the United States – to find anything to get their teeth into.'[14] Almost a decade later, Robert McCrum reiterated this view: 'there are, at present, very few truly great and original novels

---

[11] Nicci Gerrard, 'Every one's a winner', *The Observer*, 16 May 1999.

[12] Lesley Chamberlain has accused the prize of separatism, and points out that Anita Brookner refuses to participate on the grounds that it is an unfair form of positive discrimination ('Just like a woman', *Prospect* 20, June 1997, 12–13). Revealing a homophobic subtext to his misogyny, Auberon Waugh named the award the 'lemon prize' – 'lemon' being a malicious synonym for 'lesbian' (Fiachra Gibbons, 'Male perspective for Orange prize', *The Guardian*, 27 March 2001).

[13] Richard Gott, 'Review of the Booker shortlist', *The Guardian*, 10 September 1992.

[14] Richard Gott, 'Standfirst: Criticism and culture in a reactionary age', *The Guardian*, 6 February 1992.

being published in the British Isles'.[15] Chairing the Samuel Johnson prize for non-fiction (which was established two years after the Orange Prize and announces its winner in the same month as the Orange Prize, thus distracting attention from it), Andrew Marr declared the novel dead and asserted that 'British novelists lack ambition'.[16] Carmen Callil has argued that concerns about the state of British fiction can be read as a coded expression of anxiety about the decline of Britain's status as a post-imperial power.[17] In a context where colonial discourses of nation are gendered and 'woman' has long stood as a symbol of nationhood (Britannia), women's writing thus becomes both a focus of concerns about the state of the nation and a convenient pariah.

This collection of essays aims to establish a positive focus on contemporary (post-1970) British women's writing. It does not aim to demonstrate that British women writers are equal to their American counterparts, because they are not judged in comparative terms, but does set out to question the view that writing by British women is 'domestic' and 'parochial', or that it has little value because it has these characteristics. The essays gathered together here strive to challenge misconceptions and glib generalisations about 'domestic' fiction. They defend women's lives as a suitable subject for fiction and challenge the assumption that an interest in the details of everyday life means a text is devoid of depth. By reassessing texts from a feminist perspective, they examine the serious political, social and cultural issues that arise from fiction that has been dismissed as limited or trivial. Several of the essays not only seek to bridge the gulf between prize-worthy and 'piddling' literature but also attempt to contest the distinction between feminist and popular fiction, categories that establish a false dichotomy and uphold a spurious hierarchy of value. A significant degree of writing by women falls between these categories, and gets lost there. This collection aims to rescue such fiction and to give it the serious academic attention it deserves.

These essays also aim to broaden the canon of British women writers by highlighting a number of authors who are persistently overlooked in literary studies. In contrast to the renown enjoyed by nineteenth-century British women novelists (Jane Austen, the Brontës, George

[15] Robert McCrum, 'Quest for an authentic voice', *The Observer*, 11 June 2000.
[16] See Robert McCrum, 'In our philistine culture, literary prize judges have to behave like barrow boys', *The Observer*, 27 May 2001.
[17] Carmen Callil, 'Stop knocking our writers', *Daily Telegraph*, 2 November 1996.

Eliot, Elizabeth Gaskell), relatively few books have been published on British women writers of the post-war period.[18] Courses on contemporary women's writing are amongst those most in demand in many universities, but such courses tend to focus on American authors. Furthermore, over the past few years British women's writing has come to be represented, if represented at all, almost exclusively by Angela Carter and Jeanette Winterson. While their canonisation is something to be celebrated, many other British women are often overlooked. In addition to the authors discussed in this collection, Monica Ali, Kate Atkinson, Rachel Cusk, Jenny Diski, Helen Dunmore, Linda Grant, Jackie Kay, Andrea Levy, Sara Maitland, Shena Mackay, Hilary Mantel, Michèle Roberts, Jane Rogers, Helen Simpson, Ali Smith, Zadie Smith, Meera Syal, Rose Tremain, Marina Warner, Sarah Waters – to name but a few – deserve mention. Endorsing Barbara Smith's pronouncement that 'For books to be real and remembered they have to be talked about' (169), this collection of essays constitutes a plea for more serious and sustained critical attention to the neglected academic field of contemporary British women's writing.

Although certain themes and concerns emerge as particularly British in these essays (Thatcherism and the legacy of British colonialism, for example), the collection does not aim to identify or define a national literature. Women writers who live and work in Britain do not constitute a homogenous group and a significant number have a complex sense of nationality, often inflected by regional, cultural, religious or ethnic identifications, identifications that are simultaneously informed by factors such as gender, class and sexuality. This renders the singularity implied by the term 'British woman writer' problematic. Indeed, the choice of authors discussed in the following pages highlights that 'British' is no longer a stable or straightforward category, and certainly not one defined by place of birth. For the purposes of this collection, 'British' signifies the geographical location in which the writer chooses to situate herself. This understanding of the term 'British' recognises that national identity is constructed rather than innate and shaped by, to use terms coined by Paul Gilroy in *The Black Atlantic* (1993), 'routes' rather than 'roots'. This allows for a more expansive and subtle

---

[18] For three of the very few books on contemporary British women writers, see Olga Kenyon's *Women Novelists Today: A Survey of English Writing in the Seventies and Eighties* (1988), Abby H. P. Werlock's *British Women Writing Fiction* (2000) and Beate Neumeier's *Engendering Realism and Postmodernism: Contemporary Women Writers in Britain* (2001).

conception of Britishness, one that does not deny other simultaneous national or ethnic identifications. For example, Ellen Galford was born and lived in America but has lived in Scotland for nearly thirty years and defines herself as Scottish by formation. Rukhsana Ahmad describes herself as a 'British-based South Asian writer' or 'a writer of Pakistani origin living in London'.[19] Joan Riley was born in Jamaica and migrated to London with her family as a young girl, and Jennifer Johnston is an Irish woman who was born in Dublin, moved to England, but now lives in Northern Ireland.[20]

The first two essays in this collection examine literature that falls into Young's first category of British literature: fiction that is entertaining about sex but with no sense of the 'bigger picture'. These essays focus on 'singleton' literature and both discuss Helen Fielding's *Bridget Jones* books and the 'chick lit' genre they spawned. Young specifically attacked novels written in the vein of *Bridget Jones's Diary* for being 'over interested in the well worn angst of the age, the subject of young women fretting about careers, boyfriends, children and partying'.[21] Her assessment of the books which have found success following the *Bridget Jones* phenomenon reflects the scorn that many feminists feel for the 'chick lit' genre. The term 'chick lit' offers an obvious clue to the character of this kind of novel. It is marketed as fiction by women, about women and for women and, as such, upholds the ideology of gendered separate spheres. 'Chick' may be intended to signal an ironic postmodern reclamation of a derogatory term, now used to denote a strong, sassy woman, independent, confident and in control, but the implicit contrast to D. H. Lawrence's 'cocksure' New Woman, whose claims for equality and independence incited (in him at least) loathing and panic at the beginning of the twentieth century, makes it clear that, by reducing women to 'chicks', postmodern irony offers women a cheap deal in terms of available identities.

Clare Hanson argues that novels such as *Bridget Jones's Diary* constitute a kind of 'lipstick feminism' by suggesting that femininity, not feminism,

[19] See Christiane Schlote's essay in this collection.
[20] There is precedence for including an essay on Johnston in a book on British literature: James Acheson's *The British Novel Since 1960* (1991) includes an essay on 'Contemporary Irish Women Novelists' by Janet Egleson Dunleavy and Rachel Lynch. Granta's *Best of Young British Novelists* (2003), ed. Ian Jack, also includes a Northern Irish writer, Robert McLiam Wilson.
[21] Nigel Reynolds, 'Book prize judge attacks British women writers', *Daily Telegraph*, 10 May 1999.

is the route to empowerment. Yet, by focusing on the politics of reproduction, her essay also examines the way that recent non-feminist
fiction articulates feminist concerns about mothering, concerns that
have not, in fact, received adequate attention within feminism. She
optimistically proposes that such a phenomenon signals the degree to
which feminism has entered the mainstream. Hanson explores the
impact of changing patterns of kinship structures on the conditions of
mothering as represented in *Bridget Jones's Diary* (1996), *Bridget Jones:
The Edge of Reason* (1999) and Esther Freud's *The Wild* (2000), arguing
that a general move away from the institution of marriage to serial
monogamy renders relationships uncertain and intermittent. In a
situation where women are still the primary childcarers, the subsequent
emotional and economic insecurity engendered by the unpredictability
and impermanence of partnerships makes motherhood an anxious and
high-risk activity for women. From this perspective, the contemporary
heroine's apparently frivolous desire for romance (which Hanson reads
as a code for commitment) and her obsessive search for Mr Right can
be interpreted as a longing for security against the risks of reproduction
and the penalties of single parenthood. By exploring the political
context and implications of the representation of issues such as romance
and motherhood, Hanson's essay makes it clear that 'parochial' or
'domestic' fiction cannot be dismissed as 'piddling' quite so easily.

Imeldha Whelehan's essay considers why 'chick lit' is problematic
from a feminist perspective whilst also, like Hanson, arguing that such
novels provide valuable insights into the lives of a certain group of
women. Whelehan compares American 'singleton' literature of the
1960s and '70s with British 'singleton' literature of the 1990s. Through
a discussion of Helen Gurley Brown's *Sex and the Single Girl* (1962), Erica
Jong's *Fear of Flying* (1974) and Helen Fielding's *Bridget Jones's Diary*
(1996), she traces a movement from a feminist to a feminine impulse in
'singleton' literature. These novels share similar themes and concerns –
a middle-class career woman's self-deprecating obsession with
appearance, a fear of singledom, the search for a male hero, and the
problem of how to forge meaningful sexual relationships with men.
However, while Jong offers an oppositional ideology that seeks to contest
traditional ideas about gender, Bridget Jones conservatively yearns for
the more distinct gender roles and identities that characterise the
tradition of romance out of which Fielding writes. Furthermore, whereas
'singleton' literature of the 1960s and '70s exposes tensions between the
theory and practice of being a feminist, the heroine of the 1990s
ventriloquises the politics of the Women's Movement but adopts a

variant model of feminism that stresses individual choice rather than collective action, and equates empowerment with the freedom to consume. Nevertheless, Whelehan argues that although not self-consciously or overtly feminist, singleton literature expresses the concerns of feminism in the sense that it explores the changing material and social situation of the contemporary fictional heroine and highlights the contradictions in women's lives. In particular, she points to a tension between the public and private aspects of female experience. While the 1990s heroine inhabits a supposedly post-feminist world in which she is empowered by her career and enjoys the benefits of various material advances, her personal relationships with men remain governed by a system of values that encourage women to assume traditional feminine identities. Progress in the public sphere is thus in conflict with, and undermined by, more traditional struggles in her private life and personal relationships.

Maroula Joannou offers a reassessment of the early fiction of a now highly respected author, Pat Barker. While Barker's multi-award-winning *Regeneration* trilogy – which, by focusing on male experience of the First World War, is deemed to cover a broad cultural landscape and explore what are considered to be universal themes – has won considerable critical acclaim, her earlier works – *Union Street* (1982), *Blow Your House Down* (1984) and *The Century's Daughter* (1986) – have received scant attention, despite being championed and celebrated by Angela Carter. This is partly because these novels, which focus on communities of women in the north-east of England and their domestic concerns, have been perceived as parochial or 'regional'. Joannou questions this false dichotomy between the early and late work, and between the value of the universal and the particular, by arguing that the psyche of violent men and the effects of male violence – one of Barker's predominant themes – is present throughout her work. She presents Barker's first three narratives as 'Condition of England' novels which offer a critical perspective on 1980s Britain, one that simultaneously contests Thatcherite ideology and the male tradition of working-class writing. Through her emphasis on community rather than individualism, her use of the vernacular and the conspicuous absence of consumerism and the nuclear family, Barker's novels contest the values of the metropolis. In affirming regional and provincial difference, they represent a resistance to the imperatives of homogenisation and centralisation. At the same time, the attention Barker pays to the intersection of gender and class issues, together with her focus on the domestic, means that she provides a woman-centred alternative to working-class male fiction that has tended to either marginalise women or subordinate women's concerns to the primacy of class struggle. In this way, Barker combines a critique of patriarchy and capitalism, illustrating a link between sexual disorder and industrial disorder, and shows how economic hardship shapes personal relations between men and women, black women and white women, mothers and daughters.

Although an eminently 'literary' writer whose fiction has consistently received praiseworthy reviews, Maggie Gee's critical reception typifies the lack of attention received by many contemporary British women writers. John Sears argues that although Gee's novels mostly represent the ordinary and conventional aspects of white, middle-class, heterosexual life and experience, they do so in order to probe conventional social ideologies.[22] The bourgeois world of her novels is haunted by the excluded, people who populate the margins of society, the disadvantaged and dispossessed. Like Barker, Gee focuses on major historical events and their impact on individual lives and, again like Barker, explores the devastating social and psychological effects of Thatcherism and its legacy. Sears explores how the ethics of Gee's fiction, with its emphasis on social commitment and sisterly connections, is at odds not only with the fictional world she represents but also the postmodern aesthetics she employs. In this way, although Gee's novels are not always clearly motivated by a desire to deconstruct myths of patriarchy, they nevertheless articulate the concerns of socialist feminism.

The essays by David Ellis and Christiane Schlote, which focus on Joan Riley and Rhuksana Ahmad respectively, acknowledge that Britain is what Avtar Brah calls a 'diaspora space' (208–9). These essays recognise the diversity of writing in Britain and underline that racial and cultural difference are an integral part of Britishness. By challenging boundaries of inclusion and exclusion, belonging and otherness, 'us' and 'them', Riley and Ahmad decentre and reconfigure received notions of Britishness. In Brah's terms, Britishness is 'reconstituted via a multitude of border crossings in and through other diasporic formations' in their work (209).

These two essays explore the experience of Black British and Asian women (without assuming that the work of Riley and Ahmad is representative). In his discussion of Riley, Ellis locates the most published black woman writer in Britain in the context of a tradition established by male authors of the Windrush generation and African American women writers. He asks why, in contrast to the work of

[22] *The White Family* (2002), published after this essay was written, is a notable exception to this.

writers like Sam Selvon and Alice Walker, Riley's fiction has been
persistently overlooked and undervalued. Acknowledging that Riley is
committed to representing the social reality of black women in post-war
Britain and that race and gender are not equivalent social constructions, Ellis then focuses on Riley's treatment of black female identity,
paying particular attention to the politics of location and dislocation.
He highlights the painful disparity between racial mythology and the
reality of black women's lives in order to explore how existing colonial
discourses impact on diasporic identities. Riley portrays the struggle to
integrate public and private selves, and explores the destructive psychological effects of alienation, showing that female disempowerment is
often registered as a loss of control over the body. Despite this, and
although her work has been read as unremittingly negative in tone, Ellis
finds optimism located in the potential for connection and collective
strength in Riley's most recent fictions.

As a writer whose *routes* have led her to England but whose *roots*
remain in Pakistan, Ahmad explores the experience of women in both
countries, and stresses the heterogeneity of South Asian women.
Schlote's essay addresses how issues of gender, class, culture and nationhood intersect in Ahmad's work. She explores how Ahmad resists still-
available Western discourses about non-Western women as submissive
and totally subordinated by a monolithic and unchanging patriarchy
whilst also addressing the changing configurations of class relations in
Pakistan, often assumed to be static. Her essay focuses in particular on
Ahmad's representation of South Asian women's bodies as sites where
racial and class differences are inscribed, and as sites of patriarchal
repression and female resistance. Together, the essays by Ellis and
Schlote point to the inclusive and progressive character of much
current writing by British women and show that it responds to the
hybrid and multicultural society of modern Britain.

Felicity Rosslyn's essay focuses on Jennifer Johnston, 'the quiet
woman of Irish fiction'.[23] Although Johnston's identity as a woman is
not important to her sense of herself as a writer, she portrays strong
women and challenges conventional ideas about women's writing by
avoiding the theme of romantic love.[24] The 'quietness' of her work

[23] Eileen Battersby, 'Making Sense of Life', *Irish Times*, 30 September 2000.
[24] Johnston has said, 'A lot of men tell me I write awful women but I know I am
striking a chord. I create women who have the strength to move the shit aside.
Men find that threatening.' See Karen McManus, 'Prodding Republicanism',
Fortnight (April 1995): pp.36–7.

stems partly from her preference for everyday truths over 'big issues'. Nevertheless, she explores how 'big issues' reverberate through ordinary lives as she chronicles the struggles of British and Irish self-definition. Rosslyn's essay examines Johnston's commitment to a united Ireland in the context of her Protestant Anglo-Irish background. It describes her preoccupation with issues of identity, loyalty and treachery in fictions set in the First World War and its aftermath, in the Troubles of the 1970s, and in the Ireland of today. It focuses particularly on *How Many Miles to Babylon?* (1974), *Shadows on Our Skin* (1977) and *The Invisible Worm* (1991), and suggests that Johnston's theme of guilty sexuality in the last of these is part of her overall preoccupation with the distorting effects of guilt in society and politics on both sides of the border.

Eluned Summers-Bremner offers a Lacanian reading of A. L. Kennedy's fiction, one that focuses on the relationship between love, language, Scottishness and lack. Her essay examines what is often considered to be a conventional theme in women's writing – love – but, by linking issues of intimacy and national belonging, demonstrates that Kennedy's treatment of love raises crucial political questions and offers important insights into both public and private aspects of the self. She argues that while nationalism and the novel are interrelated, this relationship is historically peculiar in the case of Scotland. Because it played an aggressive role in the expansion of the British Empire, Scotland is in the paradoxical position of having generated the conditions in which nationalisms would later flourish, without recourse to nationalist fictions of lost belonging. Summers-Bremner explores this paradox of Scottish nationalism as it emerges in Kennedy's representation of the vexed landscapes of human intimacy and the complexity of feminine sexual desire.

Thanks to the success of Jeanette Winterson, and more recently Sarah Waters, lesbian fiction has won popular acclaim and received increasing critical attention since the 1980s. However, lesbian writers still struggle for visibility, particularly in an academic arena where one lesbian writer on a syllabus (invariably Winterson) is considered more than enough. Palmer's essay is thus important in turning its attention to two other important authors: Ellen Galford and Emma Donoghue. Palmer sets her discussion of recent lesbian writing in the context of a movement away from realist forms of narrative such as the 'coming out' novel and a growth of lesbian genre fiction. Drawing on a post-structuralist queer perspective, she examines the way that Galford and Donoghue offer a lesbian feminist transformation of popular genres by challenging dominant ideas about gender encoded in traditional fairy tales, and explains how a parodic reworking of the conventions of Gothic and fairy tale subverts the hetero-patriarchal image of the lesbian as grotesque, a signifier of the monstrous feminine. Palmer uses Donoghue, an Irish writer, to extend her discussion of Galford and explore Galford's influence on other authors, while investigating the intersection between lesbian feminist and national identifications. Together, the essays by Rosslyn, Summers-Bremner and Palmer emphasise that 'British' literature can no longer be seen as synonymous with 'English' literature.

Like Palmer, Gina Wisker explores how women writers play with genre. Her essay offers a historical overview of British women's horror writing and examines the ways in which Susan Hill, Emma Tennant and Fay Weldon follow the ground-breaking, revisionary work of Angela Carter in their reconception of identities that demonise women as hag, whore and witch. Whereas much conventional (male-authored) horror employs the abject to designate 'Otherness' and represents what is terrifying and disgusting in order to overpower, repress or destroy it, thus affirming the patriarchal order, Wisker argues that horror writing by women demands a recognition of the 'Other' within ourselves. By confronting or embracing rather than repressing the abject, by celebrating 'Otherness', women writers exploit the subversive power of horror and recast the genre not only as a vehicle for social critique but also as a genre that has the potential to offer a new vision of social relations between the sexes.

As Nancy Armstrong argues, domestic fiction is often underestimated because 'We are taught to divide the political world in two and to detach the practices that belong to a female domain from those that govern the marketplace. In this way, we compulsively replicate the symbolic behavior that constituted a private domain of the individual outside and apart from social history' (9–10). Women do not all write, or only write, domestic fiction. During the last hundred years, women have entered the public sphere in vast numbers and this has undoubtedly changed their perspective on the world, a change that is reflected in the subject, style and form of their fiction. Nevertheless, the domestic sphere remains a central part of the lives of most women, and it thus remains a legitimate subject of fiction. The essays gathered together here contest the established opposition between personal and political spheres of experience, seek to defend the domestic, and offer a critical reappraisal of the apparently parochial subjects and seemingly narrow focus of contemporary British women's writing. These essays propose that a focus on the domestic highlights aspects of experience beyond that realm and illustrates that 'political events cannot be understood apart from women's history, from the history of women's literature, or from changing representations of the household' (Armstrong 10). They also echo and endorse words of wisdom first uttered by Virginia Woolf almost a century ago, confirming the continued importance of her invaluable insight: 'Let us not take for granted that life exists more fully in what is commonly thought big than what is commonly thought small' ('Modern Fiction' 107).

Works Cited

Acheson, James, ed. *The British Novel Since 1960* (New York: St Martin's Press, 1991).

Armstrong, Nancy. *Desire and Domestic Fiction: A Political History of the Novel* (Oxford: Oxford University Press, 1987).

Brah, Avtar. *Cartographies of Diaspora: Contesting Identities* (London: Routledge, 1996).

Buford, Bill, ed. *Best of Young British Novelists* (London: Granta, 1993).

Chamberlain, Leslie. 'Just Like a Woman', *Prospect* 20 (June 1997): 12–13

Gee, Maggie. *The White Family* (London: Saqi Books, 2002).

Gilroy, Paul. *The Black Atlantic: Modernity and Double Consciousness* (London: Verso, 1993).

Jack, Ian, ed. *Best of Young British Novelists* (London: Granta, 2003).

Kenyon, Olga. *Women Novelists Today: A Survey of English Writing in the Seventies and Eighties* (Brighton: Harvester, 1988).

Lawrence, D. H. 'Cocksure Women and Hensure Men' in *The Gender of Modernism: A Critical Anthology*, ed. Bonnie Kime Scott (Bloomington: Indiana University Press, 1990). 227–29

McManus, Karen. 'Prodding Republicanism', *Fortnight* (April 1995): 36–7

Neumeier, Beate, ed. *Engendering Realism and Postmodernism: Contemporary Women Writers in Britain*. Postmodern Studies 32 (Amsterdam: Rodopi, 2001).

Smith, Barbara. 'Toward a Black Feminist Criticism' in *The New Feminist Criticism: Essays on Women, Literature and Theory*, ed. Elaine Showalter (London: Virago, 1986). 168–85

Werlock, Abby H. P., ed. *British Women Writing Fiction* (Tuscaloosa and London: University of Alabama Press, 2000).

Woolf, Virginia. 'Modern Fiction' in *Collected Essays*, Vol. 2 (London: Hogarth Press, 1966).

——. *A Room of One's Own and Three Guineas*, ed. Michele Barrett (London: Penguin, 1993).

——. 'Women Novelists' in *Collected Essays*, Vol. 1 (London: Hogarth Press, 1966).

(References for newspaper articles in footnotes.)

Fiction, Feminism and Femininity from the Eighties to the Noughties

CLARE HANSON

This essay argues that a shift has taken place over the last twenty years in the relations between fiction, feminism and femininity and that this shift is related to wider social and cultural changes. Throughout the 1980s, fiction and feminism seemed to go together almost automatically. All the interesting fiction (or at least, the fiction that was widely discussed in the media, and in some cases translated into film texts) was powered by feminist ideas. Fay Weldon went so far as to suggest that fiction was *the* major means by which feminism had influenced women's lives, and the iconic texts of the decade, Carter's *Nights at the Circus* (1984) and Winterson's *The Passion* (1987), triumphantly celebrated the subversive potential of their female heroes, Fevvers and Villanelle. By the late 1990s, in contrast, fiction and film had become increasingly preoccupied with femininity, the dark 'Other' of feminism. In her 1983 article 'Notes From the Front Line' Carter wrote of the way in which the 'social fiction of my "femininity" was created, by means outside my control, and palmed off on me as the real thing' (38). While she wrote, unambiguously and trenchantly, *against* femininity, contemporary fiction is far more ambivalent about it. A brief walk around Waterstones is instructive in this respect, yielding titles such as *Old Maid* (1999) and *Amanda's Wedding* (2000) among a rash of pink-jacketed books dealing with 'girlie' subjects in a comic fashion. Amy Jenkins's *Honeymoon* (2000) is another recent example of the genre, but I am going to concentrate first on Helen Fielding's *Bridget Jones's Diary* (1996), the text widely credited with capturing the mood of *fin de millénaire* independent woman.

Bridget Jones is a fiction that shares entirely Carter's understanding of the constructed nature of femininity. Fielding makes no bones about the labour involved in making oneself into a woman. So before her first date with Daniel, Bridget notes that she is exhausted by an entire day of preparation for it:

> Being a woman is worse than being a farmer – there is so much harvesting and crop spraying to be done: legs to be waxed, underarms shaved, eyebrows plucked, feet pumiced, skin exfoliated and

moisturized, spots cleansed, roots dyed, eyelashes tinted, nails filed, cellulite massaged, stomach muscles exercises. . . . Sometimes I wonder what I would be like if left to revert to nature – with a full beard and handlebar moustache on each shin . . . (30)

Through the character of Shazzer, Fielding also provides a strong thread of feminist awareness that runs through the novel: Shazzer homes in on men 'leaving their families and post-menopausal wives for young mistresses' and having sex with women 'without any niceness or commitment' (126). Nevertheless, from the start of the book ('9st 3') to its finish ('do as your mother tells you'), *Bridget Jones's Diary* seems to endorse a preoccupation with the construction of the female body in relation to the male gaze, and femininity, not feminism, is seen as the route to empowerment. The book thus seems to offer a kind of lipstick feminism that assumes that a woman's best weapon in life is a floaty white dress in a romantic setting.

This is why *Bridget Jones* has been so negatively viewed by feminist critics (and this despite the fact that high-profile feminists such as Naomi Wolf have recently written about the relation between fashion and feminist empowerment).[1] However, the question that remains to be answered is, what does the Bridget Jones phenomenon mean? I want to suggest that the extraordinary success of *Bridget Jones* is connected with a specific social issue – even though the connection may not be an immediately obvious one. A broad-brush sketch of the background of the argument would run something like this. As a result of second-wave feminism, women have a far greater degree of financial independence than ever before (although they still do not have economic equality in the workplace, and such independence is largely the preserve of middle-class women – points to which I will return). The availability of the contraceptive pill has also given women sexual freedom and reproductive choice (although, again, access to and use of the pill are class-specific). Thus, men no longer need to marry to have sex, and women no longer need to marry to gain financial security: the old imperatives that sustained the institution of marriage have gone. Moreover, the new reproductive technologies mean that we can now not only artificially prevent conception, but can also artificially produce conception. In consequence, Anthony Giddens has argued, sex has become entirely divorced from reproduction, in terms of what we might call the cultural imaginary, if not, for most of us, in immediate practical terms. Sex has

---

[1] See Naomi Wolf, *Fire With Fire* (1993), p.137.

become sexuality, something malleable and open to infinite change. The phrase Giddens coins for this is 'plastic sexuality', sex severed from 'its age-old integration with reproduction, kinship and the generations' (27).

In an era of 'plastic sexuality', reproduction becomes a fraught and difficult issue, and I would argue that this is the problem that is really being explored in texts like *Bridget Jones*. As recent research has shown, it is among same-sex couples that many of the most equitable and imaginative parenting models are currently being established.[2] However, within the heterosexual frame, it is still the case that reproduction has widely different implications for men and women. The fact that in 90% of cases lone parent families are headed up by women is a stark illustration of the fact that women are still, overwhelmingly, the primary carers of children.[3] Whether they are married or cohabiting, women will spend far more time caring and working for their children, usually at the expense of career or employment opportunities. If the relationship breaks down, they and their children will almost invariably suffer a heavy financial penalty.[4] Hence, I would argue, the return to romance, which is one of the most striking and overlooked features of *Bridget Jones*. Romance is a code for commitment, a commitment that the heroine wants not 'for herself', as in the past, but as an insurance policy against the risks of reproduction.

So, while *Bridget Jones* is punctuated by 'laddette' episodes in which Bridget, Shazzer and Jude get spectacularly and publicly drunk, the narrative follows the old romance-plot of *Pride and Prejudice* with great fidelity. Bridget first meets Mark Darcy at a party where he appears arrogant and rude, then is distracted by a Willoughby-figure (Daniel). When catastrophe strikes in Bridget's family, the wealthy Mark first blames himself (just as Darcy does in *Pride and Prejudice*), then travels off in secret to sort matters out, returning to claim Bridget and take her away from the awkwardnesses and embarrassments of her middle-class

---

[2] See Gillian Dunne, 'What Difference Does "Difference" Make? Lesbian Experience of Work and Family Life' in Julie Seymour and Paul Bagguley's *Relating Intimacies: Power and Resistance* (1999) for a detailed study of parenting patterns among lesbian parents.
[3] See Richard Berthoud, Stephen McKay and Karen Rowlingson, 'Becoming a Single Mother' in Susan McRae's *Changing Britain: Families and Households in the 1990s* (1999) for the relevant statistics.
[4] See Carol Smart and Bren Neale, ' "I Hadn't Really Thought About it": New Identities/New Fatherhoods' in Seymour and Bagguley for a comparison of male and female parenting responsibilities, especially post-divorce.

relations. Austen's Darcy is an archetypal romantic hero, if we understand Darcy and Elizabeth's romance in terms of what Giddens calls
'a meeting of souls which is reparative in character' and the creation of
a 'long-term life trajectory, orientated to an anticipated yet malleable
future' (45). Elizabeth and Darcy famously compensate for each other's
failings, so that in some sense each is made whole through the relationship that they create together. This relationship is founded not so much
on passionate physical attraction as on knowledge of each other's
character and potential. Austen's text, it could be argued, is thus part of
the wider project whereby women (writers) feminised love and brought
romantic love into the general understanding of what marriage could or
should be. However, Fielding's Darcy is, necessarily, a much more
ambivalent figure. Romantic love and marriage have long been intertwined, but now that marriage is being replaced by serial monogamy,
our conception of romance also has to change. This is underscored in
Bridget Jones through the comparison Fielding makes between the
hugely successful television adaptation of *Pride and Prejudice* and the
'real-life' relationships of the actors in it. Bridget notes the disparity
between the on-screen romance in which there are, as she puts it, 'no
goals', and the off-screen romance between the 'modern-day luvvies'
who are already sleeping together (247). Romance, or love, no longer
precedes but follows sex – and there is no guarantee of permanence in
it. This last point is underlined when Mark Darcy sweeps Bridget away
at the end of the novel, not to Pemberley but to Hintelsham Hall hotel,
where he has rented a suite where he and Bridget can play with all the
'v. posh' guest features. This is an image of fun, but also of transience
and impermanence.

Unlike Austen's Darcy, Mark Darcy promises nothing and is only
intermittently attentive, particularly in the sequel to *Bridget Jones:
The Edge of Reason* (1999). The uncertainty and intermittancy in the
relationship between Mark and Bridget suggests a connection with
'confluent love', the kind of love that Giddens claims is replacing
romantic love. In *The Transformation of Intimacy* (1992) Giddens
argues that:

> Confluent love is active, contingent love, and therefore jars with the
> 'for-ever', 'one-and-only' qualities of the romantic love complex. The
> 'separating and divorcing' society of today here appears as an effect of
> the emergence of confluent love rather than its cause. The more
> confluent love becomes consolidated as a real possibility, the more
> the finding of a 'special person' recedes and the more it is the 'special
> relationship' that counts. (61–2)

The problem is that while this new ideal of confluent love may, as Giddens suggests, presuppose more 'equality in emotional give and take' between women and men, and while it may indeed encourage more recognition of 'male emotional vulnerability' (by not requiring men to be cold and distant heroes), it has nothing to tell us about the care of children (62). Emotional equality is one thing: parenting equality is quite another, and it is not surprising that it is women who are focusing on this. Over ten years ago, a 1989 study of teenage girls found they were struggling with the effects of the severing of the link between sex and reproduction. In the past that link had underwritten companionate marriage: now there was a need to renegotiate 'the bargain between the genders' (Giddens 52). In *The Edge of Reason*, we see this renegotiation taking place through the production and reading of a plethora of self-help books on relationships such as *Men are from Mars, Women are from Venus*. Mark mocks Bridget for reading them, but ends up consulting them himself – because there are no other rules or guidelines. When Bridget is asked about the Blair government and 'New policies with Women in Mind', she suggests that Blair should draw up a code of dating practice because 'all other cultures have specific dating rituals, but we are operating in an ill-defined sea with men and women increasingly alienated from each other' (196). Bridget's identification of the problem (if not her solution) is entirely accurate, and in *The Edge of Reason* it becomes even clearer that the real crunch comes over bringing up children.

Bridget's desire to have a child is foregrounded in this novel. At one point Bridget's gay friend Tom suggests that they should have a child together, and there is some discussion of the pros and cons of single motherhood, but in the same chapter the relationship between Bridget and Mark begins to be linked to children. The Jane Austen pre-text for *The Edge of Reason* is *Persuasion*, and in the first scene with children Bridget re-enacts (under Mark's gaze) Anne Elliot's good management of her sister Mary's children. Crucially, Mark offers to help her with them. In another scene, having first had the opportunity to observe her excellent relationship with her three-year-old god-daughter, Mark releases Bridget from the grip of a six-year-old boy who has jumped on her back (just as Frederick Wentworth takes Walter away from Anne Elliot). What is significant about this is that it is not so much Bridget as Mark who has to prove his interest in children in order for Bridget to feel safe with him. However, the ending of the novel is not quite that of *Persuasion*. Bridget does not marry Mark, but only agrees to travel with him, thus continuing the theme of impermanence so evident in *Bridget Jones's Diary*.

The marketing pressures that kept Ally McBeal single may well prevail in the case of Bridget Jones, so that even if there is another instalment in the novel-series Bridget is unlikely to be brought to the crunch of marriage or pregnancy. However, if she were to move on in this way, Bridget's world would be unlikely to revolve around a well-adjusted nuclear family. It would be far more probable that the pattern of relationships would resemble those in Esther Freud's novel *The Wild* (2000). The title of this novel refers in the literal sense to some waste ground attached to the house where the nine-year-old narrator Tess is living. Metaphorically, however, it signals a wild zone that is like the 'ill-defined sea' of dating described by Bridget Jones – only this wilderness is the one in which parents and step-parents try to negotiate rules of engagement for their relationships with each other and with their children. *The Wild* is something of a projection forward from the confusions of Bridget Jones, charting the dislocations created by serial monogamy (or 'confluent love') from the point of view of the child. When the novel opens, Tess, her mother and brother are renting rooms from William, a teacher who, unusually, has sole custody of his three daughters. The seven of them form an abritrary 'family', bound together only by William's obsessive imposition of domestic rules and routines – he has rotas for cooking, cleaning, looking after the animals, even for saying grace. The rules are an attempt to impose order and stability where there are none, for the children are riven by conflicts of loyalty and haunted by ties to their absent parents. When William and Tess's mother start an affair and she becomes pregnant, the instability of this 'family' with its shifting attachments is reflected in Tess's nightmares, in which the ground literally gives way beneath her:

> [S]he was walking on a top-heavy cliff, and the hair-line cracks were opening. They were widening into gulfs, cracking just under her toes until she was stranded on one narrow, snaking ridge. 'I'll fall, I'll fall,' she fought against her pillow and suddenly she dropped like a stone into sleep. (139)

Fragments of the Norse myths that Tess is learning at school are also threaded through the novel. To Tess these suggest a turbulent world full of cruelty and perverse generation, as in the story of the Frost Giant that she recounts to her father in a letter: 'Ymir was evil, and while he slept he began to sweat. A man and woman grew out of the sweat under his left armpit, and one of his legs fathered a son with the other leg' (19). The sinister unpredictability of this world mirrors exactly that of the non-mythical world that Tess and her brother inhabit, shaped by adult desires and imperatives.

Freud also deftly invokes (Sigmund) Freud to signal the strength of transgressive desires in both adults and children. William is directing a modern version of *Oedipus Rex* while he is sleeping with Tess and Jake's mother: the fact that it is a quasi-father sleeping with his mother enrages Jake. In a sense, both he and William want to challenge the Oedipal law: 'Why shouldn't we marry who we want?' William demands of Francine and the children (55). Freud's novel would suggest that the answer to that question is complicated. On one level, it does not matter in the least whom we marry or sleep with, either within a homosexual or hetero-sexual context. Moreover – if we want to read more into William's protest – we might consider Judith Butler's analysis of the incest taboo as generative precisely to the extent to which it is repressive (76). From this perspective, William's challenge to the incest taboo has a point: the same law that prohibits incestuous desire also invites it. Nonetheless, the novel demonstrates that while the rules and laws governing kinship may be arbitrary, the breakdown of these rules in a period of rapid social change puts an enormous degree of pressure on individual parents and children. In this case, it is Jake who finally cracks when William has his cat put down. He steals a shotgun and confronts William, and in the ensuing struggle, somehow the gun goes off and Jake is injured. He misses being paralysed 'by a fraction of an inch' (247).

William's assumption of authority over Jake literally misfires, destroying the 'family' that he and Francine have created. The violent ending of the novel reflects the reality of step-parental violence against children, but the conclusion to be drawn from this is *not* that good parenting has any inevitable link with 'blood ties'. The reality is that in Britain we are increasingly moving away from traditional models of kinship based on compulsory heterosexuality and the paternal blood line, and recent studies show a widespread acceptance of this.[5] However, these changing patterns create a situation in which at best, the boundaries and forms of relationships are the subject of continued negotiation between those involved, and at worst, negotiation breaks down and conflict ensues. The weakening of the institution of marriage has brought about a 'transformation of intimacy' that has many positive features, but the negative side is that it can put too much pressure on

---

[5] See Joanna Bornat, Brian Dimmock, David Jones and Sheila Peace, 'The impact of family change on older people: the case of stepfamilies' in McRae (1999).

FICTION, FEMINISM AND FEMININITY   23

the individual to negotiate the terms and conditions of relationships. Trust and goodwill are an inadequate substitute for informed and reformed social and legal support. Without such support, motherhood, in particular, is becoming an increasingly high-risk activity. In a paper first given in 1997, Carol Smart and Bren Neale argued that:

> The risks of motherhood are becoming high again. These risks are already well documented in economic terms . . . and they are set to become higher as women realize that the cost of having children may involve an indelible contract (and extensive contact) with men whose behaviour is violent or oppressive. (137)

This is an apt gloss on the situation in *The Wild*. The economic cost of mothering is foregrounded in the novel in one of the very few moments when we have access to an adult consciousness, as William watches the pregnant Francine reading. She has been training to be a kindergarten teacher, and plans to return to the course after the baby is born: 'Francine was sitting in the garden, a teacher-training manual propped up on her knees, although it was clear to William she would not be going back. For a moment she looked peaceful' (164). In these two simple sentences we sense Francine's pliability and her anxiety, but also William's extraordinary detachment from the situation. The baby is his too, but it never occurs to him that its birth will have any effect on his career development or prospects. It is Francine who will lose the opportunity of economic independence. The emotional cost of mothering is also foregrounded, and shown to lie not so much in the relationships with the children as in the struggle to maintain contact with fathers who can be both negligent and violent.

The Wild is not a feminist text in the sense in which *Nights at the Circus* and *The Passion* are feminist. The novel is understated and unpolemical, and Freud would probably present herself as a 'gender-free' writer. *Bridget Jones's Diary* and *Bridget Jones: The Edge of Reason* are similarly not overtly feminist – if anything these are feminine texts, preoccupied with those characteristics that have been culturally linked with biological femininity. Nonetheless, these novels have all picked up on an issue that is central to feminism, and that is the politics of reproduction. As Ann Oakley has pointed out, this is an issue that has been overshadowed for centuries by the more pressing need to gain citizenship for women. As she writes:

> Nineteenth- and early-twentieth-century feminism . . . stated a variety of positions about motherhood. On the whole, the struggle to

render women citizens overshadowed the need to understand motherhood in relation to women's overall situation, psychology or future
and as differentiated by class, ethnicity and economics. (131)

Second-wave feminism has attended to the psychology of motherhood
(as in the work of Dinnerstein and Chodorow) and has also been
particularly concerned with women's rights of access to contraception
and abortion. The economics of motherhood (as mediated by class and
ethnicity) have not been a primary focus of attention. Now, however,
with the loosening of conventional family ties, economic issues are
becoming a serious cause of concern. As noted earlier, while women
have a greater degree of financial independence than in the past, they
do not have financial equality with men. Women's participation in *full-
time* paid employment has risen quite slowly over the past few decades.
In Britain in 1951, 30% of women aged 20–64 were in full-time employment: forty years later, in 1991, this figure had risen only slightly to 34%
of women aged 16–59. In the same period, *part-time* work quintupled,
from 5% in 1951 to 26% in 1991.[6] Part-time work allows women to
maintain primary responsibility for the home and children while
contributing to the family income: it can be seen, therefore, as a means
of avoiding radical change in the gendered division of labour. It has
clear disadvantages in terms of poor rates of pay, loss of promotion and
of pension rights.

The implications of this are obvious. Whereas high-earning couples
can afford to pay for childcare, even a highly-paid single parent will
struggle to do this, and may be forced out of the full-time job market
when a relationship breaks down. Whether it is through taking on the
sole cost of childcare or through loss of full-time employment, the move
to single parenthood will carry a heavy financial penalty. For those who
already work part-time, with all the disadvantages this entails, relationship breakdown and the loss of a shared income will have even more
disastrous consequences. These are the risks of motherhood in the era
of so-called 'confluent love'. Is it any wonder that young women are
anxious – and not only young women? To her great credit, in *The Whole
Woman* (1999) Germaine Greer has drawn attention to the continuing
failure of Western society to think through the politics of reproduction.
Significantly, she focuses on the figure of the single mother, noting
that '[a] woman without a partner and with children is usually a woman

[6] See Jacqueline Scott, 'Family change: revolution or backlash in attitudes?' in
McRae (1999) for these statistics and a detailed analysis of them: pp.68–99.

in trouble. The very fact that she has children will militate against her ability to provide for them' (258). Greer also highlights the culture of responsibility without rights that seems to have grown up around the single mother. She points out that:

> In Britain, despite growing national prosperity, one in four children is growing up in poverty. Whether a mother is bringing up her children on social security or on the proceeds of her waged work, she is under as much scrutiny as if she were a paid state employee. All kinds of officials have the right to inspect her, her house and her children, and assess her performance, but none of them seems to have a duty to help her. (259)

The figure of the single mother, so reviled and persecuted by successive governments, is the figure who haunts Bridget Jones, her shadowy double. (In the light of the Labour government's record, Bridget's telling a bunch of complacent lawyers in *The Edge of Reason* that 'it is perfectly obvious that Labour stands for the principle of sharing, kindness, gays, single mothers' (58) has a nicely bitter irony.) Bridget dreads becoming like Francine: her idea of hell would be to move from rented room to rented room, children in tow, forced to live in the country and peel organic carrots. And as Greer reminds us, middle-class single mothers like Francine are the tip of the iceberg: what about the thousands of others living in poverty and on benefit?

It is striking that the politics of reproduction is so clearly signalled as an issue in these non-feminist texts, which do not explicitly concern themselves with a critical analysis of patriarchy. (As suggested earlier, a counter-example of a feminist text would be Carter's *Nights at the Circus*, with its references to the New Woman and Lizzie's materialist-feminist analyses.) There are two conclusions that could be drawn from this. The first is relatively uncontroversial: that non-feminist but woman-centred texts are key sites for analysis because these are the texts that most visibly display the contradictions of women's lives and identifications. The second conclusion is more speculative. Feminism has always defined itself against femininity, at least since Mary Wollstonecraft attacked genteel femininity and 'that weak elegancy of mind, exquisite sensibility, and sweet docility of manners, supposed to be the sexual characteristics of the weaker vessel' (73). Feminism/femininity has been a foundational binary opposition, and it has been assumed that the two categories are mutually exclusive. Might it be that this binary opposition is now being unravelled, as it is recognised that the two terms are mutually dependent rather than mutually exclusive? To suggest this is not to suggest that we live in a post-feminist or post-ideological world, but to entertain the possibility that feminist beliefs may have entered the mainstream more fully than we realise. This in turn suggests the potential for more broadly based political intervention over issues such as the politics of reproduction, very much along the lines of the coalitional politics proposed by Butler some time ago. Reproduction, after all, concerns us all, women and men, gay and straight. The Blair paternity leave controversy of 2000 has something to teach us in this respect. When his fourth child was born, Tony Blair took two weeks' leave with extreme reluctance, and spent much of the time not with his wife and child but writing speeches, including a now-notorious one for the Women's Institute on community and family values. The Women's Institute rightly responded to the fraudulence of Blair's position, giving him a slow handclap: who would have thought it would be they who would make the point that so many feminists wanted to make?

Works Cited

Berthoud, Richard, Stephen McKay and Karen Rowlingson. 'Becoming a Single Mother' in *Changing Britain: Families and Households in the 1990s*, ed. Susan McRae (Oxford: Oxford University Press, 1999). 354–73

Bornat, Joanna, Brian Dimmock, David Jones and Sheila Peace. 'The Impact of Family Change on Older People: The Case of Stepfamilies' in *Changing Britain: Families and Households in the 1990s*, ed. Susan McRae (Oxford: Oxford University Press, 1999). 248–62

Butler, Judith. *Gender Trouble: Feminism and the Subversion of Identity* (London: Routledge, 1990).

Carter, Angela. *Shaking a Leg: Collected Journalism and Writings* (London: Penguin, 1998).

Chodorow, Nancy J. *The Reproduction of Mothering: Psychoanalysis and the Sociology of Gender* (Berkeley; London: University of California Press, 1979).

Dinnerstein, Dorothy. *The Rocking of the Cradle and the Ruling of the World* (London: Women's Press, 1987).

Dunne, Gillian. 'What Difference Does "Difference" Make? Lesbian Experience of Work and Family Life' in *Relating Intimacies: Power and Resistance*, ed. Julie Seymour and Paul Bagguley (London: Macmillan, 1999). 189–221

Fielding, Helen. *Bridget Jones's Diary* (London: Picador, 1996).

———. *Bridget Jones: The Edge of Reason* (London: Picador, 1999).

Freud, Esther. *The Wild* (London: Hamish Hamilton, 2000).

Giddens, Anthony. *The Transformation of Intimacy: Sexuality, Love and Eroticism in Modern Societies* (Cambridge: Polity, 1992).

Greer, Germaine. *The Whole Woman* (London: Doubleday, 1999).

Oakley, Ann. 'Feminism, Motherhood and Medicine – Who Cares?' in *What is Feminism?*, ed. Juliet Mitchell and Ann Oakley (Oxford: Blackwell, 1986). 127–50

Scott, Jacqueline. 'Family Change: Revolution or Backlash in Attitudes?' in *Changing Britain: Families and Households in the 1990s*, ed. Susan McRae (Oxford: Oxford University Press, 1999). 68–99

Smart, Carol and Bren Neale. '"I Hadn't Really Thought About it": New Identities/New Fatherhoods' in *Relating Intimacies: Power and Resistance*, ed. Julie Seymour and Paul Bagguley (London: Macmillan, 1999). 118–41

Wolf, Naomi. *Fire With Fire: The New Female Power and How It Will Change the 21st Century* (New York: Random House, 1993).

Wollstonecraft, Mary. *Political Writings*, ed. Janet Todd (Oxford: Oxford University Press, 1994).

Sex and the Single Girl: Helen Fielding, Erica Jong and Helen Gurley Brown

IMELDA WHELEHAN

This essay will offer a brief account of the main features of so-called singleton literature and then go on to explore it in relation to one of the bestselling 'feminist'[1] novels of the 1970s, *Fear of Flying* (1974) by Erica Jong, and Helen Gurley Brown's early example of a 'self-help' manual, *Sex and the Single Girl* (1962). My interest in *Bridget Jones's Diary* (1996) in particular stems from teaching women's popular fiction and from a major research interest in modern second-wave feminist thought. I was also drawn to re-evaluate Helen Gurley Brown's self-help manual because it at once pre-dates the beginnings of feminism's second wave and heralds the dawning of the new type of glossy women's magazine via her 'makeover' of the then failing US magazine *Cosmopolitan*, which she edited from 1965 to 1997. Brown's defence of the 'single girl' in her bestselling book was also a straightforward guide to marriage and what would now be called 'lifestyle'. Brown, like Austen before her, saw the material value of an appropriate 'match' and the importance, therefore, of selecting one's mate wisely. Yet, in common with the second-wave feminist arguments she precedes, Brown also champions individual self-determination and sexual freedom. Helen Fielding's *Bridget Jones's Diary* has links to both modern feminism and the glossy magazines in that Bridget is 'a child of *Cosmopolitan* culture . . . traumatised by super-models and too many quizzes' (59). When interrogated about her reading habits by Mark Darcy, she claims to be reading Susan Faludi's *Backlash*, when in fact she is ploughing her way through John Gray's *Men are from Mars, Women are from Venus*.

The truth universally acknowledged by singleton literature appears to be that singleness is an unhealthy state and any single woman who claims self-possession (or 'inner poise', as Bridget Jones would have it) is clearly deluded. Singleness can only be 'cured' by a long hard look at yourself and an adherence to 'the rules' of courtship (as outlined in

---

[1] Its 'feminist' credentials were, of course, hotly debated at the time of publication and continue to be so. See for example, Rosalind Coward (1980), Charlotte Templin (1995) and Maroula Joannou (2000).

self-help manuals such as *The Rules*), yet the heroine's eventual romance must be seen to break those rules entirely, with the man professing that he loves the woman for herself, even though all singleton heroines seem to be absorbed in creating new, better 'selves'. Helen Fielding has become the most famous British exponent of singleton literature, even though one can identify important precursors such as Kathy Lette whose novels include *Foetal Attraction* (1993).[2] Certainly this new generation of generally humorous novels with a 'confessional' flavour written by women in their thirties and often with a first-person narrative has led the media to coin the term 'chick lit' to describe writings which are seen to appeal primarily to the women readers who can recognise themselves within their pages. This gendering of novels is no new thing and feminist critics have often made the association between such a designation and assumptions about low literary value. The term 'chick' also suggests a renewed celebration of what was once considered a highly derogatory reference to women, in a new wave of what is seen as playful 'political incorrectness' – an increasingly misused and meaningless term.

Chick lit has, of course, filmic parallels in 'chick flicks' which male companions are assumed to attend under sufferance, but are targeted at women audiences and which, necessarily, include contemporary adaptations of works of literature such as Jane Austen's. Given that both Fielding's *Bridget Jones* novels freely 'adapt' Austen and at the same time capitalise upon the popularity borne out by an increasing number of such adaptations over the past decade, it is as well to be aware that a certain mode of address which proposes an ironic distance from the chief character, yet which encourages simultaneous identification with her, crosses media to become a narrative strategy within a number of popular cultural forms. Not only have novels such as *Sense and Sensibility*, *Mansfield Park* and *Little Women* been given a chick flick nuance in their 'feminist' re-readings of the texts (which also aim to give a satisfactory romance closure), but television series such as *Ally McBeal* reflect similar concerns in the ways that they at once ventriloquise feminism and yet express pleasure in embracing the unreconstructed longings expressed within classic romance formats.

[2] In her 1998 novel, *Altar Ego*, Lette has one of her characters read *Bridget Jones's Diary* as a sign that she has 'dumbed down' in order to get a man. This may suggest that Lette is attempting to distinguish her own work from what has become known as chick lit, and reminds us how arbitrary and mutable such labels are.

In 2001 the film version of *Bridget Jones's Diary* was released to imme-diate box office success and is itself testament to the hybridisation of the 'chick' product. Not only does it 'quote' the highly successful BBC adaptation of *Pride and Prejudice* by having Colin Firth play Mark Darcy in more or less the same way as he played Fitzwilliam Darcy, but it brings in Hugh Grant as the anti-hero Daniel Cleaver – previously the roman-tic lead in *Four Weddings and a Funeral* and *Notting Hill*. Despite the many ways in which the adaptation encourages us to depart from the novel (not least because of numerous accounts of Rene Zellweger's 'enormous' weight gain to play the part of Bridget encourage us to view Bridget on screen as actually 'fat'), this film version affirms one of the 'lessons' of *Bridget Jones's Diary* – that despite the changing material and social situation of the contemporary fictional heroine, a brooding hero is best left unrevised.

Given the thematic cross-overs between these media forms, it seems appropriate to recognise it as a successful product which can currently sustain any number of imitators. If none of these offer a 'true' reflection of contemporary single life for women, they perhaps present its tensions more boldly than ever. Despite all the self-help manuals that Bridget and her friends read (by the sequel, *Bridget Jones: The Edge of Reason*, she has a truckload) this genre seems, through irony, to reject any narratives of self-improvement, including those of feminism. In most cases the chief female protagonist wins over the desired male by her genuineness, her inability to operate in accordance with such 'scripts'. Narratives of self-improvement are a key feature of both *Sex and the Single Girl* and *Fear of Flying* – Brown's real-life success is measured by her marriage to film producer David Brown, and Isadora is seen trying once again to live for herself, to her own ideals. Conversely, at the end of *Bridget Jones's Diary* we are offered a tally of the year's events recorded through calorie, cigarette and alcohol intake with the ironic summary, 'an *excellent* year's progress' (310). Bridget has her man and her mother and father are reunited; this is set against a backdrop of chaos, coinci-dence and failure to live up to her own resolutions. Authorial know-ingness and humorous pastiche vie with a first-person narrative voice which for some speaks essential truths about our age.

Bridget Jones has, therefore, become part role model and part mere reflection of the fragments of themselves many readers believe they see in the novel. Moreover, 'Bridget Jones' is a term which has entered our contemporary lexicon and itself conjures up the image of a single woman of a certain age who obsesses about her body and its shortcom-ings, whilst loudly bewailing the inadequacies of men with her close friends in a bar. Although the narrative tone of *Bridget Jones's Diary* places an ironic distance between character and reader, for many readers the attraction seems to be a sense of lack of distance between fiction and experience. Whereas the feminist bestsellers of the 1970s offer flawed characters for both readerly identification and as a vehicle for a wider feminist purpose, contemporary readers of the singleton novel seem only to want to encounter themselves: 'some idealists might see such a woman as a troubling role model, but who are they kidding? I mean, we really do act like that. Bridget Jones is a fair compromise between the '70s-style feminist and the '50s debutante – the '90s woman.'[3] Needless to say in the representation of Bridget there is no suggestion of the social-political responsibility expected of the writer of feminist fiction, nor any hint of change or transformation, except from the single to partnered state. In Bridget Jones we're offered a curious double bind: a woman who knowingly absorbs glossy magazine and self-help newspeak and attempts to live up to their strictures whilst seeming to be aware that this traps her in a cul-de-sac of self-absorption and body dysmorphia.

Women's writing of the twentieth century long used the trope of recognition to draw the reader in, and *Fear of Flying* with its central character Isadora Wing uses this strategy in its representation of a flawed feminist who fails to make her politics gel with her sexual and emotional needs. As Isadora says, 'I had been a feminist all my life . . . but the big problem was how to make your feminism jibe with your unappeasable hunger for male bodies' (88). Isadora echoed some real philosophical problems for many readers because she reflects the difficulties of politicising the personal – an act so crucial to feminism. She expressed for many the frustrations of agreeing that the personal is political combined with the recognition that, day to day, you still have to muddle through your lives, living out messy, illogical relationships with real emotional investments. More than this, she demonstrates, before it was readily articulated by feminist theorists, that heterosexual desire is a minefield, and that the available 'language' of desire has remained strongly resistant to feminist heterosexual reimaginings.

Humour is a feature which unites Jong's and Fielding's work, although feminism's relationship to this kind of writing has never been straightforward: as Rosalind Coward notes, 'no one is quite sure about the political validity of the admixture of conventional entertainment

---

[3] Review by Lisa Habib on http:www.cnn.com/books/reviews/9807/04/review. bridget.jones.diary/

with a serious political message' (53). Feminists were perhaps never in agreement on how the political pill should be sugared, and in common with other oppositional ideologies expressed in fiction, such as Marxist realism, there is often a sense that without humour and the portrayal of frailty and failure, the creative imagination suffers. In *Fear of Flying* the first-person confessional narrative promises a closeness and honesty and, moreover, teases with links to the authorial voice – not least in Isadora's role as writer (this becomes more obvious in the sequel, *How to Save Your Own Life*). In *Bridget Jones's Diary*, the diary structure allows for a little distance in the confessional mode – these are confessions that are not theoretically for the eyes of others. We can therefore feel superior to Bridget and readily identify the shortcomings she is blind to, while at the same time the diary form invites us to seek truths more disarming than those uttered to another person. What may be more testing about *Fear of Flying* is that Isadora's errors are never indulged, but are accompanied by a litany of promises – to value herself, to realise her ambition to write and to love her body. Isadora's perspective on the single life is framed by her position as a serially married woman who felt that 'men had made life so intolerable for single women that most would gladly embrace even bad marriages instead' (78). As Jong has Isadora observe early in the novel, '[i]t is heresy in America to embrace any way of life except as half of a couple. Solitude is un-American . . . a woman is always presumed to be alone as a result of abandonment, not choice. And she is treated that way: as a pariah. There is simply no dignified way for a woman to live alone' (18). *Bridget Jones's Diary* suggests that single life still prompts the same kind of responses over twenty years on.

Her escape from her marriage to Freudian psychoanalyst Bennett Wing to Laingian lover Adrian Goodlove positions Adrian in the dubious role of father confessor – it is to this other man with whom she becomes sexually involved that she tells her life story, and it is Adrian who is constantly encouraging her to cast adrift from romantic ties. Her submission to patriarchal psychoanalytical explanations of her life ironically expose her continuing subjugation to the phallus, even when she attempts to celebrate her own sexual impulses. Her fear of singledom is witnessed by the fact that her escape from marriage must be by means of another man. Moreover, this is a man who flaunts his own freedom throughout their odyssey across Europe, only to be exposed as a fraud by Isadora when it transpires that he has scheduled their arrival in France to coincide with a holiday he has planned with his current partner and children. Thus Isadora's spiritual journey concludes with her recognition that her affair with Adrian was always inauthentic, and that she has simply been shoring up the ego of a man who is not even able to give her full sexual pleasure. Isadora gains insight through recognising this and moving on, albeit from the vantage point of her husband's hotel room: compare this with the close of *Bridget Jones's Diary* where Darcy and Bridget discuss the misunderstandings which have kept them apart, at once affirming the primacy of the romance narrative as well as asserting that Bridget was right to remain 'herself'. Just as Adrian Goodlove is rendered limp by Isadora's feminism, so Bridget and her ilk must accept that the single 'career girl' is both professionally and personally threatening to men. At the end of a more recent singleton novel, Melissa Nathan's *Pride, Prejudice and Jamsin Field* (2000), which again uses the *Pride and Prejudice* conceit – this time by having a production of a stage adaptation of the novel at the centre of the plot – the heroine, a successful journalist turned actress, has to learn from her friends that her 'scariness', her acerbic intolerance of male egocentrism, is repelling her prospective lover (267).

Isadora's odyssey ends up with her taking a bath in her husband's hotel room and considering her own body: 'I looked down at my body. The same. The pink V of my thighs, the triangle of curly hair, the Tampax string fishing the water like a Hemingway hero, the white belly, the breasts half floating, the nipples flushed and rosy from the steamy water. A nice body. Mine. I decided to keep it' (277). Arguably, Isadora takes ownership of herself, and accepts her own sexual destiny as the onset of her period confirms that she is not pregnant by either of her lovers. At the same time, her brush with fertility reminds us that women's heterosexuality is always to be negotiated around the facts of reproduction. While one of the criticisms levelled against Jong has been her portrayal of her character's excessive concern with her body and its effect on male desire, for the singleton heroine the body is the key to the self and, ironically or not (and that *is* the question), it literally traces the contours of the personality. Arabella Weir's *Does My Bum Look Big in This?* (1997), an obvious imitator of *Bridget Jones* in its use of the diary form, concludes with its heroine Jacqueline M. Pane determining that 'if it's the last thing I ever do, I'm going to do my best to help create a world where it's safe to have a big bum' (212). The language of social responsibility may well be used to underscore the humour and sheer bathos of her 'message', but the novel offers us a woman who cannot walk out of a room because of her obsession with her rear and is pathologically unable to recognise herself as attractive to men. Here I believe there is no space for the light-hearted recognition of the reader's own foibles in a character whose consciousness is only raised at the end to the extent that she (a size 14) joins a self-help group for the 'larger' woman. Jong's physical descriptions of her protagonists, male and female, are individuated, loving and often repugnant; chick lit more often leaves us to fill in physical details based on our conventional understandings of what is held to be physically attractive, overweight, and so forth, and Bridget herself is largely depicted by her own exaggerated sense of her self.

What feminist writing of the past few decades also attempted to do was offer a new means of depicting men – even perhaps objectifying them in order to develop a female language of heterosexual desire. But to find a way of depicting the desiring male that is not phallic can result in a bathos, which can only comment on phallocentrism rather than herald a new kind of 'hero'. What would comprise an appropriate heterosexual hero for a feminist anyway, and how could it move beyond the phallocratic order – as Isadora Wing laments, 'what could be more poignant than a liberated woman eye to eye with a limp prick?' (88). As Adrian Goodlove prophesises, 'you won't know whether I'm a hero or an anti-hero, a bastard or a saint. You won't be able to categorise me' (89). This dilemma appears to be resolved in the singleton novel by taking a hero and positioning him in rather predictable romance-narrative contexts. Take, for example, this description from *Pride, Prejudice and Jasmin Field* when the hero, about to play Darcy in a stage adaptation, enters for the dress rehearsal:

> Harry walked in. Everyone hushed.
> He was wearing a white shirt tucked into breeches. His black leather boots went up to his knees. He hadn't put his tie or his frockcoat on yet and the loose collar of his shirt revealed a beautiful chest. The words 'gorgeous', 'dead' and 'drop' came to Jazz's mind, but she couldn't remember what order they should be in. Her mind was slush. (232)

This scene clearly recalls Colin Firth's portrayal of Darcy in the BBC's adaptation of *Pride and Prejudice* which prompted the media to talk of the 'Darcy effect' upon women as he emerges from the lake at Pemberley. These intertextual links are pursued by Helen Fielding in *The Edge of Reason*, where Bridget and her friends console themselves by watching the video repeatedly and Bridget interviews Firth – disastrously – for *The Independent* (the paper in which Fielding's 'Bridget Jones' column first appeared).

If, as Lorna Sage claims, Isadora Wing is a character 'pieced together on the page, out of books' (128–9), singleton literature owes a great deal of its narrative thrust to Austen's much imitated plot. But whereas Jong uses pastiche, most notably of the eighteenth-century novel and the picaresque, to weave a subtle intertexture to her work, the constant references to Austen seem to speak of nothing less than a yearning for a plot where men's and women's roles have a distinct and different logic of their own. Singleton literature seems to be influenced by the 'Venus and Mars' logic of both the self-help manuals and recent popular scientific treatises that attempt to affirm the naturalness of distinct male and female attributes. Whereas much of the plots of the feminist bestsellers were about claiming space in a man's world, but also breaking down the boundaries of conventional gender ascriptions, the singletons seem continuously guilty about their place in the world and in the workplace – somewhere curiously lacking married women or mothers – except, interestingly, Bridget's mother, who seems to discover Betty Friedan's 'problem that has no name' rather late in the day.

Helen Gurley Brown's manual seems to fall in between these two poles. Brown is keen to affirm the right of women to meaningful careers, but also characterises marriage as a game of strategy where women need to use guile, artifice and dirty tricks to gain their prize. Her claim about her book, that '[T]his then is not a study on how to get married but how to stay single – in superlative style' (11), seems rather disingenuous given her opening gambit that 'I married for the first time at thirty-seven. I got the man I wanted. It *could* be construed as something of a miracle considering how old *I* was and how eligible *he* was' (3). Nonetheless her claim carries some weight given that she outlines a pragmatic path for single women who value their careers, which emphasises their right to self-determination and independence (she insists that the single 'girl' should get herself an apartment alone) as well as endorsing their right to sexual freedom, underlining the absurdity of preserving virginity for marriage. Brown is pragmatic about relationships in many ways (although she assumes that all sensible single girls are out to get themselves a 'prize' in financial and status terms) and remains disarmingly upfront about money, clothing, diets and make-up. The life of the driven single girl from Brown's perspective is one of supreme endeavour – sexual attractiveness is, for Brown, always reinforced by illusion. An almost monastic self-discipline, it is suggested, will pay dividends later.

These sentiments are plainly transferred to the glossy-magazine-speak of *Cosmopolitan* and its sister publications, and are found echoed parodically in *Bridget Jones's Diary* where Bridget declares that:

> [B]eing a woman is worse than being a farmer – there is so much
> harvesting and crop spraying to be done: legs to be waxed, under-
> arms shaved, eyebrows plucked, feet pumiced, skin exfoliated and
> moisturised, spots cleansed, roots dyed, eyelashes tinted, nails filed,
> cellulite massaged, stomach muscles exercised. The whole perform-
> ance is so highly tuned you only need to neglect if for a few days for
> the whole thing to go to seed. (30)

What jars more than occasionally in Fielding's work is the feeling
the although the whole process is sent up, it is deemed utterly necessary
to female identity. Here I realise I might be criticised for a rather
humourless reading of what is essentially a humorous account of the
process of beautification, but whereas Brown's position is interesting for
all its contradictions precisely because it pre-dates the women's liberation movement and its perspectives on representation and femininity,
Fielding's has thirty years of feminism to draw upon. In Brown's time
one assumes that the identity of the 'career woman' was still too
unformed and fragile to be seen to alter the dynamics of domestic life,
but perhaps the singleton novel conservatively celebrates the split
between progressive and traditional gender identities in the way that
Aminatta Forma describes:

> Many successful women therefore aim to be the boss at work but a
> traditional girlfriend in their relationships or a traditional mother at
> home. We may have laughed over Bridget Jones, but millions of
> women bought Helen Fielding's satirical tale because they identified
> with the professional, educated woman who wept over the boyfriends
> who picked her up and dumped her. And the same women thrill to the
> tales of the American television heroine Ally McBeal, another young
> woman who competes with men on equal terms at work, but who longs
> to date them according to traditional rules after work. (140)

Perhaps the dilemmas recounted in *Fear of Flying* were never seen to be
addressed by feminism for many women; or that women reluctantly
heed the voice of magazine woman, so powerfully reiterated in *Bridget
Jones's Diary* that 'there is nothing so unattractive to a man as strident
feminism' (20).

A more upbeat interpretation of the impact of chick lit might be that
offered by Francis Gilbert:

> Fiction has never seen protagonists quite like Jones before; these
> heroines are inhabiting bodies that are their enemies. To complicate

matters, the thinnists [Gilbert's term for fiction which foregrounds the heroine's obsession with her weight] tend to be wonderfully ironic and self-deprecating. Like Lola Young, they really believe that their problems are 'piddling'. The protagonists may be beating themselves up over the way they dress, what they eat and how they are perceived by others; but the thinnists don't turn their novels into leaden critiques of the world. Rather, they turn the tragedy of modern consumer society – the truth that materially we have everything we ever wanted but suffer even more than before – into an absurdist comedy: an impossible search for a mythical male hero.[4]

Earlier Gilbert suggests that this kind of fiction is the new Mills & Boon and of course they share similar origins in works such as *Pride and Prejudice*, and in the creation of a fantasy romance plot embedded in the realism of the workplace.[5] Certainly there are elements of truth in this and reading *Bridget Jones's Diary* is to study the increasing vapid materialism of our daily lives: but the subtext is more interesting than this. Bridget and her friends embrace yet are imprisoned by materialist culture; they know (especially Sharon) the language of feminism and in particular the 'new feminist' rhetoric of empowerment through individual choice rather than collective action or political transformation. They can enact empowerment through their career choices and the evidence of the handful of women who really make it, but they have also to confront a system of values about sexual difference and relationships which lags desperately behind the progressivism their material advances promise. Ideologically, women are still positioned as the makers of relationships, the people who need marriage and children-while men are the dysfunctional breakers of them – the so-called 'emotional fuckwits' who must be deceived into the 'smug married' state.

Moreover, the emotional fuckwits have their apologists in that the media are taking up the cause of the man in crisis with renewed vigour – from his reported failure to succeed at school to his anxieties about being cheated out of a career by a sassy new breed of driven women. Predictably, it has never been more fashionable to blame feminists for this and Christine Hoff Sommers's book *The War Against Boys* (2000) is

[4] Francis Gilbert, 'Why I Love Bridget Jones', *New Statesman*, 26 July 1999 – http://www.newstatesman.co.uk/199907260052.htm
[5] And, needless to say, in 2002 Mills & Boon launched Red Dress Ink, 'Stories that reflect the lifestyles of today's urban, single women. They show life as it is, with a strong touch of humor, hipness, and energy', according to the imprint's web page.

just one example of a cluster of such attacks against women's advances over the past thirty and more years. While new feminists such as Natasha Walter no longer want to politicise the personal it is already abundantly clear that it is the 'personal' – the emotional relationships and gendered perceptions of self – which steer our interpretations of the role of women in the twenty-first century, and which never emerged from the shadow of a conviction of being intimately related to our private unassailable selves. Bridget Jones and her friends recognise that while they are formally and legally acknowledged – through their jobs, their standard of education, their social mobility and their consumption choices – as men's equals, their personal lives have to abide by different rules if they are to find Mr Right – and those rules, contained in self-help manuals such as *The Rules*, encourage women to play down their rational, self-determined 'feminist' self for a retrograde unthreatening feminine one.

Their quest for monogamy and the rights of the smug marrieds who they despise is embraced because the heterosexual alternatives are still fraught with danger for the singleton. Just as Isadora Wing latterly reinterprets her fantasy of the 'zipless fuck' with a complete stranger, when she is sexually assaulted on a train, these women know that other values come between them and any quest for sexual self-determination. These women, like the characters in Candace Bushnell's *Sex and the City* (1996), flaunt their sexual independence only to prove themselves unremittingly at the mercy of men and men's power to characterise their independence as neurosis.

I agree with Rosalind Coward who asserted over twenty years ago that women-centred novels are by no means feminist ones (57), and we must be wary in the case of work by Fielding and her contemporaries of implying that we judge them by perspectives which they have not attempted to reproduce. Yet contemporary women's novels about women's lives are 'about' feminism in that if they offer any commentary on today's women's lives it is inevitably ripe for feminist interpretation and investigation – especially when a novel such as *Bridget Jones's Diary* breaks into the bestseller list and appears to have a substantial global appeal to women. While Coward is clear about the divide between political feminism and popular fiction, nowadays we might feel moved to acknowledge that the line of demarcation can blur. Sometimes 'literary' fiction has misguidedly been assumed to be more capable of the political than the popular, yet popular fiction, within the confines of often quite strict boundaries, is able to be playfully subversive. The assumptions which underpin the notion that literary = serious and/or political, and popular = sensationalist and/or exploitative have unfortunately dogged feminism in the past and resulted in a rather muted reception of those works of popular fiction, such as *Fear of Flying*, which do speak in a feminist register – if a strategically 'flawed' one.

If we recognise in the *Bridget Jones* phenomenon a new sub-genre of romantic writing, we must also recognise that it does not capitalise upon the opportunity to revolutionise the romance. If we are to identify a Zeitgeist from a tendency to portray the single woman in one particular way across several aspects of popular culture, the clear message would be that young women reject feminism for the 'empowerment' of creating oneself in the image of 'magazine woman' in a close parallel of the injunctions to women offered by Helen Gurley Brown in 1962. Yet there have to be more complicated readings than this which avoid the trap of seeing women either duped into one representation or liberated by another, and these would need to be set in the context of a new sexual politics, some would even term it a 'third wave', which attempts to remodel feminism to suit a younger generation, a generation educated into post-structuralism and with slightly more interrogative views on identity than early second-wavers, with a much more inclusive and sophisticated approach to popular cultural forms. These are women who are not duped by the glossy-magazine-speak of their day, but like their foresisters have to live out the realities of a patriarchal ideology which lags behind the progress suggested by the material gains in women's lives.

The bleak cityscapes drawn in chick lit show women inhabiting the world that today's young people are supposed to covet – careers in the media, or publishing, high disposable incomes and an active social life – yet single life does not lose its association with loneliness, or failure. This speaks to a critical gap between the ambitions of Isadora in *Fear of Flying* and the prospects for Bridget Jones. Isadora's attempts to redefine heterosexual desire and to move beyond the suffocating confines of the marital-style relationship are not yet successful by the end of the novel, always deferred; in *Bridget Jones's Diary* the ending confirms the primacy of this relationship and with it the seemingly necessary conflict of gender interests. *Fear of Flying* identified gaps and problems in the rhetoric of feminism – especially in its failure to offer a positive model of heterosexual desire which might be enabling to women who wanted to rethink their relationships, but needed help imagining what the new man would be like (and help persuading men that the new man was a good idea).

There is now even more need to offer a feminist political perspective to women which undermines the glib suggestion that it is feminism which has made women miserable singletons. Feminism as a political identity which brings with it social responsibility is set in tension with a variant model which characterises female power as residing in control of oneself and one's life choices, most notably expressed in the 'freedom' to consume, to dress in a sexually alluring way, and to continue to desire Darcy. Just as *Fear of Flying* and other feminist confessional novels exposed the tensions in the theory and practice of being a feminist, the singleton novel announces the success of feminism (through its portrayal of large numbers of university-educated women in the workplace) and simultaneously perpetuates the notion that equality, in any formal sense between the sexes, is misguided, anti-erotic and possibly against nature. In *Bridget Jones's Diary* the war between feminism (represented by references to *Backlash* and Sharon's occasional rantings) and the self-help manuals is won by the fact that Bridget and her friends embrace pragmatic solutions to their dilemmas every time. The novel is an interesting account of how women are encouraged to internalise style doctrines and calls to self-improvement, but it can only project us backwards in time as it recalls the pragmatism both Helen Gurley Brown and Jane Austen may have adopted under quite different historical conditions.

Works Cited

Bushnell, Candace. *Sex and the City* (London: Abacus, 1996).
Coward, Rosalind. ' "This Novel Changes Lives": Are Women's Novels Feminist Novels?', *Feminist Review*, vol. 5 (1980): 53–64
Fielding, Helen. *Bridget Jones's Diary* (London: Picador, 1996).
Forma, Aminatta. 'Sellout' in *On the Move: Feminism for a New Generation*, ed. Natasha Walter (London: Virago, 1999). 135–51
Gurley Brown, Helen. *Sex and the Single Girl* (New York: Bernard Geiss, 1962).
Hoff Sommers, Christine. *The War Against Boys: How Misguided Feminism is Hurting Our Young Men* (New York: Simon & Schuster, 2000).
Joannou, Maroula. *Contemporary Women's Writing: From the Golden Notebook to The Color Purple* (Manchester: Manchester University Press, 2000).
Jong, Erica. *Fear of Flying* (London: Grafton, 1974).
Nathan, Melissa. *Pride, Prejudice and Jasmin Field* (London: Piatkus, 2000).
Sage, Lorna. *Women in the House of Fiction: Post-war Women Novelists* (London: Macmillan, 1992).
Templin, Charlotte. *Feminism and the Politics of Literary Reputation: The Example of Erica Jong* (Lawrence, KS: University Press of Kansas, 1995).
Walter, Natasha. *The New Feminism* (London: Little, Brown, 1998).
Weir, Arabella. *Does My Bum Look Big in This?* (London: Coronet, 1997).

Pat Barker and the Languages of Region and Class

MAROULA JOANNOU

At the end of Kingsley Amis's novel *The Old Devils* (1986) a woman character moves to Cleveland and writes to her friends about her new life in the north to be met with disbelief: 'The theatre, what's she talking about? In Middlesbrough? It can't be the theatre as *civilised folk* think of it?' (379). Condescension of this type is predicated on the divorce of the concerns of the English regions from those of the geographical centres of power. This is not a distinction that has always prevailed and is, moreover, one that the writings of the great nineteenth-century women regional novelists, George Eliot, Charlotte Brontë and Elizabeth Gaskell, contest. In subtitling *Middlemarch* 'A Study of Provincial Life' and exploring the ramifications of the Great Reform Act on the town's inhabitants George Eliot in no way assumed the affairs of the provinces to be any less significant for the socially engaged novelist than those of the metropolis.

This essay is concerned with Pat Barker as a significant novelist of class and region. However, to designate Barker a regional novelist, a novelist whose home town of Thornaby-on-Tees is so obscure that locating it accurately would defeat most of her readers, is not to assume that she has little to say about aspects of human existence that are not associated with any particular *topos*. What follows is a reading of Barker's first two novels, *Union Street* (1982) and *Blow Your House Down* (1984), in which I depart from the critical consensus that her early works, with their 'narrow' focus on communities of women in a remote and economically disadvantaged area of the north-east of England, belie the complexity of her later critically acclaimed *Regeneration* trilogy: *Regeneration* (1991), *The Eye in the Door* (1993) and *The Ghost Road* (1995). Barker is interested in how society inflicts psychic damage on men and women, and in exploring the reverberations of violence upon the family and the community. These concerns are not only the hallmarks of her later writing, in which the reader is invited to reflect on how ideas about masculinity are profoundly altered by the experience of the 1914–18 war, but also shape and inform her fiction from the very beginning of her career.

Both *Union Street* and *Blow Your House Down* are in their different ways modern 'condition of England' novels. In the nineteenth-century the name *Union Street* was used to denote the street in which the workhouse was located and, to those in the know, was synonymous with destitution and degradation. The north-east of England where Barker's first two novels are set is emblematic of late-twentieth-century industrial decline, reflected in the demise of the traditional heavy industries like coal, iron and steel for which there is no longer a place in a new Britain in which market forces have been allowed free reign.

The character of George Harrison in *Union Street*, bereft of identity and purpose after a lifetime on the factory production line, is a compelling study of desolation. Barker's early writings offer representations of working-class communities that reflect what Habermas has termed the importance of 'vital heritages' while avoiding the dangers of an impoverished 'traditionalism' (105–8). Yet *Blow Your House Down* and *Union Street* differ radically from much working-class writing that also depicts what Raymond Williams calls 'the unpleasant, the exposed, the sordid' aspects of experience (*The Long Revolution* 301), largely because the masculinist ethos that distinguishes much of this fiction is absent in Barker's early texts, which often focus largely on women and their domestic concerns.

The publication of *Union Street* followed the election in 1979 of Margaret Thatcher's government with its famed indifference to the well-being of labour's northern heartlands and the plight of their ailing manufacturing industries. The indicators of this government's authoritarian and centralising intentions were already present at the time of *Union Street*'s appearance in 1982, the year in which Britain went to war with Argentina over the Falklands. *Union Street* was closely followed by the publication of *Blow Your House Down* in 1984. By invoking a set of class- and community-based values, which offer a marked contrast to those of the metropolis, both novels affirm the importance of regional and provincial difference, dissonance and dissent, thus counterbalancing the homogenising and centralising influence of national government.

Barker's characters are not socially excluded – it is a function of centralising cultural dominance to assume that the poor are excluded from society – but have their own society. Nevertheless, they inhabit what Carolyn Steedman terms 'the old defensive culture of poverty' in a divided Britain (108–9). They are, moreover, subjected to everyday deprivation and humiliations that will be unfamiliar to Barker's more affluent readers, and that have the power to challenge and shock those habituated to the literary representation of more privileged lives.

The prostitutes in *Blow Your House Down* have met in the Palmerston public house, with its presiding matriarch, for as long as anyone can remember. They move in a 'nightly gavotte' up and down the terraced streets named after forgotten Victorian statesmen until they reach the viaduct where they ply their trade (9). The urban neighbourhood in *Blow Your House Down* signifies far more than it can ever do in areas that lack its long and vibrant history of social cohesion. Melbourne Terrace, for example, is not the street one woman would have chosen after her divorce but it is all she can afford and 'none of her stuck-up in laws would've been seen dead walking down a street like that' (23). Though the setting is post-industrial the milieu of both *Union Street* and *Blow Your House Down* is oddly unaffected by the signs of consumerism or modernity. While the presence of the supermarket and the car distinguish the urban streets of both novels from the earlier proletarian fiction of the 1930s, there are few visible reminders on the landscape of the affluence of the 1960s.

The racial composition of the working class in *Blow Your House Down* has, however, altered somewhat although the neighbourhood is still overwhelmingly white. The few Pakistani immigrants there are appear to have no names and form no part of what Williams calls, in *The Country and the City*, a 'knowable community' (59). Moreover, applying that acid test of neighbourliness, they cannot be called on when children need to be looked after at short notice. As Stuart Hall has put it, race is 'the modality in which class is "lived", the medium through which class relations are experienced, the form in which it is appropriated and "fought through"' (341). This is exemplified in *Union Street* in which 'the constant persecution' of a black woman who seemed 'reasonably quiet, anxious to pass unnoticed' appears to be motivated by the insecurity of a white woman whose sister has 'had three to a nigger' and has been left to bring them up as a single parent on social security (82).

One way in which the challenge to the centre and its values is expressed is through Barker's use of the vernacular. As Eric Hobsbawm has pointed out, national languages are almost always semi-artificial constructs and are 'virtually invented'. He argues that they are 'usually attempts to devise a standardised idiom out of a multiplicity of nationally spoken idioms, which are thereafter downgraded to dialect' (54). Moreover, the *lingua franca* of a standardised written language and literature has often had a tenuous relationship to the speech habits of large sections of the population. The vocabulary of her native Teesside – 'scrumping', 'sodding', 'bairn', 'juddering', 'skint', 'nowt' – weaves through Barker's prose and speaks of her refusal to make linguistic concessions to a national or international readership unschooled in the vernacular.

The picture of the north that Barker offers is radically different from the anodyne impression of northern life that, according to Stuart Laing, had earlier been assimilated into the new national (southern and London-based) culture of Britain with little difficulty (219–20). There is an elegiac tone in Barker's depiction of the townscape of the industrial north-east, an area notorious for the aggrandising ambitions of local Labour politicians and their hated new developments like the Cragg Estate in *The Century's Daughter* (1986), 'trapped between two motorways with every entrance blocked by concrete bollards' (11).[1] The most famous of these municipal racketeers, T. Dan Smith, was found guilty of corruption and imprisoned. One character in *Union Street* points out that her local council had managed to do more damage to the environment in one year than Hitler accomplished in five. Yet the memory of what once existed cannot be erased. The sense of history and cultural loss that permeates working-class memory – 'We had pride. We were poor, but we were *proud*' (*The Century's Daughter* 129) – goes hand-in-hand with what are sometimes termed urban class geographies, and is invoked by Barker's older characters. In *The Century's Daughter* 84-year-old Liza is the 'sole remaining inhabitant of a street scheduled for demolition. Isolated, helpless, threatened with eviction if she did not agree to conform and get out' (1). Sadness and incomprehension accompany the wanton demolition of the familiar streets, houses and landmarks, which is depicted in all of Barker's early fiction.

The production lines of the factories in *Union Street* and *Blow Your House Down* speak of the altering nature of work and of new patterns of consumption but, above all, of the post-industrial feminisation of the labour force that has characterised late-twentieth-century capitalism. The cake factory in *Union Street* and the frozen-chicken factory in *Blow Your House Down* – used shortly afterwards and to similar effect in the film *Letter to Brezhnev* (1985) – take the place of the shipyard, the coal mine, the engineering factory, and the steel works of earlier working-class fiction. The sense of the world 'out-of-sorts' in both novels is in part determined by the mass production of items for consumption that have been traditionally been produced in the home and in the countryside. Instead of being individually baked in a domestic context the shop-bought cake becomes a manufactured industrial commodity. Instead of running around 'naturally' in a farmyard the factory-processed chicken

---

[1] Published in the United States as *Liza's England*.

becomes an inanimate object moving at speed on a conveyer belt. Although the factory women are often the main family breadwinners, their histories and values are significantly different from the traditional male workers in industry whose roles they have assumed. In *Blow Your House Down* the tedium and alienation of assembly-line work is broken not, as in *Saturday Night and Sunday Morning* (1960), by the camaraderie of male banter but, unexpectedly, by a chorus of women's voices singing. As Paulina Palmer has pointed out, the chicken factory is a microcosm of patriarchal power relations (89). But it is also a microcosm of class relations. The denaturalised woman whose poverty binds her body to the factory machine is the carrier of the generalised injuries of her class in ways that are analogous to the denaturalised woman whose poverty drives her to prostitute her body on the streets.

Women are forbidden to enter the room in which men kill the chickens. Instead, they remove the chickens' guts and force their legs inside. In *Blow Your House Down* there is a strained analogy between the prostitutes and the chickens: 'When you're just stuck there you feel like a bloody battery hen' (125). The fate of the chickens lying on a conveyer belt 'naked with plump thighs' is that which awaits the prostitutes. This is a comparison to which Barker returns later in the novel when the murderer frenziedly scoops up a handful of feathers from an old mattress on which a dead woman lies.

The historical context for *Blow Your House Down* is the 'Yorkshire Ripper' case in which a deranged serial killer, Peter Sutcliffe, murdered thirteen women and wounded seven others in cities in the north of England between 1975 and 1981, holding the nation in the grip of terror about where he would strike next and who would be his next victim. The police told Alma Reviers, who had just been arrested in a car in Sheffield with Sutcliffe and was in danger of being his next target, that they were not interested in her, they were interested in him. As Nicole Ward Jouve has pointed out, nowhere in the massive press coverage which the Yorkshire Ripper case received do women feature as people but as bodies on which male violence has left its inscription (51).

Blow Your House Down is about the murder of two prostitutes by an unidentified misogynist who mutilates their bodies in much the same way as Sutcliffe mutilated the bodies of his victims. The third section of the novel is written in the first person by the lover of one of the murdered women who extracts her vengeance. Barker's Freudian investment in understanding the psyches of men who are prompted to act violently – *Regeneration* is concerned with traumatised participants in the 1914 war – is already visible and prompts her to risk affronting feminist sensibilities by writing briefly from the point of view of her serial killer, a risk she had taken earlier in depicting the perspective of a paedophile in *Union Street*. As its title would indicate, *Blow Your House Down* is a modern urban fairy tale in which the victims who have been terrorised finally put pay to the big, bad wolf. But at this point the novel also takes on the Nietzschean overtones of the book's preface: 'Whoever fights monsters, should see to it that in the process he does not become a monster.'

What do we know of Sutcliffe's victims? One of his married victims, Emily Jackson, took to prostitution to take her mind off the death of a child. Of the others, Wilma McCann, Irene Richardson and Vera Milward became prostitutes because they were left alone to fend for their young children. Their life histories are not dissimilar to those of Kath and Brenda in *Blow Your House Down*. The early chapters of the novel describe how Brenda began soliciting in order to support her three children after her husband deserted her with 'bills stuffed away all over the place, pushed down the sides of the sofa, under the carpet' (19). Just as the public mood changed when Sutcliffe switched his attention from prostitutes to 'respectable' women so in *Blow Your House Down* it is the assault upon Maggie, a 'respectable' middle-aged factory worker going about her normal business, that signifies the change in the attitudes of the police to the rapist's victims.

Barker contests the sentimental myths of working-class life that present heroic images of men while ignoring other aspects of gendered experience. For example, working-class women may attach great importance to acquiring material goods for their children because such possessions symbolise the security, comfort and status that they were themselves denied. In *Union Street* this means Clark shoes rather than cheap rubber plimsoles and the purchase of a doll that is as large as the child for whom it is intended. If the formative class-based attitudes of warmth, supportiveness and resilience are transmitted from the mother to her child so equally are potentially damaging class-based anxieties, selfishness, jealousies, insecurities and resentments.

The psychic make-up of the women in Barker's early fictions is always derived from their own relationship to their mothers. Her women are, in the main, caring mothers, although this does not necessarily make them 'good' mothers as the term might normally be understood. However, the fact that in *Blow Your House Down* the women support their children through prostitution questions the pieties to which British cultural historians, most notably Richard Hoggart, have often been wedded, which equate the one consistent female figure in working-class representation, 'Our Mum', with sexual abstinence and moral virtue (35). In bringing up their children single-handedly, these women refuse a male-defined reality and refute the conventional notion that a woman's status and self-esteem depend on the security that men bestow. What the community values in its women in *Union Street* is their strength, pride and resilience. The 'weakest' women in Barker's early fiction, those whose behaviour incurs the disapproval of their peers, are often the women whose need for male approval is the strongest, and who are the most reluctant to challenge male authority where the interests of their children are concerned.

Barker carefully avoids any suggestion that the psychic structures of all working-class mothers are identical and is concerned with the indicators of particularity and difference. Her interest in psychoanalysis, which becomes much more pronounced in her later writing, is expressed through her probing exploration of the troubled realm of mother–daughter relationships, which Adrienne Rich once termed 'the great unwritten story', that is, the cathexis between mother and daughter that may produce both 'the deepest mutuality and the most painful estrangement' (225–6). These relationships are neither simplified nor romanticised. In *Union Street* Iris King feels different things about her daughters at different times: 'Sometimes they were her little girls who must have everything that she lacked. But increasingly too, they appeared as rivals who might be resented for having more' (195). Kelly's mother puts her own need for a relationship with a man above the needs of her daughter whom she neglects. In turn, the child feels distaste for a mother whose 'hard exterior had cracked to reveal an inner corruption' (59).

Working-class writing is still lamentably under-represented within the English literary tradition. As late as 1982, the year in which *Union Street* was published, Raymond Williams was still able to argue that 'the simplest descriptive novel about working-class life is already, by being written, a positive and significant cultural intervention. For it is not, even yet what a novel is supposed to be' ('Working Class' 111). But there is a theoretical problem for feminists about what aspects of working-class existence are represented and how. There are, moreover, dangers in invoking the old working-class solidarities without asking the question, whose work was it that kept the old neighbourhoods alive? This is a question that feminists might wish to posit as the equivalent to Brecht's famous question, who built the pyramids? In *Wigan Pier Revisited: Politics and Poverty in the 80s*, Bea Campbell's odyssey through the working-class communities of the north, Campbell retraces the steps Orwell had taken in 1937 to reveal the importance of women whose interests were never articulated within the patriarchal organisations of the labour movement or in the iconography of the working class (97).

The isolated figure walking the city streets across a range of working-class fiction from Walter Brierley's *Sandwich Man* (1937) to James Kelman's *The Burn* (1991) – the working-class counterpart of the *flaneur* or voyeuristic stroller in the city – is an unemployed or under-employed man. The usual distinction between the public and private space put forward by Habermas and others is rendered problematic by the existence of prostitutes (the only women streetwalkers in the modern city) for whom the public spaces of the city constitute a regular place of work. As one character in *Blow Your House Down* points out, 'you do a lot of walking in this job' (94). Moreover, *Union Street* and *Blow Your House Down* inflect the socialist-realist traditions of working-class fiction by their concentration on a *group* of working-class women rather than the usual male hero or even on one woman protagonist. In *Blow Your House Down* this is a stigmatised occupational group: prostitutes. The seven chapters of *Union Street* are variations on the seven ages of woman in which each story represents a part of the collective experience of the female sex as a whole. The book ends with the oldest inhabitant, Alice, and the youngest, Kelly, meeting near a park bench and symbolically reaching out to touch hands.

The figure of the prostitute, often the 'tart with a heart', has been used to expose the hypocrisies of patriarchal sexual morality in a wide variety of cultural representations from *Camille* to *Taxi Driver*. How, then, might one argue that Barker's representations are different? In the first place, Barker follows the lead of the English Collective of Prostitutes in the 1970s in arguing that there is essentially no difference between the 'respectable' woman and the woman who earns her livelihood through prostitution. Secondly, Barker insists – and perhaps insists somewhat disingenuously – that prostitution is just a job like any other, albeit more dangerous than some. The characters in *Blow Your House Down* are all represented as 'ordinary' women who have chosen to work in the sex trade for a variety of reasons. It is Brenda's shocked realisation that any one of her neighbours who works as a prostitute can earn more in a night than she has left at the end of a week which makes her abandon the chicken factory for more lucrative work. The figure of the pimp – the puppet-master behind the scenes controlling the women's movements for his own gain – is also a curious absence in the novel. The prostitutes appear to control themselves.

Only one has a partner who abuses her sexually and uses her as a meal-ticket. Neither is Barker much interested in such factors as coercion by men, low self-esteem, drug dependency, alcoholism and histories of sexual abuse that are often put forward to explain why women enter prostitution. As one woman says, 'I am not in it because I'm a poor, deprived, inadequate, half-witted woman, whatever some people might like to think, I'm in it because it suits me' (112). Moreover, the work is probably no worse than the work done by the men with whom the prostitutes consort and no more alienating than the work of their sisters on the factory production line. The compensations are the company, the excitement, and the enhanced purchasing power: 'she had the best dressed kids in the street. That meant a lot' (50).

The analogy between marriage and prostitution that the novel makes is one commonly found in feminist theoretical writing. In so far as it entails sexual services performed for one's keep, *Blow Your House Down* represents marriage as little different from prostitution:

> What got her was the hypocrisy of it all. They went on about being married, but when you got right down to it, past the white weddings and the romance and all that, what they really thought was that if you're getting on your back for a fella, he ought to pay. That was what they really thought. And where did that leave you? You might just as well be standing on a street corner in bloody Northgate – at least it'd be honest. (20)

As Peter Hitchcock has put it, 'while class is constantly being rethought *vis-a-vis* the social, it is generally undertheorised in terms of the literary, as if what is problematic for the social scientist is transparent or inconsequential for the literary critic' (20). This is certainly true of feminist literary criticism, which has often responded creatively to the challenges of race while maintaining a decorous silence in relation to the obdurate realities of class. In *Class Fictions*, an attempt to theorise the relations between gender and class in literature, Pamela Fox has argued that the private sphere is the place where 'we can glimpse the greatest anxieties and longings concerning working-class culture and writing – where we can begin to track the debilitating, as well as empowering effects of both marginality and incorporation' (200–1). In both *Union Street* and *Blow Your House Down* the most important concerns of working-class women are located in private life and especially in their concern for their children, whether or not these women have work outside the home.

The solidarity in the novel is predicated on new configurations of gender rather than the older class solidarities. The women's sense of gender solidarity is compounded in *Blow Your House Down* by the threat to life posed by an unknown, marauding man which makes *all* men (even those whom have hitherto been trusted implicitly) suspect as potential killers. The prostitutes speculate that the murderer is almost certainly someone's 'regular'. Moreover, he may be someone with an occupation like a taxi driver or a policeman to whom they have turned for protection in the past. Fear momentarily changes the character of the sexual transactions on which the women's livelihood depends. These cease to be individual exchanges and become collective arrangements whereby all the women agree to work in pairs for their mutual safety.

The image that prevails is not the familiar one of the nuclear family (which is conspicuous by its absence) in both novels but of female determination and self-sufficiency; of a single parent trying as hard as she can to bring up her children successfully on her own. Yet neither *Union Street* nor *Blow Your House Down* show communities of women formed by choice rather than necessity. Barker affirms the bonds between the mothers and children from which men are excluded at the same time as she decries their emotional consequences. It is their mother and their grandmother whom the children visit in the Harrison household in which the husband, George, is made to feel emotionally redundant. The respect for pregnant women and for children, shared by the women in this novel, contrasts markedly with the indifference of men. It is her female friends who take one woman to hospital and care for her in *Blow Your House Down* when she is abandoned on the doorstep by the man she was with just as she is about to go into labour. Another's advanced state of pregnancy offers her no protection from the indignities of a prolonged and brutal gang rape.

The privacy that allows the lower middle classes to hide behind the anonymity offered by the suburban street does not exist in poor neighbourhoods. As Williams notes in his essay 'Region and Class in the Novel', 'the isolation of private individuals, whose lives can be closely and intimately explored as if there were no wider social life, is evidently dependent on the social existence of individuals for whom power or money has created the possibility of *practical* distancing or displacement' (62). In poor communities such as those depicted in Barker's novels association is everything and there can be no such voluntary distancing or displacement.

One example of this is the rape of young Kelly Brown in *Union Street*, which cannot be kept secret from her neighbours for long. At first, the adults in the street respond collectively, showering the child with sweets and presents. The other children are carefully instructed to play with Kelly as if things were normal and to ask no questions, but the whispering by which the community polices itself internally never stops. Francis Mulhern has pointed out that '"communities" are not *places* but *practices* of collective identification' (86). In this small world the desire to be respected, the need to acquire a good reputation, or to avoid being tarnished by a bad one, are of paramount importance. In *Union Street*, Iris King 'knew she was respected and her family was respected. Her reputation mattered more to her than anything else' (196). Brenda King's furtive abortion is undertaken at her mother's behest in order to avoid the shame, disapproval and humiliation in which the infraction of the community's unwritten codes would result. What the backstreet abortionist is asked to put at risk is the life of a five-month pregnant teenager in order to keep the family's hard-won reputation intact. As Beverley Skeggs has suggested, the powerful investment in respectability that working-class women sometimes display is often their only way of distancing themselves from the sexualised images of women's bodies that imperil their safety (4). It is these images that Iris, who was brought up in a brothel area, knows only too well and which come back to haunt her as she retreads the derelict streets of her childhood to procure a kitchen-table abortionist for her daughter.

Barker explores the politics of the body with acuity. The prostitutes in *Blow Your House Down* depend for their livelihood on the availability of their bodies so the relationship of the body to these women's identities becomes a prototype for larger cultural experience and meanings. The social resonates insistently in the language in which the sexed particularities of the woman's body is described: 'If you want to run your cunt as a soup kitchen, that's entirely up to you but don't do it here' (46). One prostitute reflects wryly that she is as likely to catch silicosis (a disease from coal dust that miners contract) from one of her clients as venereal disease. Their bodies constrict Barker's characters in ways that are analogous to the constrictions imposed by the small streets in which they have grown up. In *Union Street*, for example, Alice Bell's home is 'almost an extension of her own body' (234). However, the body can sometimes distract from the hidden causes of a woman's oppression, and can be held solely responsible for problems, such as unwanted pregnancy, that have social and economic – as well as biological – origins and dimensions.

There is a particular tension in Barker's feminist corporeality between the body as maternal and the body as sexual. As one character in *Blow Your House Down* comments, 'Always remember your mouth's your own. When he's shot his muck you've got to go back and kiss them bairns' (46). Moreover, the body has the power to tell its own narrative that contradicts the written or spoken word. The fact that Blonde Dinah in *Union Street* has once given birth is not widely known in the neighbourhood, but the stretch marks on her naked body speak of a personal history that cannot be refuted or concealed. What characterises the neo-Lawrentian emission of bodily fluids that leave such a powerful impression on any reader of *Union Street* and *Blow Your House Down* is their seepage and their alarming visibility as they leak into the social domain. The substances produced by the body, such as phlegm, blood, excrement, urine and saliva, are visible as both the lubricants of sex and the indicators of sickness and are invested with power and danger in the novels because, in the age of sexually transmitted diseases, their lack of confinement threatens to contaminate the wider community.

The focus in *Blow Your House Down* is not simply on women's sexuality but on women's sexuality that is visibly paraded as deviant. This is most striking in relation to the specific sexual practices men require prostitutes to perform in the novel and that they do not require of their wives. The notion of corrupted or deviant sexuality is contained within the very definition of prostitution itself. The sexualised body is the available body of the economically disadvantaged woman. It is also the denaturalised woman's body that has been trained to behave in ways that are profitable and to desist from modes of expression that are not. One woman laments that she can no longer permit herself to laugh lest her client might think that she is laughing at him. Thus sexual disorder has a synechdochic relationship to the problem of industrial disorder in Barker's novel and a class critique is mapped upon the symbolic body of gender. Yet if the bodies of the women in *Blow Your House Down* have been abjected and reified, the focus on a woman's potential to give birth, and particularly to give birth to daughters, remains a source of hope. What Barker's early fiction illustrates is a type of biological materialism in which the power to ensure the survival and continuity of others like oneself acquires particular meanings in relation to class and nation precisely because birth takes place in the context of a well-established community. This is the 'knowable community' whose values and survival are under threat. Thus the maternal narrative intersects with the narrative of class survival and, because the survival of the community depends on its ability to reproduce itself, children such as Kelly Brown in *Union Street* represent the future and are uncritically accepted within the fold of the 'knowable community even if their mothers have transgressed. In giving birth women acquire the power and status that they are denied in the context of a declining industrial nation in which working-class men have been rendered power-less. If paid work is the *sine qua non* of Barker's male characters – Barker writes with sympathy of George Harrison choosing to go out to work as a toilet cleaner rather than to sit idly at home – fecundity endows her women their deepest significance and purpose. In impoverished com-munities the creation of new life is almost always perceived as a sym-bolic triumph over adversity.

The story of Lisa Goddard in *Union Street*, for example, registers a woman's complicated emotional responses to a birth of her new baby. This is at first an unwanted burden, incessantly demanding the love and support of which the mother is herself bereft. Yet 'the thought that inside that tiny body was a womb like hers with eggs waiting to be released, caused the same fear, the same wonder' (139). The vignette ends on a note of jubilant acceptance, the more compelling because of Lisa's former ambivalence, and because the character's identification with her baby, and the maternal role that is expected of her, has hitherto been resisted: 'My *Daughter*' (139).

Works Cited

Amis, Kingsley. *The Old Devils* (London: Penguin, 1986).

Barker, Pat. *Blow Your House Down* (London: Virago, 1984).

———. *The Century's Daughter* (London: Virago, 1986).

———. *Union Street* (London: Virago, 1982).

Campbell, Bea. *The Road to Wigan Pier Revisited: Poverty and Politics in the 80s* (London: Virago, 1984).

Fox, Pamela. *Class Fictions: Shame and Resistance in the British Working Class Novel 1890–1945* (Durham, NC: Duke University Press, 1994).

Habermas, Jürgen. 'Modernity: An Incomplete Project' in *Postmodernism: A Reader*, ed. Thomas Docherty (Hemel Hempstead: Harvester Wheatsheaf, 1993). 98–109

Hall, Stuart. *Sociological Theories: Race and Colonisation* (Paris: UNESCO, 1980).

Hitchcock, Peter. 'They Must be Represented? Problems in Theories of Working-Class Representation', *PMLA*, vol. 115 (January 2000): 20–32.

Hobsbawm, Eric. *Nations and Nationalism Since 1780* (Cambridge: Cambridge University Press, 1980).

Hoggart, Richard. *The Uses of Literacy* (London: Chatto & Windus, 1957).

Laing, Stuart. *Representations of Working-Class Life 1957–1964* (Basingstoke: Macmillan, 1986).

Mulhern, Francis. 'Towards 2000, or News From You-Know-Where' in *Raymond Williams: Critical Perspectives*, ed. Terry Eagleton (Cambridge: Polity, 1989). 67–94

Palmer, Paulina. *Contemporary Women's Fiction: Narrative Practice and Feminist Theory* (Hemel Hempstead: Harvester Wheatsheaf, 1989).

Rich, Adrienne. *Of Woman Born: Motherhood as Experience and Institution* (London: Virago, 1976).

Skeggs, Beverley. *Formations of Class and Gender* (London: Sage, 1997).

Steedman, Carolyn. *Landscape for a Good Woman: A Story of Two Lives* (London: Virago, 1986).

Ward Jouve, Nicole. *The Streetcleaner: The Yorkshire Ripper Case on Trial* (London: Marian Boyars, 1986).

Williams, Raymond. *The Country and the City* (London: Chatto & Windus, 1973).

———. *The Long Revolution* (London: Chatto & Windus, 1961).

———. 'Region and Class in the Novel' in *The Uses of Fiction: Essays on the Novel in Honour of Arnold Kettle*, ed. Douglas Jefferson and Graham Martin (Milton Keynes: Open University Press, 1982). 59–69

———. 'Working Class, Proletarian, Socialist: Problems in Some Welsh Novels' in *The Socialist Novel in Britain: Towards the Recovery of a Tradition*, ed. H. Gustav Klaus (Brighton: Harvester, 1982). 110–21

'Making Sorrow Speak': Maggie Gee's Novels

JOHN SEARS

Since 1981 Maggie Gee has been publishing novels which explore the vicissitudes of English social life from a perspective that is perhaps best characterised as that of a compassionate humanist feminism, informed by a subtle critical consciousness and by a perceptive analysis of the social and cultural effects of political changes in English society in the latter part of the twentieth century. Her work examines the lives of characters (who are, for the most part, traditionally realised) and their interactions with others, with institutions (notably social and domestic) and with social phenomena that metonymically constitute the fabric of England and motivate myths of Englishness, myths that constitute the background to and provide the texture for the novels. Gee's novels explore freedoms, individualisms, responsibilities and duties (always plural concepts, in opposition to their monological mythologisations in the wider culture) and the tensions between them, as well as the pains, triumphs, hazards and achievements which delineate and circumscribe individual lives.

Gee's novels have received little serious critical attention. They are eminently comparable to the works of writers contemporary with her career, but constitute an output that is sufficiently diverse and 'individual' to resist easy critical classification. They are not as shockingly magical-realist as the work of Angela Carter (although their political motivation and their palpable anger at injustice are similar); not as polemical as Jeanette Winterson's writings (although Gee's polemical moments carry comparable force and validity); their realism is not historically authenticated like that of Pat Barker; and they are not as clearly motivated by the need to deconstruct the foundational myths of patriarchy as the writings of the 'Tales I Tell My Mother' group (although comparisons with the works of Michèle Roberts and Sara Maitland can be made). Instead, Gee's novels, considered together, constitute a deliberate resistance to literary orthodoxies, preferring instead to ground their analyses in the socially familiar, the culturally conventional and the ideologically reassuring, in order to insistently expose and interrogate the limits of the 'ordinariness' they so meticulously detail.

From being positioned, in the early 1980s, as an 'experimental' writer, and therefore connected with the young generation at the forefront of English fictional postmodernism exemplified by writers like Julian Barnes and Martin Amis, Gee's writing (which, of course, refuses to fully conform to such a position) has subsequently been frequently praised by reviewers for its 'quality' without being fully considered in terms of its projects[1]. In *The English Novel in History*, Steven Connor not only offers a useful critical framework in comparing Gee to Virginia Woolf, but also reads *The Burning Book* (1983) as a sophisticated metafictional meditation which combines its own sense of apocalyptic historical finality (in its representation of nuclear holocaust) with an analysis of the formal fictional problems involved in such a representation (238–45). In the background of Connor's discussion lie John Barth's notions of the literatures of 'exhaustion' and 'replenishment', with *The Burning Book* falling firmly into the latter category in spite of its formal and philosophical preoccupation with aspects of the former.[2] *The Burning Book* ironically closes Connor's account of the problematics of closure, fictional and historical, in contemporary English fiction, and this gives some indication of the position that Gee's novels occupy in relation to critical assessments of English fiction of the 1980s–1990s. Her writing resists critical attempts either to reduce it to the status of 'symptom' (of postmodernism, of metafiction, of exhaustion or replenishment) or to elevate it to full exemplary status – *The Burning Book* is an exploration both of closure and of the persistence of narrative; 'writing ends' is 'writing on', and Gee's political motivations suggest that her novels are less concerned with 'the sense of an ending', and more with exploring (in T. S. Eliot's sense) how endings become new beginnings. Similarly, the overt or residual experimentalism of Gee's novels is never simply formal or formally simple, but is, in Teresa Brennan's term, 'propositional' (xii–xiii); it 'puts forward', suggests, implies and ultimately provokes a critical response or set of responses to that which it represents. Such propositional fictional acts frequently constitute challenges to the conventional projects of fictional writing, of critical reading and to the conventional social ideologies in which both, Gee's novels suggest, are inevitably grounded.

---

[1] Reviews quoted on dustcovers of *Dying in Other Words* and *Lost Children*.
[2] John Barth, 'The Literature of Exhaustion' (1967) and 'The Literature of Replenishment: Postmodernist Fiction' (1980), both essays reprinted in his *The Friday Book: Essays and Other Non-Fiction* (1984): pp.64–76, pp.194–206.

Circular Time

What if nothing is lost, never lost entirely? – If time is a circle? – If
love could return. And lack, and need; meek, mute [. . .] The
unimaginable could be imagined. (*Lost Children* 320)

The challenge that Maggie Gee's novels pose to conventional social
ideologies is articulated in two ways: through the interrogation of what
Julia Kristeva calls 'epistemophillic thought' (198), and through a
rhetoric of repetition and circularity which seeks to question and
compromise the temporality and linearity of conventional narrative
forms. Kristeva's notion of 'Women's Time' informs Gee's exploration of
human lives as experienced through the representational temporality of
narrative, and the relations between these human lives and their
expression in narrative, as encoded in the formal structures of narrative
with which Gee's novels experiment, asking questions about how
emotional experiences transcend specific historical limits and contexts,
how the effects of the past transcend its specific discursive encoding as
history, how social experience transcends any reductive or simplistic
transcription into ideological or intellectual dogmas.

Through repetition and circularity – 'What if time is a circle?' –
Gee's narratives play with structure and linearity, constructing a fictional universe in which character consciousness, narrational point of
view and narrative mode coalesce and combine into reading experiences held together by formal frameworks which allow the working
through of a series of political and aesthetic propositions and inquiries.
Hélène Cixous, in an essay titled 'Extreme Fidelity', asks a series of
questions to do with human experience as it is encoded in the binary
structures of masculinity and femininity, which she refers to as
'economies':

What can we assign as descriptive traits to these economies? Let us
consider our behaviour in life with others, in all the major experiences
we encounter, which are the experiences of separation; the experiences, in love, of possession, of dispossession, of incorporation, and
non-incorporation, the experiences of mourning, of real mourning, all
the experiences which are governed by variable behaviours,
economies, structures. How do we lose? How do we keep? Do we
remember? Do we forget? (136)

These are the questions that Gee's novels typically ask, the experiences that they explore – 'experiences of separation' like the marital

separation which structures *Light Years* (1985), or the family split caused by a runaway daughter in *Lost Children* (1994); separations which divide individual subjects from the social worlds they inhabit, or divide present 'realities' from historical contexts; experiences of love and the pain of love in *Grace* (1988) and in*The Burning Book*; of 'real mourning' in the ethical project of *The Burning Book*, which seeks in some way to account for the historical trauma of Hiroshima and the threat, in the 1980s cold-war contexts, of its repetition. 'Making sorrow speak', the title of this essay, is taken from *Dying in Other Words* (1981), and expresses the intentionality of the fictionalised writer in this novel and, I suggest, of Gee's other novels, the intention to articulate in fictional form the experiences 'of real mourning' for that which is lost, 'dying', 'burning'; Cixous argues, with explicit reference to the novels of Clarice Lispector, but with relevance to the novels of Maggie Gee, that such writing can be read as 'an *immense book of respect, a book of the right distance*' (136), and this is precisely what Gee's writing performs – the enactment of respect, of the right distance in relation to the devastating social and psychological effects of contemporary political ideologies.

Gee's novels explore entropy and loss. Her narratives centre on loss as a formative and deformative experience in people's lives, and portray individual responses to this condition. These responses are in turn structured into narrative forms that postulate and explore the viability of an alternative ontology of recuperation in order to provoke in the reader and, perhaps, in wider society, what André Breton calls, in the second Manifesto of Surrealism, 'an attack of conscience' (123). Gee studied Breton while working for an MLitt on Surrealism; she also has a PhD in Twentieth Century Literature, and lists her main influences as Nabokov, Beckett and Woolf (she wrote the catalogue guide for the British Council exhibition on Woolf in 1991). These influences situate her writing on the cusp of what are conventionally understood as modernism and postmodernism, and we can detect the influence of other key artists in her writing – notably T. S. Eliot and Pierre Bonnard (whose paintings figure repeatedly in Gee's novels), but also cited or mentioned are Mondrian, Ernst, Grosz, Vuillard, O'Keefe, Picasso and Pound, Mansfield, Proust and Wells – a range of reference which demonstrates a pervasive concern with modernist literary and pictorial art as a discursive mode through which twentieth-century history – mainly post-war, mainly the histories of big, tragic events and their effects on individual lives – can be symbolised and in some way comprehended. Gee's novels are thus engaged in part in an extension of the broad modernist project of exploring forms of representation and their commensurability with rapidly changing, and yet structurally consistent, forms of experience.

The Pattern

On 28 June 1938, Walter Benjamin recorded a dream:

> I was in a labyrinth of stairs. This labyrinth was not entirely roofed over. I climbed; other stairways led downwards. On a landing I realised that I had arrived at a summit. A wide view of many lands opened up before me. I saw other men standing on other peaks. One of these men was suddenly seized by dizziness and fell. The dizziness spread; others were now falling from other peaks into the depths below. When I too became dizzy, I woke up. (93)

Gee's first novel, *Dying in Other Words*, can be read, along with her subsequent fictions, as an elaboration and extension of the allegorical import of Benjamin's dream as representing an aspiration to a position of total vision, modernist in impetus, tempered by a perhaps postmodern sense of an ending – dizziness and falling – and waking, perhaps, like Milton's Adam, to find the dream real. Gee's novels, in short, express modernist desires in postmodernist terms, and are concerned with the failure of various totalising aesthetic or political visions, or more specifically with what is excluded, marginalised, remaindered or forgotten by the dominant culture of the period and place to which the novels refer – England in the late twentieth century. Gee's novels are, in Fredric Jameson's terms, 'cognitive maps' which chart the relations between social ideologies and that which they repress (*Geopolitical* 3). These ideologies are most commonly the various forms of bourgeois Thatcherism of the 1980s and their residual effects on subsequent political frameworks in the 1990s (Majorism, Blairism), their various social manifestations and consequences, particularly for those ideologically or economically excluded from the dominant culture. The repressed of these ideologies is that which escapes their totalising aspirations and returns to undermine or challenge their hegemony – the 'others' of social consciousness, the seedy sides of decorous liberal surfaces, all that is excluded in the name of constructing a view of the world which is self-consistent. Postmodern aesthetics – the end of history or ideology, the triumph of textuality and formal self-reflexivity – come crashing up against the historical conditions of their own possibilities, as Gee's novels insist, in the decade of 'the end of society', upon a supposedly outmoded ethic of social commitment and responsibility. Her characters, in the maps of the fictions they inhabit, seek patterns which the narrative and the narrator seem to withhold: 'I lost my view and then I lost the pattern' (221), Moira writes in *Dying in Other Words*, before she's murdered – or did she fall from her own peak, her own position of total vision? As the novel tells us earlier, 'the key was the same to them all, and she made the pattern' (195). In *The Burning Book* Frank wonders, 'There must be some kind of pattern' (264), and Henry loves 'things that would come again, rare moments that made a pattern' (103); Harold, in *Light Years*, asks 'Was there a pattern?', recognising that 'everyone wants things to come again' (281); and in *Grace*, the eponymous heroine asks, 'At what point did all the little changes blend together and overturn the structure of things?'(133). All Gee's characters search for patterns in the fabrics of their lives and the worlds they inhabit, all search for repetition and the security of a return to structure, all express a desire to return to consistency from a world of hostile, unpredictable contingency. The patterns searched for reside, perhaps, in the social ethics embodied in fictional forms which constitute the novels themselves, novels which repeatedly assert historical materiality, grounding their postmodernist formal tendencies in a firm grasp on the effects and implications of grand ideological assertions. In reply to a slogan such as 'there is no such thing as society' Gee's novels insist that individual lives are enmeshed in a social fabric which it is one of the novel's responsibilities to reify and structure;[3] to various assertions of 'the end of ideology' Gee's novels assert the pervasive material influence – always negative – of particular ideologies on the quality of lived experience, particularly for those excluded from such world views;[4] to 'the end of history',[5] Gee's novels demonstrate the persistence of historical consciousness as the unconscious of the dehistoricising 1980s, returning like the cries of the hibakusha, the victims of Hiroshima, to haunt the decade as they haunt

[3] 'And, you know, there is no such thing as society. There are individual men and women, and there are families. And no government can do anything except through people, and people must look to themselves first. It's our duty to look after ourselves and then, also, to look after our neighbour.' Margaret Thatcher, interview in *Woman's Own*, 1987; cited in Kenneth Baker, ed. *The Faber Book of Conservatism* (1993), p.94.
[4] See Daniel Bell, *The End of Ideology* (1960).
[5] See Francis Fukuyama, *The End of History and The Last Man* (1992).

The Burning Book and, in different ways, *Grace*, insisting on the eternal present of historical time – 'If you think all that stuff is history . . .' (233), Lorna warns her daughter in *The Burning Book*.

The persistence of history, the material effects of abstract ideological assertions, and the prevalence of the social as the horizon of individual experience combine to orchestrate the political aesthetics of Gee's novels. Her fictional worlds are mainly middle-class, white, heterosexual spaces in which her characters' complacency is repeatedly probed, teased and delicately dismantled by a narrating voice ironically aware of the all-too-narrow limits of such conventional positions, and of the threats posed by all that lies beyond those limits. In *Grace*, the threat is post-Chernobyl radiation, nuclear weapons and nuclear waste, but these symbolise the pernicious, damaging influence of capitalism itself, which inflicts its own total vision upon the lives of the characters; 'It's everywhere', Grace thinks, 'appalled. If only there were some way of escape' (48). In *Light Years*, Lottie enters the nightmare world of the city to retrieve her stolen possessions, and encounters the space of the dispossessed, which she can read only in Dickensian terms: 'Then it struck her. *These are slums. This is what slums are.* But the map had no different symbol for slums' (287). Such a moment can stand for a recurring experience in Gee's novels. The disorientation of the characters' recognition is figured in the metaphor of the map lacking a symbol for what is experienced, and thereby being rendered inadequate to the experience.

Lost Children

Nowhere is this situation more integral to the narrative than in *Lost Children*, the novel which occupies a central place in Gee's output both in terms of its publication date and its explicit harnessing together of themes which recur separately or in less developed form elsewhere in her œuvre. *Lost Children* explores the effects of a runaway child on her family, and draws upon contemporary themes of homelessness, the dissolution of the conventional nuclear family, abortion, and first world attitudes to third world poverty in order to frame its analysis of loss as an integral element of a culture of consumer plenitude. Gee presents a typical bourgeois reality tainted by that which it has systematically repressed, as Alma, the novel's central figure and focaliser, is forced to come to terms with the reality of her daughter's disappearance and both the discontent that this disappearance betokens, and its effects on her previously stable family and social lives.

The novel opens with a hypothesising omniscient narrative voice, vacillating between question and wish, 'What if . . .? If only . . .' (7), between interrogation and desire; the first paragraph is repeated at the novel's end, with desire modulated to postulation, not 'if only' but 'maybe . . .' (320), a shift of mood which emphasises and undermines the novel's circular structure of presence – absence – presence, departure – return. Alma and Zoe, as mother and daughter, symbolise in their names the oppositional structure through which circularity is undermined and emphasised. Alma's son Adam and husband Paul imply a biblical parallel which the novel refuses – Paul remains obstinately blind to Alma's emotional condition, Adam secretly communicates with the missing Zoe but is a rather shadowy figure in the novel. The family structure in this novel is wholly conventional, and in itself offers a symbol of continuity and connection between generations, but is shown to rely in fundamental ways on the female members whose names delimit the sequence of possible relationships from A to Z, and is thrown into disarray by the removal of one of these two women. Zoe's disappearance forces a reconfiguration of relations within the family, for which no member, least of all Alma, has a map with adequate symbols. The novel subsequently explores, through Alma's focalisation, psychological processes of grief, mourning and compensation for loss both in terms of Alma's experience of them, and in terms of their potentials as connective experiences which can be between Alma, the other members of her family, and the wider society that she inhabits. Alma's initial 'turn inward' in response to Zoe's absence is transformed (8), gradually, as the novel progresses, into a 'turn outward'; her personal grief reconstitutes itself in the form of an expanded and developing social conscience, manifest in the gradual recognition of the generality of her personal experience, and of this experience as a condition endemic to human society:

> All over London, all over Europe, Alma thought, all over America and Japan, wherever people are rich and infertile, the women are having these conversations. And all over the developing, the withering, world, where people are fertile and horribly poor, the children huddle and steal and starve, grow up without parents or food or love. (279)

Alma's insight signifies the extent, at this late stage in the novel, of her moral and intellectual development in terms of making sense of her own experience, not by internalisation but by recognising that her experience is already a constituent of the lives of others and is in no way exclusive to her; the claustrophobic middle-class milieu that she inhabits, and its concomitant narrow ideology, momentarily open up to accommodate, however sketchily, a sense of sisterhood in suffering, a momentary recognition of the self in the other. But whereas, in *Light Years*, Lottie's opportunity to assume an active role leads her through the slums of London to a confrontation which alleviates to some extent her own condition of loss, Alma is rendered, in *Lost Children*, almost wholly passive, helplessly awaiting the return of her lost daughter, a condition which enforces the development of her own responses to it. Alma's disempowerment in the face of events beyond her control enforces a learning process which is at once focused on her own responses, and on her burgeoning recognition that her condition and her responses can be, indeed must be, shared with others. *Lost Children* conforms, in this sense, to the structure of the *Bildungsroman* in its location of the individual within a complex social network of actions, histories and beliefs with which she must learn to come to terms, and Zoe's act of disappearing from her mother's and her family's life constitutes the catalyst for a transformation of Alma's ethical engagement with the world around her. Zoe's return, and the explanation for her disappearance, links the education of Alma to the novel's theme of the particularity of individual loss and its repetition, across the groups of individuals who constitute families, communities, nations, as we learn of Zoe's own experience of loss. *Lost Children* is thus exemplary of the ways in which Gee's fiction uses narrational consciousness and its refraction through the consciousness of a centrally placed focaliser as a structure through which a double symbolisation can be achieved – that of the individual, struggling to make sense of a reality which is fundamentally hostile to that individual's condition, and that of a social totality which betrays disconcerting tendencies to repeat itself in patterned forms, while resisting the individual's desire to conceptualise it in adequate ways.

Saying the Unsaid

Reading Gee's novels as cognitive maps which force her characters (and, perhaps, her readers) to encounter a 'real' rather than a symbolic social world, we can see the texts as interventions in an ideological discourse of ethical disavowal which corresponds in significant ways to the political climate of England of the 1980s. Gee's characters, and the reader who is so often directly addressed, if not figured as an actant in the narrative, are led through fictional labyrinths (like the labyrinth of stairs in Benjamin's dream) – the formal complexities of *Dying in Other Words* and *The Burning Book*, the schematic patterning and parallels of *Light Years* and *Grace* – towards the possibilities of insight, understanding and their emotional correlatives of compassion and pity offered by fictional forms and by the act of narration itself, with all the ideological and ethical responsibilities that such forms and such an act demand – possibilities of envisioning or finding an adequate symbolic form for the social totality and its manifold interconnections, of making real the impetus of the vision of Benjamin's dream, the possibility, in Jameson's terms, 'of making your way from those vivid miseries' (missiles, starvation, birth-rate, burglaries, riots and genocide, murder and violence), 'to be able to make your way through that level so as to think it together with its deeper, but non-visual systemic cause' (*Aesthetics* 2). This is one of the things Gee's novels attempt to do. As Grace reminds us, 'So many things couldn't be unsaid' (34).

The Dedication

One of the ways in which Gee's novels assert their existence in and influence upon a material social world is through the act of dedication. Each novel is, through its dedication, situated historically in a network of interpersonal relations which transcends the given text and the given historical context, suggesting an interplay between public and private experiences which resonates throughout the novels. In *A Lover's Discourse*, Roland Barthes writes of the dedication as 'an episode of language' in which, by which, 'the subject dedicates something to the loved being', 'a gift of love' situated in an 'exchange economy', 'a poetic gesture' by which language is not given but dedicated in a speech act which commits the given novel to a social and yet personal function (75–7). Gee's novels are dedicated 'with love and gratitude', repeatedly, to a female community: 'For my friend Barbara Goodwin, who has always helped me, with love and gratitude' (*The Burning Book*); 'This book is dedicated, with love and gratitude, to my friend Beverley Hayne . . . and to my daughter Rosa' (*Grace*); 'This book is dedicated to my beloved mother . . .' (*Lost Children*); 'This book is in memory of Peg Rankine . . .' (*Light Years*). The dedication is a form of speech act, a performative act of donation which constructs those named within the dedication as receiving subjects, to whom the fiction is directed and for whom the fiction functions. The social network mapped out in the dedications to a career of novels from 1981 onwards is almost exclusively female, noting relations of motherhood through generations, and sisterhood through shared experience, but also placing the whole spectrum of the social as potential recipients of the 'gratitude and love' which constitutes the emotional force of Gee's dedications. The dedication to *Dying in Other Words*, exemplifies this amplification of the circle of dedicatory recipients:

> To the people who helped me survive, with gratitude and love; my parents, and other friends who are family in Aberystwyth, Brighton, Fen Ditton, London, Oxford, St Andrews, writing from Washington or walking in the snow of the wild West Midlands: and to friends I don't know in the distant cities, standing in bus stations, shadows, long queues, or glimpsed behind glass as the curtains open and close.

The performativity of such a dedication resides in its expansion from the family specifics of 'my parents', to 'other friends who are family', the alphabetical (linguistically governed but politically neutral) listing of regions, towns and cities in Britain and America, to 'the distant cities', all-inclusive and yet non-specific, a notation of all readers, male and female, as recipients but also class-conscious – readers in 'bus-stations', 'queues', readers excluded from the mainstream of bourgeois social life – precisely the figures who populate the margins of the bourgeois worlds of Gee's novels, haunting middle-class wealth and complacency with their insistent voices and lives – the lives of the dead Hibakusha in *The Burning Book*, of the homeless and dispossessed in *Light Years* and *Lost Children*, of the murdered in *Dying in Other Words*.

If Gee's novels can be read as extended efforts at achieving a fictional version of linguistic performatives, of doing something material with words, and as expressing a complex political vision in terms of a series of interventions into the material social conditions of existence of a predominantly bourgeois group of characters, then these interventions occur in two ways – through the ironic voice of the narrator, and through the repeated encounters her characters have with the dispossessed, the socially excluded, the disadvantaged. The insistence upon dispossession and disenfranchisement as material, lived realities in contemporary Britain ultimately constitutes the defining theme of Gee's writing, and places her in a tradition of

socially conscious fiction which she nevertheless transcends through
the meticulous, significant detail which characterises both her use of
language and her thematic preoccupations. Gee's wider project is, in
this sense, comparable with that of a writer like Jane Rogers, whose
novels, similarly detailed, carefully observed and consistent in the
depth of their engagement, map a similar set of concerns with representing the unrepresented in society, from the orphan in social care
in *Separate Tracks* (1982), to the convicts colonising Australia in
Promised Lands (1996) (interestingly Rogers, like Gee, has received
little critical attention). From the world of rented bedsits, alley-way
violence and restricted ambition in which *Dying in Other Words* is
set, through the working-class families of *The Burning Book* to the
troubling encounters in *Light Years* between high bourgeois Lottie and
the homeless people of London, who return in *Lost Children* to coun-
terpoint Alma's job in an estate agent's, Gee's novels allow spaces for
the representation, from different viewpoints, of the experiences of
exclusion which are themselves excluded from the dominant ideology. Her novels are acts of inclusion, like extended narrative
embraces, again attempting to represent in some way a social totality,
to acknowledge that the privileged worlds of Alma, Lottie and Grace
exist interdependently with a social structure which demands disad-
vantage and poverty of some of its members. Gee's novels, in this
sense, articulate a socialist feminism which derives its political force
from the works of theorists like Ann Foreman, and in many ways
Gee's novels express the persistence of certain political ideologies
and values – socialist feminism, pacifism, an intellectually informed
and motivated humanism – from the 1960s and 1970s into the
1980s and 1990s, most clearly perhaps in the anti-nuclear marches
which occur in *The Burning Book* and in *Light Years*.

This 'persistence of values' as the repressed of the dominant
ideologies of England in the 1980s and 1990s is the explicit theme
that Gee's novels address. In 'Word, Dialogue and Novel' Julia
Kristeva cites the French poet Francis Ponge's rewriting of the
Cartesian *cogito* – 'I speak and you hear me, therefore we are' (45).
This dialogic reformulation expresses the social inclusiveness of Gee's
literary project as embodied in the dedications as well as in the bodies
of the novels themselves, and suggests that we read as a manifesto
statement the lines from Moira, the writer, in *Dying in Other Words*:
'Let the artist make sorrow speak for all those too timid to
speak . . . and let anger cry out on behalf of all those who bowed
down, and went without, and accepted' (65).

Works Cited

Baker, Kenneth, ed. *The Faber Book of Conservatism* (London: Faber & Faber, 1993).

Barth, John. *The Friday Book: Essays and Other Non-Fiction* (New York: Putnam, 1984).

Barthes, Roland. *A Lover's Discourse – Fragments* (London: Penguin, 1990).

Bell, Daniel. *The End of Ideology* (Harvard: Harvard University Press, 2000).

Benjamin, Walter. 'Conversations with Brecht' in *Aesthetics and Politics*, ed. Fredric Jameson (London: Verso, 1980). 86–99

Brennan, Teresa. *History After Lacan* (London: Routledge, 1994).

Breton, André. *Manifestoes of Surrealism* (Ann Arbour: University of Michigan Press, 1972).

Cixous, Hélène. *The Hélène Cixous Reader*, ed. Susan Sellers (London: Routledge, 1994).

Connor, Steven. *The English Novel in History 1950–1995* (London: Routledge, 1996).

Foreman, Ann. *Femininity as Alienation: Women and the Family in Marxism and Psychoanalysis* (London: Pluto Press, 1977).

Fukuyama, Francis. *The End of History and the Last Man* (London: Penguin, 1992).

Gee, Maggie. *The Burning Book* (London: Faber & Faber, 1983).

———. *Dying in Other Words* (Brighton: Harvester Press, 1981).

———. *Grace* (London: Heinemann, 1988).

———. *The Ice People* (London: Richard Cohen Books, 1998).

———. *Light Years* (London: Faber & Faber, 1985).

———. *Lost Children* (London: HarperCollins, 1994).

———. *Virginia Woolf 1882–1941*, British Council 1991

———. *Where are the Snows* (London: Heinemann, 1991).

Jameson, Fredric, ed. *Aesthetics and Politics* (London: Verso, 1980).

———. *The Geopolitical Aesthetic: Cinema and the World System* (London: BFI, 1992).

Kristeva, Julia. *The Kristeva Reader*, ed. Toril Moi (Oxford: Blackwell, 1986).

Rogers, Jane. *Promised Lands* (London: Faber & Faber, 1995).

———. *Separate Tracks* (London: Faber & Faber, 1983).

'Wives and Workers':
The Novels of Joan Riley

DAVID ELLIS

Why Has It Taken So Long?

'The first novel by a West Indian born woman has just been published in Britain. But why has it taken so long to happen?' (Bishop 27). This question, posed in 1985 on the publication of Joan Riley's *The Unbelonging*, was certainly a legitimate one. Nearly twenty years on, we can perhaps extend this query to, 'Why has Joan Riley not been accepted as one of the foremost contemporary writers in Britain today?' By 1996 she had published a further three novels and contributed to and co-edited a collection of short stories by 'literary exiles'. Despite a comparatively quiet period since then, Riley remains the most published black woman writer in Britain today and yet one of the least recognised and discussed.

Already, some important issues are beginning to appear. Should Riley's work merit special attention because of its contribution to one or all of the (contested) canons of black British writing, contemporary women's writing and/or black women's writing? Or should her work be judged in isolation from such compartmentalising activities? It should be possible to do both. Riley's writing does not require any special pleading, but it does sit at a point of multiple intersecting concerns – literary, historical, theoretical and social – that demand attention. One consequence of this is a tendency to read Riley's fiction as a social document concerned with issues of racism, patriarchy and national identity and this diverts attention away from considerations of its literary worth. Furthermore, this blurring of the boundary between realism and reality in Riley's work has generated anxiety due to her unflinching depictions of racial prejudice, sexual violence and psychological trauma. As will be explained further below, such passages have tended to induce defensive responses across a wide range of readers. In doing so, Riley's work raises significant questions relating to the function of literature in the modern world, the identification of reading constituencies and the role of narrative in shaping personal and social realities. By confronting such issues in Riley's work, it becomes possible to highlight the intimate relationship between the literary and the real in a manner that addresses both literary quality and contextual significance.

A Modified Realism

Joan Riley was born in St Mary's, Jamaica, in 1958 and migrated to England as a young adult, where she attended Sussex and London universities. She has since remained resident in England. This dual experience of life in both the Caribbean and in the metropolitan centre locates Riley's work within a tradition of writing established by the writers of the Windrush generation of the 1950s. Sam Selvon, George Lamming, Wilson Harris and Andrew Salkey were seminal figures in a period that saw the 'birth' of the West Indian novel as one consequence of post-war migrations to Britain. Two key modes of production and reception bind these writers together and provide clear links to Riley's work. Firstly, they employed the social realist genre established by C. L. R. James as the dominant mode of expression of the West Indian novel in the 1930s (Harris is the notable exception to this). Secondly, their writing, which employed both Caribbean and English settings, was written in exile and with a white English audience in mind. There are crucial and conjoined issues here.

Writers such as Selvon and Lamming became aware that the reality of England they encountered was very different to the Eurocentric images supplied by a colonial education. Novels such as *A Brighter Sun* (1952) and *In The Castle of My Skin* (1953) can thus be read not only as narratives of an emerging regional identity, but also an attempt to educate a largely ignorant English public who could not readily distinguish, for example, Africa from the Caribbean. This English-orientated writing also extended to those novels set in England. Books such as Lamming's *The Emigrants* (1954) and Selvon's *The Lonely Londoners* (1956) traversed the urban terrain of working-class London and can be read as responses to the new social mythologies surrounding an incipient multiracial Britain. Such narratives frequently dealt with the harsh economic realities of the migrants' lives, as well as their legal and illegal leisure pursuits. In doing so, these Caribbean writers were coincident with the growing taste for the neo-realism of the kitchen-sink drama and the 'Angry Young Men'. This genre, that exploited a notion of 'gritty realism', turned upon fetishised images of poverty, transgressive sexuality, regionality and hedonism, and themselves often incorporated black characters as a signifier for social exclusion. Whilst the Caribbean writers undoubtedly profited from this cultural trend, they also had to be cautious of reinforcing the new myths of racism which typically focused upon issues of black sexuality and criminality. What was produced, therefore, was a modified realism that was aware of the ideological context into which it would be published. In this sense, then, Riley is the inheritor of a literary tradition which has always exercised an element of self-censorship whilst employing the genre characteristics of realism.

Washing Dirty Linen in Public

A body of writing more contemporary to Riley's was that of American black women's writing. *The Unbelonging* entered the literary milieu of Alice Walker's *The Color Purple* (1983) and Maya Angelou's *I Know Why the Caged Bird Sings* (1984). Each of these texts were extremely successful, both being reprinted in Britain four times in 1984 alone. The Women's Press must have had similar hopes for Riley as the first of a developing genre of black writing in Britain by women. It is now clear, however, that Riley's work has not been celebrated, in the manner of *The Color Purple*, as a 'contemporary modern classic' (Wisker 1), despite similar concerns over the latter's representativeness of black lives within the context of racist sentiments. We are entitled to ask why this should be.

David Punter notes of *The Unbelonging* that it has 'never received its due share of praise or criticism because, I am certain, the materials with which it deals are too painful for the reader, whatever his or her cultural positioning' (163). This concurs with Gabriele Griffin's experiences of teaching the text where her students were 'quite shattered' by what Griffin herself describes as the 'unremitting negativity' of the novel (24). In response to this, one might suggest that Walker and Angelou have enjoyed greater success than Riley, because there is a sense of redemption or salvation in their writing. Put simply, Celie learns the significance of the colour purple and Marguerite understands why the caged bird sings. By contrast, Hyacinth – as I shall discuss in more detail later – is every bit as dispossessed at the end of her narrative as she was at the start. Perhaps, however, reading positions, despite Punter's assertion, *are* important.

Riley is herself quite pointed about the relationship between the setting of her work and its popular and literary reception: '(e)verybody read the black American writers and were moved, but at least it couldn't happen in Britain'. She continues, '(i)t was only when black writing was about the British backyard, that it started to get uncomfortable' ('Writing' 550–1). In essence, what Riley's work does not permit is a sense of distance whereby a white English readership can take comfort that the American Deep South is no more closely related to them than, say, the poverty and misery of Dickens's London. Neither does Riley's work contain the redemptive potential of the American texts, where the success of the central characters can be read as a signifier for the progressive liberalisation of society.

These 'absences' can be read as a manifestation of Riley's commitment to reality rather than realism. Providing the sense of closure typical of realism would, she says, 'allow my readers to retreat back to their comfortable world and not accept their collective part in solving issues that did not go away with the final full stop'. It would be a betrayal of the 'community of women who give unstintingly of their lives to flesh . . . (her) creative world' ('Writing' 552). Thus, while Riley does recognise that she is working with fictional narratives she is also conscious that such narratives have an important social function in expressing a social reality and providing points of identification for people within that social order. Upon the publication of *The Unbelonging*, Riley noted, '(i)f we (black women) don't write our stories, someone else will, and we're not going to like what they're saying' (Bishop 27). For Barbara Burford, the requirement to engage with this field of representation was made all the more urgent by the success of novelists like Walker and Angelou. As she remarks, 'I am interested in the lives and realities of Black people living in other cultures' she says, 'but I am reluctant to have their lives read into the record as my reality' (37).

This commitment to recording black women's reality through fiction distinguishes Riley's work from that of the 1950s writers. Their work was undoubtedly a seminal intervention in the global map of literary production and crucial to the rise of national self-confidence in a period of approaching decolonisation. However, they were male-generated accounts that were accorded an unwarranted authenticity. As Riley puts it, '(w)hen I was a black undergraduate, accepted definitions of black women, came out of the perceptions of black men. . . . After all, they were black, they should know. No-one seemed to notice the irony' ('Writing' 548). Other 'second generation' writers, such as Caryl Phillips, have also written their own accounts of the migrations of the 1950s and these have included a greater emphasis upon female characters, (who were typically secondary to the narratives of the earlier generation) and include a greater critique of black patriarchy.[1] For Riley, however, this has become an elevated focus of concern. Her por-trayal of black men as abusive, unreliable and – in the case of *The Unbelonging* – incestuous, are images which, it was felt, would only fuel racist sentiment. Her commitment to reality rather than realism has consequently been described as 'washing dirty linen in public' from the outset by black readers, and this has again acted against its success (Bishop 27).

This reaction speaks again of the intimate link between narrative and lived reality. If Wisker was concerned that *The Color Purple* would cause 'uproar amongst Black males' (2), for the reasons described above, one can understand a deeper concern for narratives set in Britain – particularly ones which do not carry the historical buffer zone of a forty-year retrospection. Whilst Riley is sensitive to the political realities of producing black fiction in the context of social racism,[2] this should not take precedence over the role such writing can play as a source of communal self-reflection and the construction of an 'independent and representative black critique' ('Writing' 551). Such a critique could not be truly representative without the contributions of black women. In this regard, however, black women find themselves with potentially multiple concerns.

Two Kinds of Women

If some black men have been resistant to black women's narratives, a further significant reading position that has contributed to Riley's critical reception is the response from white feminism. Riley notes that 'white feminists (are) angered that racism is given precedence over what they see as the more important gender issues' ('Writing' 550). In essence, many of the debates described above could find resonance with the struggle to establish women's writing within the patriarchal order of Western literature, and with similar concerns for the relationship between literary production and social formations. Perhaps, however, it is from this point that developments in the field of theory provide a means of reading Riley's work outside of the negative responses outlined above.

---

[1] See *The Final Passage* (London: Faber, 1985) and Phillips's early drama, especially *Strange Fruit* (1981) and *Where There is Darkness* (Oxford: Amber Lane Press, 1982).
[2] Gabriele Griffin (1993) recounts Riley's unwillingness to discuss incest in an all-white gathering (24).

Throughout the 1980s, the black feminist critical project sought to carve out concerns that could not be subordinated to apparently more totalising theories of race and gender. A central document to this endeavour was Hazel Carby's 'White woman listen! Black feminism and the boundaries of sisterhood' published in 1982.[3] Carby's work articulates some important distinctions which respond to 'common-sense' parallels between race and gender as equivalent social constructions, and which can provide a meaningful approach to Riley's work.

Carby identifies the three central concepts of feminist theory as being the family, patriarchy and reproduction. In each of these concepts, she argues, 'the way the gender of black women is constructed differs from constructions of white women because it is also subject to racism' (46). One specific construction she describes is particularly pertinent to Riley's fiction. Carby quotes Elizabeth Wilson's notion that in post-war Britain, work and marriage were viewed as alternatives for 'two kinds of women', wives and mothers *or* workers. It was a widely debated issue occasioned by the employment of women as part of the war effort and which would lead to a popular concern over 'latch-key kids' by the 1960s. It was, however, a concern that did not extend to the women recruited into the labour force from the colonies. Rather, as Carby claims, 'the state produced common-sense notions of . . . (the black family's) inherent pathology: black women were seen to fail as mothers precisely because of their position as workers' (49). Wendy Webster, however, has argued more recently that black women were not typically viewed in this way. Conversely, she says, 'migrant women were not assigned the primarily relational identity embodied in the notion of a "working wife". Wanted as workers, they were not wanted as people who would establish family life in Britain' (146).

Webster's adjustment on Carby is an indication of the (often ambivalent) position occupied by women within the black British experience. Black women could be recruited into positions such as nurses, cleaners and other service providers, but they were not viewed as requiring any such services for themselves. This is a comparatively under-explored aspect of migration within this period where the focus has been typically on the male experience. What it specifically conceals is the disparity between constructions of black women and the realities

---

[3] First published by the Centre for Contemporary Cultural Studies, Birmingham, in *The Empire Strikes Back* (1982), pp.212–35. Reproduced as a series of excerpts in Heidi Safia Mirza, ed. *Black British Feminism: A Reader* (1997). Subsequent references relate to this latter volume.

of their lives. This can be discerned via notions of the personal and public spheres – black women were assigned to various kinds of public roles that were at variance with common perceptions of their personal lives. That is to say, they could be cleaners, but black districts were notoriously dirty: they could act as midwives, but they were bad mothers; they lacked familial responsibility but threatened the white population's access to housing, employment and benefits. Carby has noted how black women's critique of history is not only concerned with absences, but also with 'the ways in which it has made us visible' (45). It is this notion of in/visibility that can provide a point of entry into Riley's fiction. Her fictions provide both a point of identification for a black women's readership in Britain, and they explore the effects of being the subject of representation in a differentiating order of otherness. Specifically, they engage with psychological effects of being alienated from the self through a set of ideological productions that project a 'reality' incommensurate with one's own lived experience.

This can be encapsulated by Webster's formulation of wives and workers in so far as this reflects conflicting private and public identities. This should not be taken as a safe binaristic pairing, however. In his analysis of the neo-realism of the 1950s, Jonathan Dollimore describes these terms more as an intimate, but concealed, web of relationships:

> to see the full extent of patriarchal power in the personal sphere is to see how pervasive it is in the public sphere and so, finally, to collapse the distinctions between the two. Thus both the family unit and sexual relations are disclosed to be, not havens of retreat from the world of power relations, but two primary sites of their operation. (70)

It is thus in the confused overlap between private and public identities – between identities of wives and mothers, or workers – that the significance of Riley's fiction can be discerned.

An Agonised Dependence

In her introduction to *Leave to Stay: Stories of Exile and Belonging* (1996), Riley writes that, 'the experience of being a migrant was not an easy one. It was an isolation, being cut off from the most basic aspects of cultural norms' (2). While not all of her characters are migrants, their positioning within the black community and the sense of embattlement that this brings with it does mean that isolation is a recurring theme in her writing.

In *The Unbelonging*, Hyacinth Williams's life with her father and stepfamily is one of physical isolation as she will be beaten by her father for being away from her house for longer than is absolutely necessary. This physical confinement is reinforced by his reiterated assertion, '(t)hey don't like neaga in this country' (30, 51, 64, 69, 95). While Hyacinth's experience of bullying at school certainly seems to confirm this, it also prevents her from accepting offers of help from one teacher and her doctor, and leaves her with a pathological distrust of white authority. In *Romance* (1988), too, isolation is a key theme. The action is set in Croydon – an area significantly removed from the Brixton heartland of the sisters' earlier lives. Desiree's strained marital relations with John are set in contrast to the earlier period of hope and promise there, when he was politically active in black politics. This engagement has been physically debilitated by the move into a pre-dominantly white neighbourhood, where the street becomes an arena for surveillance, embodied by Nosy Dora, rather than community and collectivity. This sense of isolation is also manifest in the sisters' loss of familial links back to Guyana.

Riley's assertion, though, clearly indicates a correlation between physical isolation and its consequent effects upon the interpellated subject. The absence of cultural norms appropriate to the location of the self into a social order renders the subject vulnerable to alternative and often damaging social scripts. In *Romance*, Desiree responds to the narrative of a black activism that insists upon the passivity of black women in an appropriately disengaged manner. For example, while she liked John to talk about the struggle, 'it didn't matter that she never really understood the concept' (84). Any attempts either of the sisters *does* make to engage with politics are thwarted by a lack of genuine action on the one hand and a dismissive attitude towards women on the other. Notably, when they attend a meeting of the Black United Front following Jay's arrest, they are greeted by 'a hostile-looking woman who pointedly turned her back on them while joining eagerly in a discussion about the role of the African woman' (127). This role is premised upon the expectation that 'women should support their men' (10, 55). Such support is both emotional and physical and is based upon the subjuga-tion of women's needs to those of men and is thus an expression of domestic power. Acting as a service provider in this regard not only conflates the roles of wife and worker, but also prevents female collect-ivity by containing women in the domestic arena.

Often in Riley's fiction this exposure to prohibiting narratives or dictates leads to more extreme forms of delusion. Typical of this is Hyacinth's mental reconstruction of her life in Jamaica as a Utopian space that provides a source of refuge from the wretched misery of her life in Britain. These fantasies and dreamscapes are self-delusory in so far as they are accorded an almost willed existence. After being threatened with eviction from her care home, it is described as 'inevitable that she should dream that night, escape to a Jamaica which seemed to be slipping away from her in her waking life' (86). As Griffin has noted, this suggests an element of control over her unconscious that somehow compensates for the lack of agency in her waking reality (21). If this were the case, Hyacinth's desire for emotional refuge should diminish as she successfully progresses through secondary and into tertiary education. But this does not occur. Hyacinth is not merely taking refuge in memories of a happier time – she is falsifying her memories. Thus, she dreams of attending pleasurable events such as the Independence Day parades or of trips to tourist attractions, which increasingly become revealed as places to which she has never been. Such mental constructions remain stubbornly in place – despite increasingly sinister images entering her dreams – hence her horror when she finally does return to Jamaica, to be reconciled with her aunt.

Similar acts of self-delusion take place elsewhere in Riley's work. In *Romance*, Verona responds to being raped at the age of thirteen by one of her sister's (black) boyfriends by maintaining a bulky frame and dating older white men. Each of these acts gives her the illusory sense that 'she was in control . . . She needed that control. It was her second line of defence, along with her huge size' (19). This illusion is fed by Verona's avid consumption of romance fiction and her – again, willed – identification with the idealised, typically European, characters and scenarios found therein. For example, during her first sexual experience with Steve – who would later assault her for being pregnant – she forces herself to view this unsatisfying reality through the images and linguistic register of romantic fictions:

> She ran her fingers through his untidy blond hair, along his narrow back and flat bottom, fantasising that in response he was tenderly caressing her quivering white flesh . . . that the fingers tweaking at her short hair were really tangling in her imagined long golden tresses. (174)

In *A Kindness to the Children* (1992) Jean's (self-)consciousness has also been damaged by similarly phallocentric texts linked to her religious upbringing. As Riley explains, '(r)eligion is very essential to Jean's rural Caribbean past; religion for me has always been male, it's either a white Jesus or a black Jesus but which ever way it is, Jesus is a man' (Hussein 17). Jean's perceived sense of her own failure is always measured in relation to men – her failure as a Christian, a daughter, a wife and a mother. Her attempts to integrate her successful professional life with her personal life are undermined by this sense of failure as a family member. One by-product of this delusion is a lack of community with other women, particularly Sylvia, whom she perceives as a threat to her status as wife and mother by presenting a source of competition. In this respect, also, she is an isolated figure and vulnerable to patriarchal norms which thoroughly undermine her sense of self-worth and contribute to her mental breakdown. Her subsequent paranoid episodes lead her to acts such as absconding with her children or associating with Ras Peter, a Rastafarian who lives on the squatted ground near Pearl and George's house, as false gestures of independent action.

For both Punter and Griffin these internalised states of mind and associated behaviours are indicative of a deluded sense of agency in the context of overwhelming subjugation. As Punter puts it, 'Hyacinth's dreams of Independence Day parades are reduced to its opposite, the lineaments of an agonised dependence' (131). Such dependence in Riley's work is typically registered in the loss of control over the body. Thus, Hyacinth's apparent agency in her dreams is negated by attendant bed-wetting episodes, which continue into her adulthood (albeit much less frequently). This is also manifested in the uncontrollable shaking that occurs at other moments of perceived threat throughout the novel. Similarly, Jean's alcoholism and experiments with marijuana represent a lack of control over her body, which results in violent acts towards her children. It is similarly evident in the sexual exploitation of her body as different men take advantage of her confused state, ultimately resulting in her rape and murder at the end of the novel. This lack of bodily control is, perhaps, most clearly evident in *Waiting in the Twilight* (1987).

Dedicated to the courage and loyalty of 'a whole generation of women, who took ship and sailed into the unknown' (Foreword), the narrative is centred upon the life and death of Adella Johnson. The novel begins with Adella as a 58-year-old woman partially disabled by a stroke, and now working as a part-time cleaner for the council. Her partial paralysis can be read in parallel with Hyacinth's bedwetting and shaking – it is an expression of a lack of control or sovereignty over the body. Christine Wick Sizemore argues that Adella's physical state puts her in the 'ninth stage of life biologically' (129), and this encourages her to interpret Adella's recurrent lapses into memory as both a way of coping with shame and a 'process of mourning' for others, and for her anticipated 'dead self' (134). However, like Hyacinth, Adella's lack of control over her body had begun at a much earlier age.

This can be registered through the series of enforced migrations that punctuate Adella's life. The first of these, chronologically, is from her childhood village of Beaumont to Kingston. It is occasioned by the increasing sexual interest in her of the local pastor who 'had an eye for the young girls' (33). This apparently common knowledge is dealt with by removing Adella from the source of threat. In Kingston, Adella is obliged to adopt the religious practices of her cousin and his wife who are both devout Seventh-day Baptists (103). It is her sense of frustration with the circumscriptions and demands of such devotion that leads her to a dance-hall tryst with Beresford, a policeman who meets her – significantly, again – after she is attacked and robbed in West Kingston. Adella becomes pregnant from the ensuing sexual encounter with Beresford and is consequently forced, by her disapproving cousin, into her second migration to a yard in one of the poor areas of Kingston. At this stage, she is dependent upon Beresford and, unaware that he is married, is forced into concubinage in exchange not just for money, but also his protection:

'Yu tink yu can jus live by yuself dungya? Well yu betta learn dis fram now. If yu doan have a man fe proteck yu, yu gwine have plenty trouble . . . tru everybady know me roun ya yu gwine safe long as dem know yu is my woman.' (113)

Riley is typically forthright about this scenario; 'If you get pregnant in Jamaica you are finished. You are fair game' (Sizemore 131). In effect, however, Adella already was fair game by dint of her sex within a Jamaican patriarchal social structure, and this sense of entrapment follows her to England. Here she is again a service provider – of sex, accommodation, food and childcare – for her husband, Stanton, and then other men after Stanton deserts her. Her final forced migration occurs when her house in Britain is the subject of compulsory purchase and she is obliged to move into council accommodation. It is the final sign of the defeat of her attempts at a physical independence and is mirrored by her continued and deluded belief that Stanton would ultimately return to her.

Suspended in Discourse

Griffin has argued that *The Unbelonging* has 'essentially a linear structure and belongs to the tradition of realism'. Furthermore, she proposes
that in this novel, 'dream is always identified as dream, and "reality" as
"reality"' (25). For Punter, 'the fantasy is all too present . . . but its relation to the real undergoes a disastrous and traumatic transformation'
(168). These problematised navigations of fantasy/reality/realism are
recurrent themes of Riley's work. At their basis lie conflicting images of
the self within characters who lack secure points of identification. Just
as Dollimore's formulation can be used to erase the public/private
distinctions implied in the roles of wives and workers, so Riley's characters find themselves disorientated without the stability that the
(apparent) authenticity of a personal/private role could provide. Instead,
their increasing inability to discern reality amongst multiple layers of
representation becomes symptomatic of their alienation.

For instance, in *The Unbelonging*, Hyacinth's very first attempts
to identify her father are mediated through the hyperreality of
Hollywood: '(s)he had always imagined her father would be a cross
between Sidney Poitier and Richard Rowntree' (14). The collapse of
this celluloid image is not solely replaced by a brutal material reality
alone, but by further layers of social myth. Her father's reiterated
mantra on 'neagas', as noted above, is both a social truth *and* a pan-
optic act of linguistic terrorism – it does not have to be entirely true to
succeed in policing Hyacinth's behaviour. Furthermore, even where
racism *is* a truth about British society, it is typically based upon the
constructions of colonial discourse or what Edward Said has termed,
'textual attitudes' (92). That is to say, the (very real) prejudice that
Hyacinth experiences is itself the product of racial mythologies and
stereotypes, rather than actual or real personal characteristics. Viewed
in this way, Hyacinth's relationship with the material world is a profoundly discursive one. Consequently, what agency she can achieve
during her waking life can only be enacted at the level of narrative.
Thus, she can successfully deceive her father, conceal the truth of her
home life from teachers and doctors and create false identities for
herself at university. Having no sense of her 'real' identity, she can
exploit this freedom to create new ones. As a coping strategy, however,
this has profound limitations.

One might argue that Hyacinth is held within an ambivalent
position in language that renders her in a state of constant deferral.
Here, she is simultaneously dependent and independent: dependent

upon her father and subsequently the state for her accommodation, but independent of these through a strategy of concealed truths and deferred identity. However, this ambivalence ultimately severs Hyacinth not just from society but from herself. Consequently, she identifies, first of all, with the characters in romance fiction – as a precursor to Verona – and latterly with the Asian students at sixth-form college. In each case Hyacinth is held within a deferred space of presence and absence. This is alluded to in a further recurrent phrase of the novel: Charles's warning that '(t)here is no harm in it [romanticising one's country], so long as I know the reality' (121, 122, 139). The difficulty that Hyacinth endures is a radical inability to find a position of certainty from which to distinguish between fabrication and reality at both a personal and social level.

Similar incapacities are evident elsewhere in Riley's fiction and again crucially depend upon the characters' acts of self-censorship and thus self-isolation. For example, Verona does not reveal her rape and its after-effects to Desiree out of a sense of shame that simultaneously impels her towards romance fiction. Equally, Adella is unable to tell either her daughters or Lisa that she cannot return to Jamaica because of her reliance upon 'menfriends'' gifts after Stanton leaves and the knowledge that she has been condemned in church for this. She is thus impelled towards the romance of Stanton's return which, as Isabel Carrerra Suarez ironically notes, 'would correct her failure as a wife' (292).

A consequence of being suspended in discourse for these characters is a lack of quantifiable progress – their sense of self is deferred in a freeplay of meaning which has to continually refer back to, and revise, the past in order to achieve coherence in the present. In Riley's first two novels, this unsuccessful search for certainty is enacted at both a formal and metaphoric level.

In *The Unbelonging*, Mr Williams's incestuous activities in the past and his increasing threat to Hyacinth is mediated through the recurring quotation from *Cider With Rosie*, '(i)ncest flourished where the roads were bad' (48, 62, 91, 106, 131, 137). Hyacinth is too inexperienced to understand what this means, and her own psycho-sexual development has been arrested by the association of her father's erection with anger and violence. Therefore, what this phrase also comes to suggest is the impossibility of linear progress – the road continually meets an impasse before which the individual must retreat only to return to its implacability at later stage. It is from this notion of cyclical repetition that Griffin's notion of unremitting negativity emerges. What Riley has done is refuse the more traditional quest form where physical restraints can be relieved through a form of spiritual, emotional or intellectual progress. Rather, where one might normally expect the entrapment of a cyclical narrative to be addressed by a linear dream narrative which suggests the potential for individual progress and the possibility of escape, both Hyacinth's reality and her dreams remain trapped within a cycle of oppression and subjugation.

Waiting in the Twilight has a similarly cyclical movement. At the conclusion of the novel, Adella is again at the physical mercy of others. Having suffered a further stroke she is in a hospital corridor waiting to be moved into a ward, but in a bitterly ironic twist, this final enforced migration never occurs and she dies before a space is found for her. Similarly to *The Unbelonging*, this physical journey is mirrored by a mental journey through Adella's recollected past and, again, it is cyclical, beginning and ending with the death of Mada Beck in Beaumont and the phrase, '(a)ll dat respeck' (8, 165). Adella's memories are not delusory in the same way that Hyacinth's are, but they do exist as a source of refuge from the present and frequently operate as a justification for Adella's persistent belief that Stanton will return to her. Adella is thus held in suspension on the cusp between two accounts of her life – a twilight existence that remains a circular trap with no possibility of progression. It is this sense of narrative entrapment in Riley's texts that clearly distinguishes her work and its reception from that of the black American writers alluded to earlier.

Dialogues with the Reader

Suarez describes Riley's novels as being 'woman centred' (292), and this is certainly true. However, her accounts are notably different from other white gynotexts. For example, Sue Anderson describes the depiction in Pat Barker's *Union Street* (1982) of 'an emotionally secure life created between the women "on the street", in public, as a means of support and a way of coping with an unsatisfactory "private" life' (182). There is a clear demand for similar security and support in Riley's novels, but the isolated and narrative-bound nature of her characters clearly mitigates against this occurring. There are, however, some signs of optimism in her two most recent novels.

In *Romance*, despite Desiree's hysterectomy, Clifford's death, Ruby's failed hip operation and Verona's experiences of sexual violence, some evidence of progress is in place. Desiree has accepted that supporting

John is not her principal function, and this is achieved through dialogue with Mara and also through the arrival of John's grandparents from Jamaica who exhibit a mutual interdependence. Ultimately these twin forces leave Desiree 'more optimistic about their learning to communicate better with one another' (196). This phrase, while specifically concerned with Desiree's marriage, is also relevant to her relationship with Verona. Such dialogues have not resolved all of the social issues which impact upon the family members, but they do signal an escape from isolation and therefore the possibility of achieving points of connection and stability.

This potential for collective strength is also evident in *A Kindness to the Children* where there is a sense of female community in the search for Jean once she has absconded into the ghetto districts with her children. Sylvia accepts the responsibility for finding her, but when her enquiries around the districts are met with suspicion, she is compelled to seek the assistance of Pearl. Pearl has previously had an exaggerated dependence upon her husband, symbolically represented by her inability to climb the steep slope to the provision ground. With Jean irredeemably divided from herself by her inability to reconcile the roles of both worker *and* wife and mother, the narrative pairing of Pearl (wife and mother) with Sylvia (worker) is suggestive of the positive potential for women to help overcome these alienating projections. Ultimately, this is what occurs. Sylvia is able to find Jean and rescue the children through a combination of the collective help of the women in the neighbourhood and Pearl's willingness to overcome her fears about the dangers of the ghetto and accompany Sylvia in her search. In the former case, this collective action is in stark contrast to the predatory nature of gossip that Sylvia has previously encountered and which has clear links to the condemnation of Jean by the church community. In the latter case, Pearl uses her experiences with Sylvia to gather the courage to climb to the provision ground. Again, this elevates her position from one of supporting George, to one of a more effective partnership.

These are, perhaps, minor successes but Riley's fiction constantly guards against any unproblematised notions of romance or nostalgia. If this has had, and continues to have, an inhibiting effect upon the commercial success and critical reception of her work, then Riley has maintained a modest intended constituency for her work: 'my writing's almost a dialogue with myself. . . . And I want to take my dialogue and put it in the ring with other people's dialogue . . . I also like to make dialogues with the reader' (Hussein 19). This finds resonance with Burford's intended readership also: '(t)o whom do I want to tell this story? Firstly to myself, then I want to talk to one hypothetical Blackwoman . . . For me it is as simple as that: sharing on a one to one basis with another woman' (37). This intimate sense of communication finds parallels with the potential for progress – or its inhibition – within Riley's novels as the wives, mothers and workers try to achieve communication. It also has a clear relevance for dialogues at the point of reception. The absence of a substantial body of black writing in Britain by women continues to detract from the possibilities of such dialogues taking place and the need for these accounts continues to be as pressing at it was in the 1980s. Why is it taking so long?

Works Cited

Anderson, Sue. 'Life on the Streets: Pat Barker's Realist Fictions' in It's My Party: Reading Twentieth Century Women's Writing, ed. Gina Wisker (London: Pluto Press, 1994). 181–92

Bishop, Marla. 'Interview with Joan Riley', Spare Rib (July 1985): 27.

Burford, Barbara. 'Landscapes Painted on the Inside of my Skin', Spare Rib (June 1987): 36–9.

Carby, Hazel. 'White woman listen! Black feminism and the boundaries of sisterhood' in Black British Feminism: A Reader, ed. Heidi Safia Mirza (London: Routledge, 1997). 45–53

Dollimore, Jonathon. 'The Challenge of Sexuality' in Society and Literature 1945–1970, ed. Alan Sinfield (London: Methuen, 1983). 51–86

Griffin, Gabriele. 'Writing the Body': Reading Joan Riley, Grace Nichols and Ntozake Shange' in Black Women's Writing, ed. Gina Wisker (Basingstoke: Macmillan, 1993). 19–42

Hussein, Aamer. 'Joan Riley talks with Aamer Hussein', Wasafiri, vol. 17 (Spring 1993): 17–19.

Punter, David. Postcolonial Imaginings: Fictions of a New World Order (Edinburgh: Edinburgh University Press, 2000).

Riley, Joan. A Kindness to the Children (London: Women's Press, 1992).

——. Romance (London: Women's Press, 1988).

——. The Unbelonging (London: Women's Press, 1985).

——. Waiting in the Twilight (London: Women's Press, 1987).

——. 'Writing Reality in a Hostile Environment' in Kunapipi, vol. 6:1 (1994): 546–52.

Riley, Joan and Briar Wood, eds. Leave to Stay: Stories of Exile and Belonging (London: Virago, 1996).

Said, Edward. Orientalism (Harmondsworth: Penguin, 1978).

Sizemore, Christine Wick. Negotiating Identities in Women's Lives: English Postcolonial and Contemporary British Novels (Connecticut: Greenwood Press, 2002).

Suarez, Isabel Carrerra. 'Absent Mother(lands): Joan Riley's Fiction' in
    *Motherlands: Black Women's Writing from Africa, the Caribbean and South
    Asia*, ed. Susheila Nasta (London: Women's Press, 1991). 290–309
Webster, Wendy. *Imagining Home: Gender, Race and National Identity 1945–1964*
    (London: UCL Press, 1998).
Wisker, Gina, ed. *Black Women's Writing* (Basingstoke: Macmillan, 1993).

Confrontational Sites: Cultural Conflicts, Social Inequality and Sexual Politics in the Work of Rukhsana Ahmad

CHRISTIANE SCHLOTE

> In a way, it's an awful thing to confess, but I find it really difficult to find solutions. There aren't solutions. There are only dilemmas. Or, you can try to play the hand that you've been dealt as best as you can and with as much dignity as you can and with as much humanity as you can.[1]

In recent years, a group of British and American writers, artists and film-makers, loosely categorised as 'of South Asian descent', has gained enormous popularity.[2] This phenomenon has been accompanied by an increasing commodification of postcolonial cultural expressions. South Asian British popular culture, in particular, has become 'all the rage for late capitalism' (Sharma et al. 1). Although Indian British and Indian American literature remains dominant, fiction by British writers of Pakistani descent has also benefited from the 'postmodern fetishization of otherness' (Schwarz and Ray 15).[3] The work of prolific writers such as Tariq Ali, Zulfikar Ghose, Hanif Kureishi and Bapsi Sidhwa, as well as that of the newer voices of Ayub Khan-Din and Kamila Shamsie, not only belies the hitherto narrow conception of South Asian British literature but also demonstrates the heterogeneity of Pakistani migrant literatures.[4]

[1] Author's interview with Rukhsana Ahmad, London, April 1999.
[2] I would like to thank Emma Parker and Anshuman Mondal for their careful comments and Felicity Hand for providing me with her essay 'Gentle Anthropology'. Thanks are also due to the *Berliner Programm zur Förderung der Chancengleichheit für Frauen in Forschung und Lehre* for their financial support. An earlier version of selected parts of this essay was presented at the triennial Conference 'Bodies and Voices' (European Association for Commonwealth Literature and Language Studies) at the University of Copenhagen in March 2002.
[3] Also witness the recent success of the first novel by the Bengali British writer Monica Ali, *Brick Lane* (London: Doubleday, 2003).
[4] For recent anthologies of Pakistani literature in English see Muneeza Shamsie ed., *A Dragonfly in the Sun: An Anthology of Pakistani Writing in English* (1997) and Aamer Hussein, Mumtaz Shirin and Jamila Hasmi, *Hoops of Fire: Fifty Years of Fiction by Pakistani Women* (2000).

Within this necessarily arbitrary group, postcolonial women writers, in particular, have begun to address the multiple conflicts that face their mostly female characters. Thus their cultural-national origin, their class background, and their gender function as primary sites to be negotiated. This essay will focus on the work of the Pakistani British novelist, playwright and translator Rukhsana Ahmad who defies easy categorisation. Ahmad might be situated within the context of an international group of women writers and feminist critics operating with the conviction that categories such as race, class and gender have to be understood, as Rose Brewer puts it, as 'simultaneous forces' (16). According to Muneeza Shamsie 'feminist consciousness permeates the fiction of many South Asian writers ranging from the Pakistani Bapsi Sidhwa and Rukhsana Ahmad to the Indian Sashi Despande, Sunetra Gupta and Arundhati Roy'.[5] In this essay, I will examine Ahmad's representation of South Asian women's bodies, particularly with regard to the bodily inscription of racial and class differences and explore Ahmad's questioning of Western notions of female sexuality, family relations and politics. I will discuss her work within the framework of the renewed interest in South Asian fiction but also in terms of the 'burden of representation' put upon writers from 'their own communities'. The discussion will focus on Ahmad's work as a novelist as well as her work as a playwright and translator.

Of Roots and Routes: From Karachi to London

In *Cartographies of Diaspora: Contesting Identities* (1996) Avtar Brah asks, 'What are the implications for late twentieth-century Britain of certain ways of imaging "Englishness" . . . It is centrally about our political and personal struggles over the social regulation of "belonging"' (192). Ahmad was born in December 1948 in Karachi and taught at the university there before fleeing 'the restrictions that you would have as a Muslim girl of a middle class, very conservative family' by means of an arranged marriage in London. She describes her own story of 'political and personal struggles' as follows:

> I felt very burdened when I first came here . . . It really bothered me, if somebody got abusive on the road . . . I then had my children and

I didn't work for three years. . . . I started looking for opportunities to write . . . the Islamisation [in Pakistan] began and this caused me great distress . . . I went home and . . . started a series of articles about women's issues and I started getting published in Asian magazines.[6]

Ahmad can be seen as part of a group of expatriate Pakistani writers. However, compared with Pakistani British writers such as Kureishi and Khan-Din who, according to John McLeod, using Paul Gilroy's terms, had to replace the 'grounded certainties of *roots*' with 'the transnational contingencies of *routes*' (215, his italics), Ahmad has had both experiences at her disposal. Whereas 'Kureishi's family history in South Asia may appear to him as just stories . . . very removed from his own' (McLeod 215), Ahmad has experienced these stories at first hand. She describes herself as a 'British-based South Asian writer or a writer of Pakistani origin living in London'.[7] Nonetheless, her self-identification by no means implies a straightforward feeling of belonging to the Pakistani community in Britain. Rather, her relationship with this community, in itself a very heterogeneous group, is marked by the ambiguity already identified by Stuart Hall in his seminal essay 'New Ethnicities' (1989), in which he discusses the need for essentialised black communities versus the need to acknowledge their heterogeneity. In contrast to a local Pakistani community leader who proclaims, 'A person cannot exist outside the community, as a wave cannot exist outside the ocean' (Werbner 240), Hall has emphasised that this kind of pan-ethnic rhetoric does not necessarily cut across all national, religious or class lines and is clearly gendered. Thus, any categories of so-called 'communities', whether based on national, cultural, religious or gender affiliations, need to be seen as constructed and context-specific. As Ahmad herself explains: 'I find that quite useless . . . for the writer to seek a location in the canon . . . for either a community or a nation state or a category such as gender. I . . . feel that in the end you're speaking for yourself.'[8]

In her play *Song for a Sanctuary*, Ahmad makes a point of questioning any kind of exclusionary identity politics based on cultural or national origins: Kamla, one of the social workers in a women's refuge, replies to the accusations of an Indian woman by asserting that she [Kamla] might be black but is certainly not Asian: 'You can't deny me my identity. . . .

---

[6] Author's interview with Rukhsana Ahmad, London, April 1999.
[7] Ibid.
[8] Ibid.

You people with your saris and your bloody lingo and all your certainties about the universe, you don't have a monopoly on being Asian. You can't box it and contain it and exclude others' (183). As a writer whose *routes* led her to England but whose *roots* remain firmly anchored in the socio-political realities of a postcolonial country, Ahmad can also be seen as part of the group of so-called 'postcolonial writers' whom critics often assumed to be more motivated by their presumed political agenda than their aesthetic visions. In England, Ahmad was eventually invited to join the Asian Women Writers' Collective.[9] As she states in her essay 'In Search of a Talisman': 'It was an exciting discovery – a group of women from the subcontinent who were all interested in writing, in feminist politics and in each other's work' (110). As Martina Ghosh-Schellhorn demonstrates, this group of Asian British women writers, set up in 1984 by the writer and activist Ravinder Randhawa, has also been portrayed in terms of a strict 'binary distinction between the aesthetic and social engagement' (37). Writers such as Ahmad 'write against' such simple, binary notions, not least because they question certain postcolonial theorists' refusal 'to connect a cultural politics of identity and difference to a social politics of justice and equality' (San Juan 12). The narrow path Ghosh-Schellhorn describes as 'the fine balance the Collective achieves between its self-consciousness as an activist group and its refusal to force activism to any kind of closure' (40), also marks Ahmad's work which is characterised by the aforementioned feminist consciousness coupled with an acute awareness of social and political conditions.

Ahmad has been working as a novelist, playwright, screenwriter and translator since 1986. She started her playwriting career with the pioneering theatre company Tara Arts, co-founded in 1977 by its artistic director Jatinder Verma. In 1990, Ahmad and Rita Wolf founded the Kali Theatre Company to promote new writings by Asian women dramatists. Their inaugural production was Ahmad's play *Song for a Sanctuary*. Subsequent productions by Kali include Ahmad's plays *Black Shalwar* (1999) and *River on Fire* (2001). *Black Shalwar* was Ahmad's adaptation of the short story 'Kali Shalwar' by the Urdu writer Saadat Hasan Manto. Apart from her stage and radio plays, translations and adaptations form an important part of Ahmad's œuvre. Even though Ahmad's parents were both Punjabis, they taught their children to speak Urdu because, as Ahmad explains, Punjabi has the status of a 'peasant language' whereas Urdu is spoken by upwardly mobile

[9] Originally called the Asian Women Writers' Workshop.

Pakistanis. Ahmad has edited and translated a collection of feminist Urdu poetry called *We Sinful Women* (1991), which consists of a larger number of poems by the two well-known Pakistani writers and poets, Kishwar Naheed and Fahmida Riaz, as well as featuring work by the younger contemporary poets Ishrat Aafreen, Saeeda Gazdar, Zehra Nigah, Neelma Sarwar and the late Sara Shagufta.[10] Ahmad also translated Altaf Fatima's Urdu novel *The One Who Did Not Ask* (1993). Ahmad's own first novel, *The Hope Chest*, was published in 1996 and a second novel is forthcoming. She has also edited (together with Rahila Gupta) *Flaming Spirit: Stories from the Asian Women Writers' Collective* (1994) and her short stories appear in various collections.[11] The following analysis of Ahmad's interrogations of how women, particularly in Pakistan and Britain, are affected by racism, poverty and patriarchy is mainly based on *The Hope Chest* and *Song for a Sanctuary* with further references to *We Sinful Women*.

Body Politics

After a long neglect of the body in academic discourse, economic, social and cultural transformations have fostered a vast increase of literature on the body over the last few years. Discourses, particularly in gender and cultural studies, on the cult of the body and on 'body politics' (whether understood in terms of early Western political theory or as formulated by feminist movements as a woman's right to control her own body) have positioned the body as 'a central object of personal concern, as well as a key social issue' (McDowell 36). However, despite efforts to deconstruct binary notions of sexuality and terms such as 'male' and 'female', women's bodies continue to be seen as inferior.

In the context of postcolonial literatures, analyses of the bodily representations of female protagonists are further complicated by the fact that in many countries women writers have encountered great

[10] First published in Pakistan as *Beyond Belief: Contemporary Feminist Urdu Poetry* (Lahore: ASR Publications, 1990).
[11] See *Prose and Poetry by the Asian Women Writers' Workshop* (1988), *The Inner Courtyard: Stories by Indian Women*, ed. Lakshmi Holmström (1990), *The Man Who Loved Presents: Seasonal Stories*, ed. Alison Campbell, Caroline Hallett, Jenny Palmer and Marijke Woolsey (1992). Ahmad has also edited *Dreams into Words* (1991) and *Daughters of the East* (1991) for the community publishing series Durham Voices.

difficulty when trying to address issues of sexuality, gender oppression and inequality (Loomba 229). Françoise Lionnet declares that 'in post-colonial literature the gendered and racialized body of the female prot-agonist is consistently overdetermined; it is a partial object on which are written various cultural scripts and their death-dealing blows' (87). In the West, this has partly led to very one-dimensional images of South Asian women, and particularly of Muslim women, who have been mainly constructed as submissive, dependent and oppressed victims. According to Alison Shaw, South Asian women residing in Britain have furthermore been described as 'doubly oppressed, subordinate to men at home and the victims of racism in the wider society' (132).

Regarding the situation of women in Pakistan, it has to be pointed out that under General Zia-ul-Haq (1977–88) the state, in con-junction with Islamic fundamentalists, clearly used religion as a means of exerting control over women and passed laws which reduced women's status. But Pakistani women have not remained silent in the face of these discriminations. This is exemplified by the formation of the Women's Action Forum (WAF) in 1981. The WAF addressed legal as well as social issues, such as the enforced segregation of women, stricter dress codes and new laws regarding adultery, rape and prostitution. Nonetheless, Ania Loomba's insistence that it is important to homogenise neither 'First World' nor 'Third World', women but to bear in mind that women's movements have been divided by different class, religious, sexual or political affiliations, remains important. The WAF is a case in point. Since its activists mainly came from an upper middle class of professional women, it has been criticised for failing to include more women from lower classes and rural backgrounds (Bano 205).

Regarding South Asian women in Britain, Shaw emphasises that their situation has improved. Her research shows that women have more control within as well as beyond their households and that increased female education and employment among South Asian British women not only mirrors Western values but changes within Pakistani society itself. Challenging one of the most persistent and most contested issues taken up in Western discourse on Muslim women, Noshin Ahmad explains:

> There is concern that the veil inhibits women from expressing their sexuality. . . . [but] the Muslim woman . . . critically engages with the veil, her body . . . as she sees fit. Women negotiate and use different strategies to lay claim to their bodies. (80)

Ahmad's work is strongly situated within this tripartite framework of women's conditions in Pakistan and Britain and the racialised representations of Pakistani women in the West. Ahmad's treatment of these issues is poignantly anti-essential in that her female protagonists, both in *The Hope Chest* and in *Song for a Sanctuary*, are vivid examples of the various ways young women in Pakistan and Britain construct their identities and claim their bodies (including the decision to wear a veil, for example). One of the reasons Ahmad gives for her work on *We Sinful Women* is that she wanted to 'dispel the assumption that women in the developing world are passive, voiceless and hopelessly conformist' (*WSW* 8).[12]

Up to a certain point *The Hope Chest* can be characterised as a female *Bildungsroman*, as Ahmad charts the journey from girlhood to womanhood of the novel's three young female protagonists, Rani, Reshma and Ruth. Bapsi Sidhwa describes the *Bildungsroman* as 'the dominant mode for Third World Literature' (Jussawalla and Dasenbrock 201).[13] However, while the 'Third World' *Bildungsroman* has usually been written from a male point of view, *The Hope Chest* offers a distinctly female perspective. Even though very different in terms of their social, socio-economic and cultural background, all three protagonists find that their bodies play a crucial role in the search for identity, whether illustrated by their experiences of resistance and subjection or physical and psychological illness. Rani and Reshma are both Pakistani, yet separated by their very different social and economic status: Rani comes from a wealthy upper-class family in Lahore. Reshma, a friend of Rani's younger sister Shehzadi, is the daughter of the poor gardener employed by Rani's family. When Rani is sent to a hospital in London for the treatment of her supposed anorexia, she becomes friends with the Londoner Ruth in the exclusive clinic. While Rani and Ruth try to come to terms with their psychological problems, Reshma's family force her, out of poverty, at the age of thirteen to marry a widower who is twice her age and has two small children. The second part of the novel shows its female protagonists five years later. Rani, now an art student, returns to the London clinic after having been

---

[12] For an account of contemporary Pakistani womanhood see Shahla Haeri's collection of interviews with six professional Pakistani women: *No Shame for the Sun: Professional Pakistani Women: Gender, Culture and Politics in the Middle East* (2002).

[13] For a discussion of the use of the *Bildungsroman* in postcolonial literature, see Anupama Jain, 'South Asian Women ReWrite the American Novel: Meena Alexander, Bharati Mukherjee, Bapsi Sidhwa and the Bildungsroman' in *Asian American Writing, Asian American Fiction vol. 2* (2001).

unhappily married to a man who was chosen for her by her mother. There, once again, she meets Ruth, now with a little daughter, who has also had to return to the clinic. Reshma's life has been dominated by the birth of her three children and is changed completely when she decides to terminate her fourth pregnancy. With the help of Shehzadi, now a medical student, she undergoes an abortion and a sterilisation, upon which her husband throws her out of the house and she has to return to her own parents without her children.

In her play *Song for a Sanctuary* Ahmad also foregrounds the relationship between a mother (Rajinder) and her daughter (Savita) and the subjugation of both to Pradeep, Rajinder's husband and Savita's father. The play is set inside a women's refuge in London to which Rajinder and Savita have escaped because of Pradeep's violence towards his wife and the sexual abuse of their daughter. Again, in *Song for a Sanctuary* Ahmad emphasises the conflicts evolving from the different national, cultural and socio-economic positions of the residents and refuge workers.

Gendered Spaces

In the novel as well as in the play (and also in various poems in *We Sinful Women*) the lives of women seem to be determined and confined by restrictive spaces from which there seems to be no escape. In *The Hope Chest* the characters mainly move between hospital rooms in Pakistan and London, their parents' houses and, later on, those of their spouses' families. The settings for *Song for a Sanctuary* consist of the claustrophobic and overcrowded refuge and an excursion to Rajinder and Savita's former home, now haunted with the memory of Pradeep's physical abuse and violence. From a geographer's perspective, Doreen Massey emphasises that 'the home may be as much a place of conflict as of repose. . . . Many women have had to leave home precisely in order to forge their own version of their identities' (11, 164). Anthropologists have pointed out the manifestation of privacy, and with it the attempt to protect the family's – or more precisely, its female members' – honour in the physical spaces of Pakistani households such as presented by high walls, concealed doorways or the practice of purdah, that is the spatial separation of women and men who are not closely related.[14] The media

---

[14] See Hastings Donnan's 'Family and Household in Pakistan' and Alison Shaw's 'Women, the Household and Family Ties: Pakistani Migrants in Britain', both in *Family and Gender in Pakistan: Domestic Organization in a Muslim Society* (1997).

campaign of General Zia called 'Chadur aur Chardiwari' (the veil and four walls) reflects this exact spatial seclusion of women (Ahmad 10). This strict dichotomy between the female's 'domestic' and the male's 'public' sphere, however, cannot be upheld in the face of social and economic transformations, such as labour migration and urban growth which has resulted in redefinitions of gender roles. This is reflected in Ahmad's novel: 'All the young men and boys seemed to have gone away to places like Saudi Arabia and Dubai. Only the women were left behind, to make trips to the post office, mostly waiting for money orders' (40–1). Also Reshma's father, Ajaib Khan, 'had moved South in search of a better job' (84).

Despite these developments, traditional gender roles remain a decisive factor in women's lives. Throughout history women have been seen as restricted to their bodies, whereas men have been associated with the disembodied mind. In this respect, their bodies can be seen as the ultimate spaces of confinement, marked by the way they are appropriated predominantly by men, but also by their own families. The motif of shame plays a dominant role in South Asian literature and is based on the traditional concepts of *izzat* (honour) and *sharam* (shame). As already mentioned, in reference to Ahmad's ambiguous relationship with Britain's Pakistani community, Pakistani women are expected to adhere to the strict terms laid down by traditional Pakistani society. Any nonconformist behaviour or failure in their duties as daughters, wives or mothers reflects on their family's honour. This extends to an expectation that domestic violence should be tolerated. As Shaminder Takhar points out, the 'importance of notions of shame (*sharam*) and honour (*izzat*), often used to explain the limits to [South Asian] women's participation in social and public arenas, has been challenged' by South Asian women's projects (216). Nevertheless, the repercussions of these traditional concepts reverberate throughout Ahmad's work. After having been banished from her husband's home after her abortion, Reshma is also cursed by her own mother with the words, 'You should have died before you had a chance to disgrace us like this' (272). In *Song for a Sanctuary*, Rajinder's sister Amrit warns that Rajinder's divorce would kill their parents: 'the shame of it all, the disgrace!' (171). The metaphor of the imprisoned body is also ubiquitous in the poems in *We Sinful Women*. In her poem 'She Is a Woman Impure' Fahmida Riaz portrays 'a woman impure / imprisoned by her flowing blood' (97), and in 'Akleema' she describes Cain and Abel's sister Akleema as 'Imprisoned by her own body' (99). Ishrat Aafreen likewise talks about 'the prisons of our bodies' in her poem 'Liberation' (155).

In *The Hope Chest*, Reshma's concluding thought summarises the condition of Ahmad's female characters: 'Whatever she had sought had involved only her own body. She had innocently assumed that that, at least, was her own' (274).

Each character's story reflects the ambiguity of spaces such as 'home' and 'body' as sites of repression *and* resistance. The first few sentences of *The Hope Chest* already indicate the limitations and the possibilities available to its female cast. During Rani's appendectomy the following surreal incident takes place:

> Rani's soul escaped and floated close to the ceiling directly above the operation table. It was a little outraged at the casual disregard with which her inert body was being treated. . . . Seemingly indifferent to the blood and gore stemming from the incision across her belly, the group of medics around the table were animately discussing whether Benazir Bhutto had had her nose 'done' or not. (3)

As if to indicate that issues such as a disembodied woman and patriarchal concepts of beauty are too complicated to be dealt with in realist terms, Ahmad resorts to what might be perceived as 'magic realism', a literary mode seen by some critics as characteristic of postcolonial literature. In view of the term's problematic association with exoticism, however, I would argue that Ahmad uses such Márquezian supernaturalisms as levitation in order to capture a specific human experience similar to what the Puerto Rican American playwright, José Rivera, in reference to his play *Each Day Dies With Sleep* (1992), explains as follows: '[T]here's the sad human urge to escape . . . unhappiness by diving into deep interior worlds where dreams are real and nightmares may somehow be tamed. . . . Those odysseys into the inner world of the imagination are journeys of survival' (163). Thus Rani's out-of-body experience, which she describes as 'a miraculous release for my soul, from the confines of my body' (220), recurs frequently and allows her to 'survive' unwanted experiences such as her wedding night: 'The spectre stood silent, outside her body, away from both of them, impassive and firm, waiting for him to finish, refusing to return' (186). Returning to her first out-of-body experience during her appendectomy, the medics' 'casual regard' eventually results in accidentally burning a little patch on Rani's thigh. Significantly, a young nurse called Meena notices the accident first. The ensuing commotion points to two of the novel's dominant and interlinked themes: the increasing social stratification of Pakistani society and the commodification of women's bodies. Thus, the male surgeon, Dr Samad, is not so much worried about Rani's injury but first and foremost about his reputation with future wealthy patients. He 'looked dismayed as though he had been cheated out of winning a sizeable lottery by a single digit' (5). While he is mainly trying to find someone to blame, Meena calls for action: 'she was the only one, Rani's soul decided, with some gratitude, who appeared to have any concern for the body' (6). Reshma undergoes a similar experience before her abortion when she feels that 'Her body was taken over and duly prepared for the "clinical procedure"' (215). Even though Rani recovers from the appendectomy, it leaves her a changed person, symbolised by her dwindling appetite, caused by the memory of the smell of her own burning flesh: 'that unforgettable odour . . . began to haunt her every waking moment' (7).

Eventually, Rani's condition is diagnosed as anorexia nervosa. Bryan Turner points out that 'social and collective practices operating on the body of the anorexic should not detract from its political feature of anorexia as a domestic rebellion. . . . a contest . . . over the control of the individual's body' (194).[15] Rani's parents take her to an exclusive clinic in London. Their motives for this move are ambiguous and reflect the balancing act of negotiating tradition and change within Pakistani society. Her mother's vision of a woman's life is very traditional: 'What's a woman's life without marriage and children . . .? Nothing if you ask me' (246). Shahana's overriding ambition is to acquire 'two wonderful sons-in-law' (7). Anything threatening her plans has to be fought accordingly, especially a psychological illness. Similar cultural and parental attitudes have been addressed in the work of other South Asian British writers, as when Saleem Sinai in Salman Rushdie's *Midnight's Children* (1981) realises that he lives 'in a country where any physical or mental peculiarity in a child is a source of deep family shame' (216). Similarly, Karim Amir, Kureishi's Pakistani British hero in *The Buddha of Suburbia* (1990) declares that 'In my family nervous breakdowns were as exotic as New Orleans' (11). But Shahana's decisions are also governed by an increasingly stratified Pakistani society. Sabra Bano explains that the transformation of Pakistani cities into consumer societies resulted in higher competition for consumer goods and the prestige attached to them (197).

[15] For an analysis of anorexia as protest and rebellion (often in conjunction with an identity crisis), see Kim Chernin, *The Hungry Self: Women, Eating and Identity* (1985) and Susie Orbach, *Hunger Strike: The Anorectic's Struggle as a Metaphor for our Age* (1986).

When faced with Rani's sudden appendectomy, Shahana's main concern is not only her daughter:

> If it had not been an emergency . . . they would have taken her abroad for surgery. Money was not a problem for Shahana and Saeed. The bigger problem would be explaining to all their friends why poor Rani should have been subjected to the dangers of major surgery at a government hospital in Lahore. (3)

Rani responds to her mother's traditional demands for a suitable marriage through her body: 'A deep feeling of depression had settled on Rani's spirits. Something was awfully wrong with her own life . . . she exptected . . . Shahana . . . [was] at the heart of the problem. . . . Her breakfast tray revolted her . . . She made a dash for the bathroom as her stomach heaved helplessly' (67). In this context, Rani is exemplary of many Pakistani upper-middle-class women who, according to Hastings Donnan, display an often 'outright hostility towards idealized female domestic roles' (15). In the second part of the novel, faced with her arranged marriage, Rani experiences a relapse of her anorexia. Even though she agrees to marry the man her mother has chosen for her, on her wedding night she recalls her mother-in-law's eyes when they first met: 'A strangely cold, assessing look had sized her face, her body, her person, for what it was worth' and recognises the same look on her husband's face (183). She realises that her mother's control over her has been replaced by that of her husband, Kamal, and her mother-in-law, Punni. Ahmad situates inter-generational conflicts such as these, particularly between mothers and daughters and mothers-in-law and daughters-in-law, in the broader context of social and cultural restrictions faced by Pakistani and South Asian women in general. Loomba emphasises that women's political participation in postcolonial societies does not always necessarily reflect a feminist agenda: 'women are objects as well as subjects of fundamentalist discourses' (226). Similarly, Anita Desai observes that in Indian society 'women are as responsible as men are for all those old orthodoxies and traditions having been kept alive through the generations' (Jussawalla and Dasenbrock 165).

The inter-generational conflicts between Ahmad's female characters must thus be seen within the context of traditional notions of womanhood held and enforced by an older generation of women and the younger women's tentative attempts to challenge these 'mountains of dead traditions / mountains of blind beliefs / mountains of cruel hatreds', as Ishrat Aafreen describes them in her poem 'Liberation' (*WSW* 155). As she says in 'Ghazal', 'Enough poison there is of traditions to last us a / lifetime' (*WSW* 163). Again, it is the concepts of *izzat* and *sharam*, in particular, which – not least because they guarantee a daughter's (and in extension a family's) financial future – are regarded as absolutely essential by mothers and mothers-in-law and through which young women's lives are monitored and controlled. Depending on their class background (economic and educational status), young women react differently to the restrictions and expectations (specifically in terms of marriage and the birth of sons) imposed on them by their families. Rani reacts to the commodification of her body by her family and her husband with a renewed refusal to eat.[16] As anorexia also has negative effects on a woman's ability to conceive, Rani remains childless and eventually separates from her husband. After another consultation with her London psychiatrist, Rani finally realises that she has to take responsibility for her life, that her refusal to eat is only a temporary means of gaining control over her own body, and would eventually lead to its gradual destruction, and that her marriage lies at the core of her problems: 'I have to decide for myself what I want from life and . . . to fight for it. I have to stop running away from things' (255). Although both Rani's and Reshma's marriages end, Rani's economic position enables her to tell her unfaithful husband to leave her house and she is able to pursue her ambitions as a painter and refuse a life as wife and mother. She realises that in contrast to Reshma, who is thrown out of her husband's house and is denied access to her children, 'I will manage. This should be easy for me, easier than it is for any of them . . . at least I have a place of my own where I might begin to find myself' (306).

For obvious reasons, Reshma's strategies of resistance are very different. She comes from a very poor family and has 'understood the vagaries of inequality very early in her life' (213). But when, at twenty-one, Reshma is faced with the pressure of adding another child to the other five, she also claims control over her own body. She asks Shehzadi for help: 'I want to get . . . the operation . . . they stitch up the womb? So I don't have any more children . . . I must . . . get rid of it . . . this new . . . one' (209). Referring back to Noshin Ahmad's notion of a

---

[16] For Kamal, Rani had been 'the most sensible choice, rather than the most desirable one'. Upon entering 'the smart bungalow, a part of Rani's dowry, he had felt a distinct sense of triumph; for it was, he knew, a price tag which honoured him, confirmed his own desirability as a son-in-law' (181).

critical engagement with the veil, the figure of Reshma also illustrates the issue's complexity. In contrast to Western representations of veiling as an exclusively oppressive mechanism of male control over women, Ahmad emphasises an individual Muslim woman's agency, which might also result in using the veil defiantly, as seen in Reshma's case: before she enters the hospital, there was an 'almost invisible shudder, and Reshma pulled her *chadur* tightly around herself in a defensive gesture' (213).[17] Nonetheless, Ahmad also points out how women's choices, particularly in the non-Western world, are still mainly dictated by what Brah describes as the 'socio-economic, political and cultural conditions' of their migratory journeys (182). As Ahmad explains, 'I suppose I'm always preoccupied by that subject of divisions between people. . . . *The Hope Chest* is about that, how you know that the context that you are born into completely separates you from all other people and all other experiences.'[18] In *Song for a Sanctuary* Ahmad painfully shows that a common, terrible experience such as domestic violence does not necessarily lead to the construction of a 'strategic community' of women. Rajinder is not only portrayed as her husband's victim, but also as being trapped within her own prejudices, which make it impossible for her to feel any kind of solidarity with her fellow refuge residents, as when she tells Kamla that 'I'm not one of your illiterate working class women to be managed by you' (174). As Brah points out, 'female cultures are not devoid of contradictions, tensions, rivalry or inter-generational differences that may spill over into conflict' (82).

Although an analysis of the third female protagonist in the novel, Ruth, Rani's British friend in the London clinic, exceeds the scope of this essay, Ruth also uses her body in a way which counters her mother's aspirations, who had hoped that she would become an independent, educated young professional. Instead, Ruth deliberately becomes a single, young mother. All three women engage in physical rebellions against the expectations of their environment, most poignantly symbolised in the metaphor of the 'hope chest', which, again, marks the fundamentally different life-plans as envisioned by mothers and daughters. Thus, for Shahana, the metal trunk, full of 'linens and quilts, saris and rolls of silk and chiffon . . . priceless collectables' represents 'years of saving, and years of hope . . . so that when the time comes (and it always does) to produce a respectable dowry to wed her daughter

---

[17] See also Katherine Bullock, *Rethinking Muslim Women and the Veil* (2002).
[18] Author's interview with Rukhsana Ahmad, London, April 1999.

there would be a sense of abundance' (246). Rani, on the other hand, experiences the trousseau as follows: 'A palpable image of the trunk ballooned in her imagination, gripped her senses and weighed her down. . . . It was . . . as if . . . someone had locked her inside that silver trunk and thrown away the key' (247).

Through the juxtaposition of such different biographies as Rani's and Reshma's, who come from opposite ends of Pakistan's socio-economic stratum, Ahmad challenges the often too simplistic contrast between the warmth and community of Rani's home country and the grey and cold city life during her residences at the London clinic, often found in analyses of postcolonial literatures and in works of older male postcolonial writers, where the narrative shifts between Western and non-Western settings. Whereas fiction by male migrants is often characterised by nostalgic notions of an idealised Caribbean island or an Indian village, Ahmad portrays the harsh conditions for women, both in Britain and in Pakistan, where it is possible, for example, that a locust storm ruins Reshma's family's crop, and she is forced to marry at thirteen for the survival of the family. In 'In Search of a Talisman', Ahmad herself concedes that her relationship with Pakistan has considerably changed over the years and that 'sentimental visits home' taught her a better understanding 'of the political structures that operated against the poor' (111).

Conclusion

Ahmad's work is characterised by a complex poetics of gender, race, class, religion and place. The often explicitly Western assumption of a conflict between aesthetic and social engagement is of no avail in the reading of Ahmad's work and in extension that of many other postcolonial women writers. Her work as a writer and feminist activist is firmly situated within the tradition of Pakistani, and particularly Urdu women writers, who have escaped 'the stranglehold on aesthetic values' (WSW 1), who have extended 'the frontiers of form and thought' and developed a progressive tradition of Urdu writing 'with a strong commitment to political action' (WSW 7). In the case of the women poets Ahmad selected for We Sinful Women, this meant that in order to address contemporary Pakistani women's lives through Urdu poetry (traditionally still largely known as 'love poetry'), conventional (that is, traditional) representations of women were abandoned and language was 'modernised': 'Poems . . . are not only deliberately political, they are also consciously averse to the stilted, formal diction popular with earlier Urdu poets. . . . [they] not only refuse to conform to the notion of the ideal woman, they set out to defy it and to claim a new identity. Fahmida Riaz . . . finds greater vitality in the language of peasants and working people' (*WSW* 3). Similar choices (for example, emphasis on the heterogeneity of Pakistani women, flexible forms of identity, representation of an increasingly stratified Pakistani society through linguistic differences, incorporation of taboo subjects such as anorexia) are reflected in Ahmad's own work. Even though she describes her work on the whole as 'quite die-hard realistic', she finds 'phantasy very useful as a device', particularly in her work for the stage.[19] Her emphasis on polyphonic voices finds its stylistic expression in her polyglot abilities as a writer *and* translator. As she states in 'In Search of a Talisman': 'This is a major concern of my writing now – a concern that crosses borders and feels the iniquities within societies and across frontiers . . . Pakistan, or India or Britain, become merely the context of the scenario I choose for my work' (111).

Ahmad's female protagonists are clearly marked by their gendered identities and their circumstances of class and place. True to Susan Bardo's explanation that 'women engage in self-destructive behaviour in order to compensate for their lack of social power' (Lionnet 95), all three women in *The Hope Chest* partly succeed in their rejection of traditional gender roles through bodily resistance and subversion: at the end of the novel, Rani becomes a painter, Reshma trains as a midwife and Ruth cares for her daughter, tellingly named Faith. In view of the fact that all three women have also attempted suicide, however, Ahmad seems to advise caution in overemphasising any strategies of bodily resistance. Whereas her novel at least indicates the possibilities inherent in the breakdown of family structures under crisis through the female characters' newly found agency, in *Song for a Sanctuary* she painfully illustrates that female bodies continue to be controlled and even destroyed by male power. The play ends with Pradeep stabbing his wife, and his words: 'This is not murder, it is a death sentence . . . She can't leave me, she's my wife' (186).

The epigraph of *The Hope Chest* – 'Why do women keep their jewels locked in trunks / To whom will they bequeath their legacy of grief?' – is taken from one of the *ghazals* in *We Sinful Women*,[20] called simply

---

[19] Ibid.

[20] As Ahmad explains, the *ghazal* is one of 'the most popular conventional' forms in Urdu poetry: 'It requires an ornamental style of writing. . . . In common with the sonnet it has a structured rhyme scheme and carefully controlled rhythm' (*WSW* 3).

'Ghazal' (171), by Ishrat Aafreen, about whom Ahmad writes: 'She identifies how that which is upheld as heroic, pure and virtuous womanhood actually destroys and consumes women' (*WSW* 27). Rani's mother, Shahana, realises this herself in a moment of clarity: 'The hopes she had pinned to the prospect of a baby had nothing to do with Rani herself. They were part of a collective dream, one of those dreams which had not been dreamt by her but had been handed down to her, by her own mother. Dreams woven into songs and stories . . . Songs which mock the failure of that dream with cruelty, or the ones which recount the pain of that failure with tears' (258). Some of the later lines of the same poem could be an appropriate epigraph for *Song for a Sanctuary*: 'When tragedies strike behind a closed door / Why do the walls often seem to know? . . . Why are the nights armed with daggers when they come?' (*WSW* 171). Returning to this essay's epigraph, it is important to note that in Ahmad's work – to borrow Reshma's words – 'the contradictions never resolved themselves easily' (84). There are indeed no easy solutions to the complex cultural, political, economic, sexual and religious issues (that is, traditional values versus modern lifestyles) addressed by Ahmad. In the face of the confrontational sites negotiated by Ahmad's characters, perhaps Rani's realisation, after she has asked her husband to leave, is no small success to strive for: 'You did it, Rani! You didn't disgrace yourself, you came out of it with dignity, all by yourself, and without breaking down. Well done!' (305).

Works Cited

Ahmad, Noshin. 'Hijabs in Our Midst' in *Young Britain: Politics, Pleasures and Predicaments*, ed. Jonathan Rutherford (London: Lawrence & Wishart, 1998). 74–82.

Ahmad, Rukhsana. *The Hope Chest* (London: Virago, 1996).

———. 'In Search of a Talisman' in *Voices of the Crossing: The Impact of Britain on Writers from Asia, the Caribbean and Africa*, ed. Ferdinand Dennis and Naseem Khan (London: Serpent's Tail, 2000). 101–115.

———. *Song for a Sanctuary* in *Six Plays by Black and Asian Women Writers*, ed. Kadija George (London: Aurora Metro Press, 1993). 159–86.

——— ed. *We Sinful Women: Contemporary Urdu Feminist Poetry* (London: Women's Press, 1991).

Asian Women Writers' Workshop, ed. *Prose and Poetry by the Asian Women Writer's Workshop* (London: Women's Press, 1988).

Bano, Sabra. 'Women, Class, and Islam in Karachi' in *Family and Gender in Pakistan: Domestic Organization in a Muslim Society*, ed. Hastings Donnan and Frits Selier (New Delhi: Hindustan Publishing Corporation, 1997). 189–207.

102   CHRISTIANE SCHLOTE

Brah, Avtar. *Cartographies of Diaspora: Contesting Identities* (London: Routledge, 1996).

Brewer, Rose M. 'Theorizing Race, Class and Gender: The new scholarship of Black feminist intellectuals and Black women's labor' in *Theorizing Black Feminisms: The Visionary Pragmatism of Black Women*, ed. Stanlie M. James and Abena P. A. Busia (London: Routledge, 1993). 13–30

Bullock, Katherine. *Rethinking Muslim Women and the Veil* (London: IIIT, 2002).

Campbell, Alison, Caroline Hallett, Jenny Palmer and Marijke Woolsey, eds. *The Man Who Loved Presents: Seasonal Stories* (London: Women's Press, 1992).

Chernin, Kim. *The Hungry Self: Women, Eating and Identity* (London: Virago, 1985).

Donnan, Hastings. 'Family and Household in Pakistan' in *Family and Gender in Pakistan: Domestic Organization in a Muslim Society*, ed. Hastings Donnan and Frits Selier (New Delhi: Hindustan Publishing Corporation, 1997). 1–24

Ghosh-Schellhorn, Martina. 'Cyborg Goddesses? Some Thoughts on the Asian Women Writers' Collective', *Hard Times*, 67/68 (Autumn 1999): 38–42.

Haeri, Shahla, ed. *No Shame for the Sun: Professional Pakistani Women: Gender, Culture and Politics in the Middle East* (Syracuse: Syracuse University Press, 2002).

Hall, Stuart. 'New Ethnicities' in *Black British Cultural Studies*, ed. Houston A. Baker, Manthia Diawara and Ruth H. Lindeborg (Chicago: The University of Chicago Press, 1996). 163–172.

Hand, Felicity. 'Gentle Anthropology', *Cuadernos de Filología Inglesa*, vol. 7:1 (1998): 41–52.

Holmström, Lakshmi, ed. *The Inner Courtyard: Stories by Indian Women* (London: Virago, 1990).

Hussein, Aamer, Mumtaz Shirin and Jamila Hasmi. *Hoops of Fire: Fifty Years of Fiction by Pakistani Women* (London: Zed Books, 2000).

Jain, Anupama. 'South Asian Women ReWrite the American Novel: Meena Alexander, Bharati Mukherjee, Bapsi Sidhwa and the Bildungsroman' in *Asian American Writing, Asian American Fiction vol. 2*, ed. Somdatta Mandal (London: Sangam Books, 2001). 123–33

Jussawalla, Feroza and Reed Way Dasenbrock, eds. *Interviews with Writers of the Post-Colonial World* (Jackson and London: University Press of Mississippi, 1992).

Kureishi, Hanif. *The Buddha of Suburbia* (London: Faber & Faber, 1990).

Lionnet, Françoise. *Postcolonial Representations: Women, Literature, Identity* (Ithaca: Cornell University Press, 1995).

Loomba, Ania. *Colonialism/Postcolonialism* (London: Routledge, 1998).

Massey, Doreen. *Space, Place, and Gender* (Minneapolis: University of Minnesota Press, 1994).

McDowell, Linda. *Gender, Identity and Place: Understanding Feminist Geographies* (Cambridge: Polity Press, 1999).

McLeod, John. *Beginning Postcolonialism* (Manchester: Manchester University Press, 2000).

Mumtaz, Khawar and Farida Shaheed, eds. *Women of Pakistan: Two Steps Forward, One Step Back?* (London: Zed Books, 1987).

Orbach, Susie. *Hunger Strike: The Anorectic's Struggle as a Metaphor for Our Age* (London: Faber & Faber, 1986).

Rivera, José. *Each Day Dies With Sleep, Studies in American Drama 1945–Present*, vol. 7:2 (1992): 167–239.

Rushdie, Salman. *Midnight's Children*. 1981. (New York: Alfred A. Knopf, 1995).

San Juan, Epifanio, Jr. *Beyond Postcolonial Theory* (New York: St Martin's Press, 1998).

Schwarz, Henry and Sangeeta Ray, eds. *A Companion to Postcolonial Studies* (Oxford: Blackwell, 2000).

Shamsie, Muneeza, ed. *A Dragonfly in the Sun: An Anthology of Pakistani Writing in English* (Oxford: Oxford University Press, 1997).

Shamsie, Muneeza. 'At the new threshold', *DAWN* (the internet edition): http://www.dawn.com/events/century/cul7.htm, 2000.

Sharma, Sanjay, John Hutnyk and Ashwani Sharma, eds. *Dis-Orienting Rhythms: The Politics of the New Asian Dance Music* (London: Zed Books, 1996).

Shaw, Alison. 'Women, the Household and Family Ties: Pakistani Migrants in Britain' in *Family and Gender in Pakistan: Domestic Organization in a Muslim Society*, ed. Hastings Donnan and Frits Selier (New Delhi: Hindustan Publishing Corporation, 1997). 132–55

Takhar, Shaminder. 'South Asian Women and the Question of Political Organization' in *South Asian Women in the Diaspora*, ed. Nirmal Puwar and Parvati Raghuram (Oxford and New York: Berg, 2003). 215–226

Turner, Bryan S. *The Body and Society: Explorations in Social Theory* (London: Sage, 1996).

Werbner, Pnina. 'Essentialising Essentialism, Essentialising Silence: Ambivalence and Multiplicity in the Constructions of Racism and Ethnicity' in *Debating Cultural Hybridity: Multi-Cultural Identities and the Politics of Anti-Racism*, ed. Pnina Werbner and Tariq Modood (London: Zed Books, 1997). 226–56

'The Nonsense about Our Irishness':
Jennifer Johnston

FELICITY ROSSLYN

Jennifer Johnston (b.1930) lives in Derry, Northern Ireland, and is the author of thirteen novels, most of them concerned with Irish political and human dilemmas. She grew up as a Protestant in Dublin, in an artistic and secular family, and studied at Trinity College before settling in London for twenty years at the time of her first marriage (1951). Surprisingly, however, she returned to live in Derry at the time of the Troubles, which was also when her writing career began (she was first published in 1972). Her claim to inclusion among 'British' women writers would be that no-one has represented more convincingly the ongoing presence of English Protestantism in Ireland (and its painful relations with Catholicism) than Johnston. It was probably as important for her to live in England in her twenties as it was to return to Ireland in her forties; and the detachment of many of her narrators from either British or Irish nationalism may well be what Johnston herself achieved by her decades in London. In her many fictions since 1972 (she has published almost every other year) Johnston has built up a comprehensive picture of the struggles and counter-struggles of British and Irish self-definition in the twentieth century.

Her determination to be in Ireland at the time of the Troubles may be the key to the unusual seriousness and dedication of her career as a writer. She has recently said in interview, 'When the country is going through upheaval I feel one ought to be there. I found it splendid and awful to come back.'[1] This instinct to locate herself in the eye of the storm has also shown itself in her outspoken and increasingly prominent career in literary Ireland, where she stirs quite conflicting feelings. She is a difficult figure to pigeon-hole, either politically or culturally. Her pride in her Protestant roots, for instance, does not prevent her from hoping one day to see a united Ireland: 'It's terribly silly a country this size can be divided. I think, God, we are all being insane.'[2] She openly

[1] Gail Walker, 'Interview with Jennifer Johnston', *Belfast Telegraph*, 24 October 2002.
[2] Ibid.

expresses an impatience with the separatism of the North that must
have cost her many of her natural admirers: 'We must look to reality and
decide that we want to be part of this heritage and stop looking at it as
oppression . . . This is one of the things I try and sell and perhaps
I don't succeed and this maybe accounts for the lack of enthusiasm for
my work on literary circuits' (McManus 36–7).

But, at the same time, she takes an equally sceptical view of the
culture of the Republic. When an interviewer suggested she wrote in
a 'demythologising' spirit both about the Troubles and the struggle for
independence, she was happy to agree. Her subject, she continued,
was 'all the nonsense between Protestants and Catholics. It includes
the extraordinary way in which over the last seventy years we've had
nonsense instilled in us about our Irishness. All this has to go, and
there are still quite a lot of people clinging on to the vestiges of that
which I think is really rather a pity' (York 44–5). One source of this
robustness about religious issues ('the nonsense between Protestants
and Catholics') is a freethinking home background that left Johnston
to share in the family life of the Catholic housekeeper for most of her
childhood and omitted to christen her until she asked it herself, when
she was twelve, for fear of going to limbo (Quinn 52–3). Her position
on the 'nonsense instilled in us about our Irishness' may similarly
derive from the unorthodox milieu of her parents, who were both
controversial figures in Dublin's theatre life. Her mother was Shelah
Richards, an Abbey Theatre actress who became a freelance director
and withstood the ire of the Catholic church and bomb threats to
keep a production open for the first three days of Holy Week in the
1940s (Longley 18). Her father was the playwright Denis Johnston,
whose brilliant first play was rejected by the increasingly conservative
Abbey and became the opening success of the experimental Gate
Theatre. Its title cheerfully reflects the offence it gave to Lady
Augusta Gregory, the gatekeeper (with Yeats) of Irish national drama:
The Old Lady Says No. Jennifer Johnston was born seven months after
the play opened, in 1930.

The 'nonsense' about Irishness that Johnston's parents were combat-
ing in their generation was the end result of the Literary Revival and its
backward-looking concern with mythology, peasantry and the Irish
language. They also struggled with the cultural defensiveness of the new
state, as it expressed itself in increasing xenophobia and censorship. In
Johnston's lifetime ('over the last seventy years') the 'nonsense instilled
in us about our Irishness' she deplores is the whole political, legal and
cultural effort to create an Irish nation as a separate entity – an entity

currently distinct from Northern Ireland, where a very similar-seeming population claims to be as 100% British as the Republic is 100% Irish. Johnston's own position on the realities of Ireland's history is probably reflected in the remarks made by a crusty character in her latest novel, who calls the Anglo-Irish abandoning Ireland in the 1920s 'fools': 'This is an infernal bloody country,' he says, 'but it's my infernal bloody country and I hope my children feel the same about it. For better or for worse. It's like a marriage' (*This Is Not a Novel* 113).

Johnston's sense that the cultural 'marriage' of Britain and Ireland is at least as substantial a fact as their twentieth-century divorce (and probably, that she herself is the daughter of that marriage) would explain what is otherwise a bewildering fact about her, that in spite of being widely acclaimed at different times in her thirty-year career, she is far from famous. She has passionate readers in both countries, and has won the Whitbread Prize – for *The Old Jest* (1979) – while *Shadows on Our Skin* (1977) was shortlisted for the Booker. Several of her books have been dramatised for film and television, they are translated into French, German and Italian, and they are well entrenched in the school syllabus. In spite of this she has nothing like the iconic status she would surely have acquired had she spoken up in favour of only one party to the political divorce. Writers like Bernard MacLaverty and William Trevor have enjoyed much more publicity, while handling very similar historical and political themes.[3] Molly Keane and Edna O'Brien are much more familiar names among women writers, though Johnston has written about the same female dilemmas and dramatised the price of social and sexual hypocrisy in modern Ireland more sharply than either.

Perhaps a wider public appeal is what Johnston is willing to sacrifice to retain her position of scrupulous detachment. She will not grieve over the Irish predicament without analysing the reasons why it is so prolonged and repetitive, and there are no sentimental pleasures to be had from her fictions, however well disguised. Her brief and elliptical novels do not yield all their depth on first reading, and she might say (with her favourite Jane Austen) 'I do not write for such dull Elves / As have not a great deal of Ingenuity themselves' (*Letters* 202). Those who appreciate her, however, rate her very

---

[3] MacLaverty's *Cal* (1983) has much in common with *Shadows on Our Skin* (1977) and Trevor's *The Story of Lucy Gault* (2002) is not dissimilar to *Fool's Sanctuary* (1987), but Johnston's handling of the materials is more restrained and credible than either.

highly indeed. Among her admirers have been the late Anthony Burgess, who spoke of her 'unique and perfect art',[4] and Derek Mahon, who calls her 'a poet' (104). In Sebastian Barry's forthrightly partisan preface to a recent omnibus edition of three Johnston novels, he represents her as a key figure for Ireland's artistic health:

> There is nothing official about Johnston, she is subversive, conservative, innovative and deeply traditional all at the same time. She is solitary and unique but completely integrated into the general geist and flavour of her country. She is in a way the most benign of Irish writers, in the way Tolstoy was the most benign of Russian. She is helpful to the emergency and healing of the heart. She does the air good for having breathed of it, and she has done the general good health and will of Irish writing and writers a ferocious service, forcing the stakes high. ('Preface')

Barry's sense that Johnston is 'helpful to the emergency' of contemporary Ireland and is contributing to the 'general good health' of its writing may turn out to have been prescient. The general bearing of her fictions is that the two parts of Ireland need one another, and indeed, belong together. This is in a sense a conservative position; but after decades of bloodshed it has all the force of innovation, and if Ireland should ever reunite politically, Johnston will have been one of those who paved the way.

Part of Johnston's contribution is to undermine the clichés of self-definition in Ireland (by religion, geography, heritage). Her characters are typically impatient with their social roles and are searching for better ways of living than are offered them. Perhaps as a result of her early exposure to the theatre, she represents characters chiefly through their voices, without authorial commentary. She uses just a few in each novel and shows great respect for their autonomy:

> One of the reasons I don't like my first book [*The Gates*[5]] is that I was able to cope with my main characters, but I had a lot of characters who were just furniture. It's terribly easy just to have people as props, and I think this is one of the differences between people telling stories where wonderful, exciting things can happen, but the people

---

[4] Quotation taken from reviews printed in the Flamingo edition of *Shadows on Our Skin* (London: Fontana, 1966).
[5] *The Gates* was Johnston's first novel, though *The Captains and the Kings* was the first accepted for publication.

are not real in any way. It's a sort of imponderable, it's a very difficult
thing to explain to people who are writing first, that if you're going
to be a serious writer you've got to teach yourself somehow or other
how to make a character breathe, how to make a character appear to
have a life, even when you turn the page over and they're not there
any longer. I can't explain how it happens, I just know that's one of
the differences between good writing and just storytelling.[6]

The typical structure of a Johnston novel has a fully 'breathing'
character like this retelling the story of the past, usually after some key
event (a killing, an operation, a burial or a scandal of some kind). The
dramatic denouement is not the point of the novel. It has already
happened; the point is to understand how the narrator arrived there,
and so the usual tone of narration is tentative, questioning, ironic and
curious.

The complication in Johnston's fictions that leads to the disastrous
outcome is most often a friendship across the political and social divide.
She shows two people developing a profound loyalty in private that is
then challenged, and wrecked, by their public obligations. It is the
variety and unexpectedness of these unofficial bonds that justifies
Barry's sense of her 'subversiveness': in *The Captains and the Kings*
(1972) it is the whisky-soaked inheritor of the big house and the boy
sent to work in his garden, in *Shadows on Our Skin* it is the schoolboy
poet and the hard-smoking woman teacher, and in *The Old Jest* it is the
daughter of the house and an ageing terrorist. The motif shows itself
capable of infinite variations across her fictions, but its value for
Johnston's purposes is that it sets off with great clarity the contrast
between the originality of human beings in their personal relations, and
the coerciveness of the social and historical forces they live among.
These are the everyday truths she wants to engage with; as she has said,
'I don't care about the big issues. What I care about is how we manage
to live with the big issues going on around us and how we manage to
face ourselves' (McManus 36).

But it is also striking that none of these involvements is romantic or
sexual (although other people sometimes suspect they are, thereby pre-
cipitating the disaster). Johnston's scepticism extends to the representation of love in fiction too: 'The power of friendship . . . I think can be
sublime. Friendship is a much more interesting notion to me than the

---

[6] Quotation taken from an Australian radio interview, 'Writers on Writing'.
See www.abc.net.au/writers/radioep6.htm

interest of love, unless you're talking about love in a sort of religious way, which is something totally different. But the notion of love that we all have in our heads, you . . . grow up, you fall in love with somebody, you get married to them, you go on loving them forever; I think it's a sort of fairy story that we have to disabuse people of.'[7] By avoiding 'romantic interest' and the implication that personal happiness can be some kind of solution to historical grief, Johnston stays close to her real target: the representation of how closely the two halves of Irish identity fit together – whether the parties are young or old, men or women, northerners or southerners – and what is lost by each generation when the two are forced apart.

Johnston's thirteen novels have disparate historical and social settings, but for the sake of clarity we might group them in the three historical periods they deal with: the early twentieth century, the Troubles, and Ireland as it is now. In the most acclaimed fictions of her early career her imagination goes back to the Ireland her parents grew up in: the Ireland of decaying Big Houses, the carnage of World War I and the bitterness of the Civil War.[8] In *How Many Miles to Babylon?* (1974), *The Old Jest*, and *Fool's Sanctuary* (1987), she investigates in different ways what made the birthpangs of the new Republic so prolonged and so painful. A bullet brings a shattering end to each narrative, but it comes from varied sources. In the first, it is an Anglo-Irish officer killing his best (Republican) friend; in the second, the British execute the Anglo-Irish organiser of a Republican terrorist attack; and in the last, it is the IRA themselves who are executing their own agent for his loyalty to his Anglo-Irish friends. The stories Johnston tells are not of the struggle of coloniser and colonised, but the struggle each character undergoes to know on what side he or she belongs, and what loyalty would mean under such confusing circumstances. The main characters in each fiction are fighting with what they call 'honour' and for a cause they take to be 'honourable', but they die with the counter-accusation of dishonour ringing in their ears.

Between writing these intensely imagined stories of the past, Johnston has written about a more familiar Ireland, the one she has

---

[7] Ibid.

[8] At this point in her career Johnston was suspected of being an apologist for the dying Ascendancy culture (for example, by Seamus Deane); see Ann Owens Weekes, *Irish Women Writers: An Uncharted Tradition* (1990). More recent critics have acknowledged her unusual mixture of 'sympathy and objectivity' (Mortimer p.213; see also Weekes pp.193–8).

inhabited since the 1970s: *The Gates* (1973), *Shadows on Our Skin* (1977), *The Christmas Tree* (1981), *The Railway Station Man* (1984), *The Illusionist* (1995) and *The Gingerbread Woman* (2000). In these novels the Troubles are often brutally present, in shootings, bombings and accidental deaths. But true to her concern with 'how we manage to live with the big issues going on around us and how we manage to face ourselves', she keeps ordinary Irish lives in the foreground. The Big Houses have been sold off for hotels and nursing homes; all the narrators of these stories are women, financially vulnerable and only residually Protestant, but their narratives show them to be courageous and questioning. They have modern decisions to make, about marriages and professions, and they waver between painful choices that Johnston knows from the inside: between loyalty to the past or the present, England or Ireland, and between domesticity or the life of an artist. Several of these fictions show women discovering their creativity late in life and against the odds (*The Christmas Tree, The Railway Station Man, The Illusionist, The Gingerbread Woman*) and the seriousness of her handling of their predicament doubtless reflects Johnston's own experience, as someone who discovered her vocation while leading a life of domesticity in England, bringing up a family of four children. (Her return to Ireland coincided with her second marriage and made her the stepmother of five children more.) If the word that chimes through her novels about World War I and its aftermath is 'honour', the word that chimes through these novels is 'freedom'. What freedom might be, what kind of freedom would be worth having, by whose definition – these are questions that concern the heroines of these stories as much as they preoccupy the bomb-makers and 'freedom-fighters' who bring sudden death into these women's lives.

The third and final period of Ireland's development that Johnston has responded to is the tentative normality that has been achieved since the cessation of political violence in the 1990s. With the political emergency no longer dominant, social issues are rising into public view, and Johnston has begun to open up the Pandora's box of past suppressions about sexual behaviour in Ireland. In three of her most recent fictions she meditates on the legacy of sexual hypocrisy and emotional suffocation bequeathed by religious censorship and puritanism, of both the Catholic and Protestant variety. Stifled voices articulate the experience of paternal incest, hidden homosexuality and a mistaken vocation for the priesthood in *The Invisible Worm* (1991), *Two Moons* (1998) and *This Is Not a Novel* (2002). In these fictions we feel the force of Johnston's sense that she does not invent her characters but merely listens intently for their voices: 'I very much feel this person wants to speak, this person wants to be released from a prison of some sort, and I have the key to let this person out of prison. And I just sort of stagger along from there really until I get a little confidence, and I see what this person has on their mind, what their problem is, what their secret is, because again, writing is to a large degree about secrets . . .'[9] The word that echoes through these novels is 'betrayal' and the focus is on the many kinds of emotional betrayal that human sexuality makes possible (incest, marriage under false pretences, bisexual infidelity, broken vows). But Johnston is concerned with a yet more essential form that betrayal can take, which is the way a culture can make it so hard for human beings to acknowledge their own sexuality that living itself begins to seem a crime. These novels are studded with self-abusive acts and suicides.

Barry's tribute to what Johnston has contributed to the Irish 'emergency' and the 'general good health' of its writing could be applied to all three kinds of novels. In an important sense, they are all part of the same work – indeed, one way of viewing them would be as thirteen instalments of one undertaking, not wholly unlike the fifteen stories that go up to make Joyce's *Dubliners* (1914). Just as Joyce aimed to tell a large truth through small specifics, and insisted that his work made 'a chapter of the moral history of [his] country' because Dublin was the centre of its 'paralysis' (*Letters* II 134), so Johnston has addressed key issues in Irish life as they have arisen in her lifetime, with the detachment of someone whose first loyalty was to tell the truth as she finds it. As with the Joycean short story, she allows her protagonists to speak for themselves without authorial intervention. Her novels are the terse structures that remain after the elaborations have been thrown into the wastepaper bin, and her strong reliance on dialogue leaves the reader with much of the work of inference to do, leading to a common complaint among critics, that they are 'never quite the full shilling' (Lubbers 222). But when all thirteen of her fictions are viewed in the same frame they cast fascinating sidelights on one another, and each individual novel radiates implications for her central concern: how to live honestly in the presence of the distorting past.

Perhaps the best way to demonstrate this interrelatedness is to take an example from each of the three periods described above and show how Johnston's art works in detail. We might begin with what, by

[9] Quotation taken from an Australian radio interview, 'Writers on Writing'. See www.abc.net.au/writers/radioep6.htm

common consent, is a classic from the first period, *How Many Miles to Babylon?* The subversive friendship in this novel is between Alex Moore, the son of an Anglo-Irish landowner, and Jerry Crowe, the Catholic boy he meets in the stables and with whom he spends the only happy hours of his boyhood.

The social background to their 'unsuitable' friendship is the exhausted Ascendancy culture. Alex's father has made a conventional marriage to a society beauty who despises him and resents his passion for the land he feels he holds in trust. His attitude reveals both guilt and responsibility: 'Here, the land must come first . . . We took it from the people. I would like to feel, that it will, when the moment comes, be handed back in good order' (47). The mother's boredom and suppressed rage – on their beautiful estate she has nothing to do but feed sponge cake to the swans and play the piano to the air – lead to her keeping her one son, Alex, with her at home. In the loneliness and tedium of his childhood, his secret friendship with Jerry is his one experience of warmth and mutuality, as they swim, fight, ride and plan to race horses together. And though the friendship is broken off by his mother's ferocious snobbery, it is re-established when they both volunteer to fight and are shipped to France.

Johnston's account of the Big House culture is unsentimental: there is no vitality to its elegance and its days are numbered for good reason. Unusually, though, for a modern novelist, she enters into the Ascendancy's preoccupation with questions of masculinity and honour with insight and sympathy.[10] Mr Moore's commitment to the land is one kind of honour, and when Alex goes to war, his whole struggle is to define honour for himself, in the teeth of the military version. (Johnston is well aware, however, that women did not have the luxury of doing the same; the viciousness of Alex's mother is part of her frustration as a genuine musician.) Alex asserts his values by ignoring the difference in rank between himself and Jerry, and taking him fox-hunting behind the lines at every opportunity. Their joint refusal to 'play the game' militarily exasperates their commanding officer, Major Glendinning, and turns him into Jerry's persecutor, so that when Jerry asks for leave to go looking for his father, missing in action,

---

[10] See Shari Benstock's 'The Masculine World of Jennifer Johnston' in Thomas F. Staley, ed. *Twentieth-Century Women Novelists* (1982). The dead young men of World War I haunt Johnston's fictions, most recently *This Is Not a Novel* (2002) where an apparently fictional letter from the front is a letter written by Johnston's uncle before he was killed in 1915 (Longley 14).

Glendinning is glad to refuse. When Jerry takes leave anyway (in obedience to his own sense of honour, because his mother wrote and begged him) Glendinning orders his execution for desertion – and in a last attempt to teach Alex the meaning of duty, puts him in charge of the firing squad.

Johnston expertly uncovers the British attitude of the period to the hope of Home Rule, as Glendinning impales Alex on the horns of this dilemma. In his view, the Irish cannot subordinate their emotions to long-term goals, and have no understanding of public responsibility. Alex asks:

'I would very much like to know what happens if I say no.'
He looked surprised.
'I am amazed you ask . . . I have no desire to have you tried. It can all become most distasteful. You are pushing me very far, I warn you. How you damn Irish expect to be able to run your own country when you can't control your own wasteful emotions, I can't imagine.'
. . . 'Where did you learn to be so evil?'
'The world taught me. The world will teach you. You will never understand me until the day you are faced with responsible decisions to make. People's lives, people's deaths. The crumbling world waiting for your word.' (156)

Alex pre-empts the firing squad by finding Jerry in prison and quietly shooting him as he sings an old Irish song. He thus puts himself in Jerry's place, and explains the nature of the story we have been hearing him tell. It is his last testament before he is shot, hence the opening lines: 'Because I am an officer and a gentleman they have given me my notebooks, pen, ink and paper. So I write and wait' (5). Alex has, in a way, proved Glendinning's point: two people will now die instead of one, and neither of them in the cause they actually enlisted for, which is preparing a giant spring offensive as Alex writes.

Through this plot Johnston allows us to glimpse the impending horrors of the 1920s and the fault-lines of the future Republic. The callous militarism of Glendinning is what the Irish Republican Army will successfully mimic, and the 'enemy' will continue to be the only one the Irish acknowledge (while European issues disappear from view, leading eventually to Irish neutrality in World War II). Although Jerry and Alex's friendship is the best thing either knows, and they dream of racing horses together after the war, Johnston does not allow us to imagine any happier future for them had they lived: Ireland would not have had room for both of them. Part of Jerry's motivation for joining up is to be 'one of the fellas [who] really knows what the hell he's doing when it comes to fighting' (106) and he gleefully anticipates Ireland's becoming a giant battlefield without quarter: 'Every town, every village will be the front line. Hill, rock, tree. They won't know which way to look' (115). When Alex says, 'I hate your vision', Jerry's reply is, 'Hate away, man' (115). In this spare exchange, Johnston uncovers the impending disaster for Ireland and Irishness – the ideological definition of belonging that will drive divisions between North and South, Protestant and Catholic, and in cases like Alex's, through the heart of someone who loves both the land and Jerry. Jerry's conviction that 'the only way to get them out is to shoot them out', makes Alex protest, 'I can't believe there are many think as you do.' Jerry ripostes, 'There will be. Maybe even yourself' (107). Here Johnston catches the authentic note of the future IRA (killing the Anglo-Irish is not a matter for conscience: the British occupation is too great a crime) and the agony awaiting those, like Alex, who have no other home or identity to claim.

Shadows on Our Skin belongs to the second historical period of Johnston's fictions: it is set in Derry, Northern Ireland, two years into the Troubles of the 1970s. The central theme is still the way the coerciveness of the past destroys the possibilities of the present, but Johnston's choice of characters for the cross-border loyalty that leads to catastrophe in this novel is quite different. Kathleen Docherty is a freethinking schoolteacher in Derry, with a Protestant mother and a boyfriend in the Army; and Joe Logan, through whose consciousness Johnston focuses the story, is a boy who finds her sitting smoking after school on his favourite wall. (Joe's age is not given but he appears to be twelve or so.) The previous Troubles of the 1920s are barely a folk-memory (although they are vivid to Joe's invalid, self-dramatising elderly father) – the current crisis is a violent new phase in the modernisation of Ireland, where the seventeenth-century arrangement between triumphalist Orange forces and defeated Catholicism in six of the counties of Ulster is finally being renegotiated in the name of social justice and civil rights.

The foreground of the novel is undramatic. Joe hates school and his alcoholic father, and scribbles rhymes in his geometry book; the friendship that grows out of talking to Kathleen as she smokes leads to her taking him on trips, lending him books, and buying him buns. The tension under which they live only emerges from Kathleen's frenzied smoking habit, and the furious smacks Joe's mother gives him whenever he comes home late after enjoying this friendship he cannot name.

What raises the emotional temperature of the story is the return from England of Joe's elder brother Brendan – the brother who identifies with the father's heroic Republican past. Brendan's ready anger at the British Army presence quickly involves him with the Provisional IRA. His position is still Jerry Crowe's – 'There'll be no decent life for anyone here until we get the British out' – and Alex's pacifism is now Joe's mother's: 'What good does killing do? . . . I see only sadness.' Brendan responds, 'If Ireland was free . . .', but to her these are just 'Words, Words. Words' (66–7).

Brendan also becomes interested in Kathleen, whose loyalty to his kid brother he cannot interpret. (Joe writes promising poetry, and he recompenses her for her friendship with poems.) Her genuine concern for the trouble she sees Brendan sliding into, and the difficulty of saying whose ring it is she wears on her finger, leads them into a rapid intimacy – and when Brendan begins to fantasise about their future together, Joe is goaded into destroying that hope. With all the fury of a jealous adolescent whose brother has encroached on his special friendship, he tells him triumphantly: 'She's going to be married to someone else . . . A British soldier. She wears a ring, you know. And she tells him everything' (182–3). Brendan's happy confidences – 'That's a great girl . . . She listened' (181) – are now disastrous: he escapes to England, but his unit of Provisionals take their vengeance. Knocking on Kathleen's door, Joe finds her packing for Dublin, battered, with her head shaved, and an angry landlady impatiently waiting for her to leave.

Brutally violated as Kathleen is, and bewildered by Joe's betrayal – '"Why did you do it? You?" . . . He wanted to tell her that he had done it because he loved her, but he didn't know how to' (190) – she remains true to their friendship. She makes peace with Joe and leaves him her copy of *A Golden Treasury*, with its childhood inscription:

> Kathleen Doherty is my name,
> Ireland is my nation,
> Wicklow is my dwelling place,
> And heaven my destination.   (191)

The verse rings ironically from the last page of the book:[11] the Irish 'nation' that would include Kathleen, the one Jennifer Johnston would

---

[11] It also carries with it an echo from *A Portrait of the Artist as a Young Man* (1916), where it is inscribed in Stephen Dedalus's schoolbook.

want to see, does not yet exist. And having a good Catholic name like Doherty – Joe says 'My Mammy's name was Doherty' (31) – is not qualification enough. The Irishness required to be Irish is seemingly so pure as to be always disappearing over the horizon. If Kathleen does not have it, neither do Joe and his mother, who hate the violence that surrounds them, and neither too does Brendan, on the run from the Provisionals. Perhaps only the decaying father, who goes nowhere and does nothing, is capable of the 100% Irishness the Cause demands.

In Joe's family life Johnston deftly touches on the underlying factors that make violence endemic to Northern Ireland. The father is unemployed, as is Brendan when he returns from England; it is the mother who keeps the home together, skivvying for others and scrubbing her own home in a frenzied search for some kind of cleanliness. The father squanders what she earns on bottles of stout, the reward due to him for past sacrifices, and refuses to move out of the squalid streets he knows, although there is better housing elsewhere. The toxic brew of social conservatism, poverty and unexpressed anger looking for an object is well caught in his triumph over the death of two British soldiers at the end of his street: 'That's as good as a tonic' (152). His feeling of innocence is unshakeable, because the nation has been wronged so badly, for so long, and he sings an old Republican song in celebration: 'A nation once again . . .' (154). His wife, in contrast, sees the dead soldiers as 'children. Younger than Brendan' (153), and focuses on the actuality of her work-damaged hands: 'the swollen joints, the scraped look of the skin, the white flecks on her ridged nails' (154). The carnage looks very different to someone struggling to live in the present rather than the past:

> She dragged her eyes away from her hands and looked up at him.
> 'It's old buggers like you should be shot, with your talk and your singing of glory and heroes.'
> 'Freedom . . .'
> 'What's freedom? . . . Have they any more freedom down there [in the Republic] than we have up here?'
> 'You misunderstand . . .'
> 'Is there a job for every man? And a home for everyone? Have all the children got shoes on their feet? Are there women down there scrubbing floors to keep the home together because stupid, useless old men are sitting round gassing about freedom? Singing their songs about heroes?' Her voice had risen almost to a scream. He looked at her in silence for a very long time. Then he started to move towards the door, crippled with pain. The pain she had

inflicted on him. The pain of the world of forgotten heroes. At the
door he turned. 'You are disgusting. Disgusting.'
'Did they even give you a pension?'
'I talk about freedom. You talk about shoes and pensions.'
'Take your bloody fairy tales out of this house before I . . .' She began
to cry hopelessly. That's two people have cried today, thought Joe.
I wonder how many more. (154)

Johnston indicates here how easily the Troubles replicated themselves
across generations. She also sketches in the ambiguities of the 'freedom'
so ferociously fought for. Social disorder was a prime factor in delaying
necessary economic improvement ('jobs' and 'shoes'); and the word
itself begs the question of whose freedom, and how defined (the
detested British Army presence was initially needed to protect the
Catholic minority from the violence of the Protestant majority.
Catholics wanted to be free to enjoy civic rights; Protestants wanted to
be free not to share them). She also hints at the special role women like
Joe's mother played in the abortive peace movement.

Meanwhile, in the character of Joe, she also suggests where a generation of Northern Irish poets came from. Trapped between economic
hopelessness and political anarchy, Joe's one world of coherence and
creativity is the realm of language. Although he is only a child, he
brings an adult passion to the hope of making meaning amidst the chaos
he sees:

What is there for me, he wondered, if I can't make words dance, as
the birds are dancing? A man with a brush and tubes of colour can
put these patterns on a page so that you can recognise them. Say,
ah, yes. Can I, with a biro pen and a string of words? Where? How
do you start? What are the rules? Do you just find them out as you
go along? Trial and error. I don't want to drive the dry cleaner's
van or be an electrician. There should be someone you can talk to.
One day my head will burst and words will spill out and be
blown away by the wind and get caught in the branches of the
trees. My words. (140)

In this fever to put 'patterns on a page' like an artist in colour, Joe is
aligned with many other of Johnston's narrators. We sense from the way
Alex cherishes lines of poetry and nursery rhymes (like that of the title,
'How many miles to Babylon / Three score and ten') that he too is a
writer in embryo, and other narrators of her novels are often artists in
paint or words. In these characters Johnston evokes the seriousness of

the decision she herself made when she came back to Ireland; these narrators reproach themselves with how late they have left the effort to express themselves, and often the novel we are left with is the only thing they will achieve. But Johnston implies that artistic effort is never wasted. Semtex and bullets continue to find their targets, but the happiness of wrestling the temporary stuff of life into the permanent stuff of art is profound, and in its own way it is the best answer that can be made to those who violently destroy life rather than create it.

Perhaps the most explosive of the plots in the third group of fictions, those set in the relatively peaceful Ireland of the 1990s, is that of *The Invisible Worm*. In this novel the story of a daughter's rape is played off against that of an embittered 'spoiled priest' turned schoolteacher. It is their friendship across the social and religious divide that makes the structure of this novel, and enables Johnston to realistically evoke the coerciveness of patriarchal forces in Ireland, even in their final decay. It is typical of her that even when focusing on the most extreme example of abuse, paternal incest, she takes a male illustration of a type of violation too; deeply concerned as she is with women's lives, she has always resisted being labelled feminist. For her, feminism denotes something limiting, another unwelcome form of separation between human beings, like class divisions.[12]

The focusing consciousness of this story is Laura's, and it takes us back to her famous politician-father's pompous funeral. Her thoughts are invaded by insistent memories – his deathbed appeal for forgiveness, the grip of his hand on her arm, her neck – and it is her struggle to avoid another breakdown that keeps much of the story in suspense. This first-person narrative is interwoven with a story told in the third person about her life in the present, where she has a frigid, childless marriage to a rising public man not unlike her father. It is when she meets the angry, lost ex-priest Dominic that she finds herself able to tell the story of her incoherent life for the first time, and to clear the twenty-year growth of shrubs and trees that hides the summer-house at the bottom of her garden – the place where her father trapped and raped her.

Laura's consciousness is a particularly dazzling illustration of Johnston's concern with the way the emotional legacy of the past can distort the present. Because she is what the world calls 'mentally ill', Laura cannot keep past and present separate in her mind; the pressure

---

[12] See Ann Owens Weekes, pp.30–1.

of unfocused emotion makes her a kind of phantom to herself, hence the opening:

> I stand by the window and watch the woman running.
> Is it Laura?
> I wonder that, as I watch her flickering like blown leaves through the trees.
> I am Laura.
> Sometimes I run so fast that my legs buckle under me; ungainly, painful.
> This woman runs with dignity.
> I have to say that for her. (1)

But the 'dignity' of this phantom also points to the saving power of narrative and its ability to make coherence out of chaos: on the last page, when the story is told and the summerhouse burned down, Laura can assert, 'She will not run again' (182).

It is not only Johnston's understanding of the price of violation for mental life but the grasp of its family dynamics that makes this novel so intelligent on such a potentially sensational theme. What Laura's father does is monstrous, but Johnston suggests he is not a monster, and we are made aware through Laura's eyes of the contribution her mother made to the disaster. She was a Protestant heiress who chose a Catholic Republican hero – and immediately regretted it: 'He was of course the new nobility . . . Energetic. Powerful' (111). She occupies herself with her boat, sailing dangerously around the coast, and keeps her husband at bay both sexually and emotionally. He is a pious, priest-fearing Catholic, for all his Republicanism, and Laura remembers that he always hoped his wife might 'turn':

> 'Divil a bit of it,' she said. 'Haven't you got my house and my land and my beautiful body? What makes you think you should have my soul as well?'
> He hated such irony.
> She was the only person in my world who didn't succumb to his enormous charm. Perhaps I shouldn't say that; perhaps she had indeed succumbed, and thereafter had to protect herself from it. (6)

Everyone, including Laura, loves her father: 'He was my warm and lovely god . . . My High King . . . I was a part of his glowing life' (116–17). We can glimpse through Laura's memories of how he begins to trespass on her body as a child what is the likely source of such

immense charm – the unconscious seductiveness of the violator who
cannot bear to admit the nature of his longing. The fires of hell are
kept burning for this crime; and it is her father's intolerance of the
potentially annihilating guilt, his refusal to know himself, that turns
him into a Jekyll-and-Hyde figure: popular statesman, and incestuous
father. When Laura's attempt to leave home for boarding school
provokes him to act, the terrible violation is followed by an
extraordinary somersault of displaced guilt. Someone is guilty of a
crime, and if it is not him, it must be Laura herself:

> Laura stood up and pulled at her clothes. There was blood on her
> skirt, there was a black painful hole in her body. She could see noth-
> ing, only hear the whine of the dog and the shocking sound of her
> father's breathing.
> 'Why did you do this to me?'
> His words startled her. He looked up at her. His eyes were full of tears
> and cunning.
> 'Think of your mother.'
> She walked across the room and opened the door.
> 'This will have to be our secret.' (157)

Laura does manage to whisper the word 'rape' to her mother, whom she
trusts to protect her; but she has imagined her stronger than she is. She
sails out in her yacht and deliberately capsizes it on the rocks. Laura is
left with her father's accusation, designed to madden her for life: 'You
killed your mother. I warned you. Warned you, warned you' (38).

The fact that Dominic is being accused of something similar – of
'killing' his old father by leaving the priesthood – suggests that the
'invisible worm' of Johnston's title is not so much sexuality as guilt.
Dominic has been made into a sacrificial offering for his whole family's
sense of Catholic obligation. He is given no choice about entering the
seminary – 'I was the chosen victim' – though his brother is allowed to
be a merchant banker and 'serves Mammon with a magnificent
Thatcherite enthusiasm' (26). The readiness of his father and siblings to
disown him completely when his personal integrity makes him break his
vows suggests the same pattern of conflict hinted at in *How Many Miles
to Babylon?* and *Shadows on Our Skin*. By Johnston's showing, twentieth-
century Ireland has been tormented by incompatible definitions of
'honour', military, nationalist and religious. The 100% purity of these
demands has left a widespread experience of guilt among the 'failed'
loyalists, and among those who do not recognise their guilt for what it
is, the habit of finding scapegoats to carry their burden.

One manifestation of the pressure of hidden guilt would be the dubious borderline between an impossible innocence and an irredeemable evil that makes the fight for Independence so intoxicating to Jerry Crowe. The same excuse simplifies life for Joe's brother Brendan: in a contest between the British Army and the 'freedom-fighting' Provisionals he knows where his duty lies. And with the cessation of public violence, Johnston implies, the weakness of the old social and religious solutions to guilt (each family dedicating a son to God and celibacy, like Dominic, all sexual scandals being suppressed and unacknowledged, particularly those that call patriarchy into question) has finally risen to the surface. If they do not work any longer, what can be put in their place?

Johnston's thirteen novels suggest her faith in the role fiction can play in helping her audience accept the nature of human experience, in all its astonishing, invigorating complexity. There is no simple cure for the habit of scapegoating others, any more than there is for self-dislike, but her novels have a wonderful potential for extending the reader's sympathy and making it impossible to think in terms of 'sides' and 'parties', 'right' and 'wrong'. Indeed, her central device of bringing together two people who should not be friends, her confidence that friendship 'can be sublime', means that conventional self-definitions based on class, country or religion are something to combat rather than submit to in her work. And although her novels offer no happy conclusions in the usual sense, they do offer the sense of a new beginning. What was mysterious is now clear, what tied the characters to the past has lost its power of coercion. The narrator, and the reader, have won a new kind of freedom – a freedom of mind, which one suspects is the only one that Johnston considers obtainable.

Works Cited

Austen, Jane. *Letters*, ed. Deirdre Le Faye (Oxford: Oxford University Press, 1995).

Barry, Sebastian. Preface to *The Essential Jennifer Johnston* (London: Review, 2001).

Benstock, Shari. 'The Masculine World of Jennifer Johnston' in *Twentieth-Century Women Novelists*, ed. Thomas F. Staley (Basingstoke: Macmillan, 1982). 191–217

Johnston, Jennifer. *The Captains and the Kings* (London: Hamish Hamilton, 1972).

——. *The Christmas Tree* (London: Hamish Hamilton, 1981).

———. *Fool's Sanctuary* (London: Hamish Hamilton, 1987).

———. *The Gates* (London: Hamish Hamilton, 1972).

———. *The Gingerbread Woman* (London: Review, 2000).

———. *How Many Miles to Babylon?* (New York: Avon Books, 1975).

———. *The Illusionist* (London: Sinclair Stevenson, 1995).

———. *The Invisible Worm* (London: Sinclair Stevenson, 1991).

———. *The Old Jest* (London: Hamish Hamilton, 1979).

———. *The Railway Station Man* (London: Hamish Hamilton, 1984).

———. *Shadows on Our Skin* (London: Fontana, 1986).

———. *This Is Not a Novel* (London: Review, 2002).

———. *Two Moons* (London: Review, 1998).

Joyce, James. *A Portrait of the Artist as a Young Man* (London: Cape, 1916).

———. *The Letters of James Joyce*, Vol. II, ed. Richard Ellmann (London: Faber & Faber, 1966).

Longley, Edna, ed. *Culture in Ireland – Division or Diversity?* (Belfast: Queen's University, 1991).

Lubbers, Klaus. ' "This White Elephant of a Place": Jennifer Johnston's Uses of the Big House' in *Ancestral Voices: The Big House in Anglo-Irish Literature*, ed. Otto Rauchbauer (Hildesheim, Zurich and New York: Georg Olms Verlag, 1992). 221–37

MacLaverty, Bernard. *Cal* (London: Cape, 1983).

Mahon, Derek. *Journalism 1970–1995* (Dublin: Gallery, 1996).

McManus, Karen. 'Prodding Republicanism', *Fortnight* (April 1995): 36–7

Mortimer, Mark. 'Jennifer Johnston and the Big House' in *The Big House in Ireland: Reality and Representation*, ed. Jacqueline Genet (Kerry: Brandon Books, 1991). 209–214

Quinn, John, ed. *Portrait of the Artist as a Young Girl* (London: Methuen, 1986).

Trevor, William. *The Story of Lucy Gault* (London: Viking, 2002).

Walker, Gail. 'Interview: Jennifer Johnston', *Belfast Telegraph*, 24 October 2002.

Weekes, Ann Owens. *Irish Women Writers: An Uncharted Tradition* (Kentucky: University Press of Kentucky, 1990).

York, Richard. 'A Daft Way to Earn a Living' in *Writing Ulster (no. 6): Northern Narratives*, ed. Bill Lazenblatt (Ulster: University of Ulster, 1999). 29–47

'Fiction with a Thread of Scottishness in its Truth': The Paradox of the National in A. L. Kennedy

ELUNED SUMMERS-BREMNER

In an interview with Cristie March in 1999, A. L. Kennedy responds to a question regarding the situation of the women in her fictions, which suggests that they suffer from 'a self-imposed entrapment', with the following statement:

> I think most of the men are trapped as well. I mean, most of my people are in situations outside of their control. I'm always drawn to the border between what you want and what you want to say and what you need to say and what's actually possible – the interior life and the exterior life . . . So if I've got any kind of agenda at all it's this: the people who come to me tend to be people who can't say what they want to say, so I say that they can't say what they want to say. And the people who are in English novels, I mean they say everything anyway. . . . They say things when they have nothing to say. And there's all these other people in the great world of Jungian synchronicity with things hanging around waiting to be expressed. There's a whole cast out there that isn't getting a look in. (March 117)

This response makes a number of interrelated points about the Scottishness of Kennedy's work and the fraught emotional situations in which her characters find themselves, and, although Kennedy underplays it, about the relation of these to issues of gender. The first point to note is the overdetermined figure of the border. Separating desire in general from desiring speech ('what you want and what you want to say') from expressive need and from the again general but necessarily specific conditions of possibility, this border, which multiplies rather than remains two-sided, may be read as a figure for the contrariness animating Scottish literary history, and the relation of women writers to that history more particularly.

The border between Scotland and England that was politically effaced by the 1707 Act of Union gave rise to further doublings within the larger but largely unaccommodating whole of the United Kingdom that led Norman MacCaig to characterise the Scot as possessing 'a large capacity for containing in himself elements that contradict each other' (vii).[1] Kennedy's work – three novels, four collections of stories, one non-fiction prose work and a number of scripts for stage, radio and screen – is arguably filled with more contraries than most. In the early fiction a compelling realism gives us grim Glasgow scenes that are frequently undercut by surreal episodes, while the latest novel and stories are less clearly tied to a geographically recognisable place, emphasising instead the vexed landscapes of human intimacy and the related travails of the anxious or neurotic mind.

Noting Kennedy's reluctance to identify her work as peculiarly Scottish, Eleanor Bell in a recent article observes that it is, nonetheless, 'ethically and politically focused', and connects this with the journeys the characters make in and out of amorous relationships (107, 109). In this essay I want to extend this investigation but also to take issue with the positivist gloss Bell offers whereby, as she claims, the novel *So I Am Glad* (1995) and the novella *Original Bliss* (1997) for example, 'highlight th[e] importance of love and the ways in which it can generate an "ethics of respect" at the individual, conscious level of the text' (109). If we read Kennedy's work as a whole, we find there is a far greater emphasis on human vulnerability, miscommunication and aggression within relationships than on happy, rationalised solutions, and on the unconscious level where desire's chief characteristic is the troubles it encounters and sometimes finds a way to adapt to or accommodate, but often does not. Furthermore, Bell is unable to offer an explanation regarding the mechanism through which love, as an abstract universal concretely treated in the fictions, speaks to the construct of polity and nation, and so to the ethical mandate of private or intimate relationships within it.

Kennedy's take on the entrapment, wilful or otherwise, of her characters, whereby her role is to communicate, in words, the failure of words to express their desires, gives us a clue as to the way love, and language, function in her fictions. I will return to the relation of this dynamic to femininity shortly. Kennedy's characters frequently suffer from incommunicable feelings that have an intimate relation to language while not being expressible within it. The feelings themselves are often of impotence and lack, which increases relative to attempts to use words to convey them, or of a promissory fullness whose comforts cannot be reached. It is as though language, through which the body gains a useful, if ill-fitting, means of communication, fails to silence the body's inarticulate response to this arrangement in the flesh. Language

---

[1] Quoted in Marshall Walker, *Scottish Literature Since 1707* (1996), p.15.

thus becomes symptomatic, an index of a larger or more diffuse mortal suffering that is tied to the entrapments of language itself.

The stylistic marker of this dynamic in Kennedy's fiction is often the use of free indirect thought, as in the following example from 'A Bad Son', in the collection *Indelible Acts* (2002):

> She was there with his father and no one to help and you couldn't trust him. Ronald understood that and she didn't, not until after. She was on her own there and something bad would be happening.
>   *Please make her safe.*
>   **Fuck.**
>   *Please make her safe.*
> It was part of his head now, his word, the way it was his father's.
>   **Fuck.**
>   *Please make her safe.* (81)

Ronald's love for his mother as it is expressed in the words in his head declares its impotence. The reality of his mother's brutalising at the hands of his father exceeds the healing or communicative power of words, and fractures Ronald's thoughts between identification with his mother in helpless prayers or pleas and with his father in the incorporation of his violence through the claiming of his word. The power of the story lies in the gradual revelation of the horror of Ronald's home life, delivered solely through his interactions with others during an afternoon and night he spends away from home at the house of a school friend. The sense of menace increases relative to its absence in the words of the text. The third person narrative gives us the state of things, but only from Ronald's childlike point of view. The story's effect lies in the gathering sense that the words thought or spoken by Ronald, his friend Jim and members of Jim's family, and Ronald's father, are merely the markers of the human drama they exclude. The inadequacy of language to account for, or alter, the complex reality of Ronald's home life is brought home at the story's end, where the child's future appears set. Stranded between the helpless goodness of his mother and the powerful badness of his father, Ronald will reproduce both the passivity and the violence of language which, confronted with the trauma of the brutalised body, itself shears off and fractures into stricture and division, the murderous nomenclature of Calvinist law:

> *Please not a thing.*
> But, in time, fear always changed to something different, you just had to wait. He would show her.

It wasn't about wishing, or pretending, and there were no miracles. It was about concentrating until you can turn into somebody new, somebody your father won't expect. Ronald would wait to get older and stronger and then it would happen, he'd make it: he'd be a bad son. (87)

In 'A Little Like Light' from the same collection, a man who feels that although he was never meant to be a school janitor he has, by some accident, become one, experiences this lack of fit between who he is and who he is for others at the point where words fail in relation to his wife, his son, and the teacher with whom he embarks on a failed affair. The inadequacy of language translates into inadequacy of feeling, the sense that flesh marked by the word does not, as it should, suffer or enable communication but becomes a block on intimacy instead, an inert symptom to which the failures of language and love attest. As in 'A Bad Son', the child's and the parent's role are imbricated with each other, as a kind of education for future disappointment is carried out between father and son:

Any treat in each other's company is no treat at all: we are not enough. We are the only real friends that we have and, as a pair, we are a continual, mutual disappointment, frequently prey to these sad, small pauses for thought. After which we hug and hold hands for a while, because we are truly sorry for each other, but sharing sympathy is not the same as love. Then we begin again with what we have to: being a father and a son. (172–3)

The father's role at work as a janitor and at home as a husband fail to compensate for the alienation of each. He wears his janitor's uniform while having sex with his wife – this being the only way they can approach intimate satisfaction – and attempts to begin a relationship with a teacher at work. This, predictably, fails, as both parties are united not so much by happiness as by their impotent wish to achieve it. The janitor tells his son about the failure of love in the same way he tells him about the physics of light, and magic, 'the way the world works' (186); 'This is love. This terrible feeling. This knowing I would rather see her than be content. Even the way that we are is so near to being enough. This is love' (191).

This 'almost, but not quite' grammar of love, where happiness is close to the wish for it, but not close enough, is, nonetheless, love's reality, a state of mind and body marked by conflict and the proximity, through trust and its companion, vulnerability, of possible abandonment and pain. The problem with claims for love's benevolence such as that made by Bell is that they ignore the way that love itself is a communication via the objectifying and alienating power of language, which makes the illusion of knowing another intimately more likely than the reality, and tends to fail, by itself, to awaken an individual or polity to the costs of thoroughgoing change. To ignore language's determinations is particularly problematic in relation to Kennedy because she identifies Scottishness, as in the interview response above, with the frustration of not being able to distinguish one's own reality from that of others who share one's language, in this case the English who 'say too much', who 'say things when they have nothing to say', whose profligacy with words ought not to limit their use by others but which appears to do so, nonetheless (March 117).

Yet Kennedy does not want to yield – to the English, or to any cultural or sexual or ethnic group in particular – sole ownership of universals such as love and truth. Indeed, her position regarding the Scottishness of her writing takes hold of both of these and makes them part of the dynamic contract between writer and reader, a dynamic in which their promise is not mined and expended, but remains opaque. In her essay 'Not Changing the World', a move away from overt nationalism, and from the restrictions following on identificatory labels of all kinds, is presented, thus, as a question: 'I am a woman, I am heterosexual, I am more Scottish than anything else and I write. But I don't know how these things interrelate' (100).

Noting that identity, as an external intervention into the complex reality of being a person, has intimate effects, Kennedy states her belief that 'writing is the most intimate of the media' offering a person a working sense of how she or he might appear ('Not Changing the World' 102). The intimacy of writing, and reading, makes both acts, in a sense, works of love, since each partner is giving to the other, consciously or otherwise, their questions, their lack. To write, to read, and to love is to temporarily cede to another the power to glimpse or to startle awake in one an instance of uniqueness, a uniqueness one cannot see or otherwise lay claim to in oneself (an account of love's obliquity developed by Jacques Lacan).[2] This uniqueness, importantly, operates not as content but in and

---

[2] See Jacques Lacan, *Séminaire VIII, Le Transfert* (1991); Miran Bozovic, 'The Bond of Love: Lacan and Spinoza', *New Formations*, 23 (1994), p.69; Jean Michel Rabaté, *Jacques Lacan: Psychoanalysis and the Subject of Literature* (2001), p.139.

as relation, and it declares that, just as no act of writing or reading will ever be quite the same as any other, so the working blindness of love, where each lover offers up their lack, is ethical to the extent that this offering amounts to an acceptance, rather than a refusal, of the conflict with language on which depends each person's unique complexity.

Women, of course, have historically been placed on the side of romantic love and a range of related operations from self-sacrifice to linguistic incompetence to presumed excess of feeling – the latter two often conflated. And it is in relation to this history – which is also part of the history of the novel, and the often disregarded flipside, or unhomely inside, of the novel's reading as *bildung* or teleological narrative of the nation – that Kennedy's claims for love and truth and their fictional correlatives become most interesting. 'I believe that fiction with a thread of Scottishness in its truth', she writes, 'has helped me to know how to be myself as a Scot', and adds that, 'if I respect my reader and am willing to enter into a relationship of trust, if not love, with them, I would prefer not [to] be labelled and categorized in return' ('Not Changing the World' 102).

I do not think we need resort to categorising to relate the precariousness of the relationships in Kennedy's fictions to the Scottish novel's history as a vehicle for national imagining. It is as a narrative of unidentifiable borders that the Scottish novel has, historically, distinguished itself, as is fitting for a nation which, as Tom Nairn claimed in the 1970s, may have invented nationalism by first succeeding independently and then joining itself to the forward arm of British expansion around the globe. Having proceeded from barbarism through the Scottish Enlightenment to significant industrial success in the nineteenth century, Scotland's ready participation in British colonialist endeavour not only changed the world, but returned to haunt it, as other nationalisms arose and changed the world still further, giving rise to 'the "void"' of Scottish production 'which cultural and literary historians so deplore' (Nairn 114).[3]

As a symbolic region of national belonging, Scotland today is split between wide geographical dispersal and success and the cultural underdevelopment of the country which, since 1707, has been subsumed within the larger body of Britain. Consequent on Scotland's wide dispersal coupled with an absence of national singularity (and excepting the tourist-Tartan versions that, like all such commodifications,

[3] See also Linda Colley, *Britons: Forging the Nation 1707–1837* (1992; 2003), pp.120–45.

belong to the visitor to the country more than to the Scottish themselves), the Scottish novel frequently engages the themes of unhomeli-
ness and haunting. Paradoxes of space, in which Scottishness is figured
as abiding in more than one region simultaneously, are common, as in
the surreal under- and overworlds of the work of a Robert Louis
Stevenson or an Alasdair Gray. Writing of Stevenson, Cairns Craig
observes that 'narrative, which holds together national identity in the
historicist mode, is disrupted by the multiple spaces into which the
nation has entered, the plethora of other narratives with which it is
entwined' (237). And if, as Bell suggests, Kennedy's protagonists only
come to rest with their Scottishness by leaving Scotland, literally or
metaphorically, and if the temporally extended equivalent of this
journey is the public history of the nation, its spatial equivalent is the
sexually intimate or love relationship which proceeds *through* loss and
the mutual yielding of subjective borders for no finally verifiable or predictably comforting end (Bell 107).

Like other recent Scottish writers, Kennedy transects present-day
narratives with past ones, which create a vertiginous sense of place,
where history as narrative is little comfort. This is undoubtedly related
to the national paradox whereby Scotland was once:

> the centre of the world's largest Empire and a mere periphery of
> Europe, a place at the core of history's technological drive towards
> the future and, at the same time, a place set apart, a space unbounded
> by history, an opening upon eternity, 'as you might say there was
> another world than this'. (Spark 143)[4]

Scotland, in other words, is 'the space within Britain which remains an
image of the "wild" districts of the borders of Empire' (Craig 238), just
as the intimate realm within the public life of the nation can, too, turn
decidedly unhomely, and, in Kennedy's fictions, frequently does.[5] That
it is not easy to separate the precarious nature of human intimacy from

---

[4] Quoted in Craig Cairns, *The Modern Scottish Novel: Narrative and the National
Imagination* (1999), pp.240–1.
[5] David Punter has taken up this theme in reading the work of recent Scottish
writers, including Kennedy, through the paradigm of the Gothic, the mode of
fiction whose territory is the haunted underside – or more correctly the exter-
nally created inside, the uncanny – of Enlightenment fictions of narrativity as
forward-moving, rationalised endeavour: see 'Contemporary Scottish Gothic:
Reconstructing the Absent Nation' in *Postcolonial Cultures and Literatures:
Modernity and the (Un)Commonwealth* (2002).

questions of national belonging in Kennedy's work is what saves it, in my view, from easy categorisation. Yet at the same time its vexed treatment of the inter-imbrication of public and private does bring to bear on the paradox of Scottish nationality an internal pressure, as though the expansionist gesture of nationalist history and its attendant hauntings were being made to operate in a much more localised yet just as intemperate space.

In Kennedy's three novels to date, different aspects of this history are in play, with the latest, *Everything You Need* (1999), notable for its conjoining of the Grail myth of the wasted land – brought to public attention by a Scot, James G. Frazer – to a question regarding the worth and role of literary production. Kennedy's first novel, *Looking for the Possible Dance* (1993), is structured around a series of physical journeys as metaphors for the journey from adolescence to adulthood made by its central character, Margaret, who leaves Scotland at the novel's end for London with a promise, to her lover, to return. But if that is the metanarrative of identity structuring the book its theatre is that of conflict-ridden love: Margaret must accommodate both her love for the father who brought her up and her love for a man, Colin, by means of an eventual truce with herself and her own (Scottish?) contrariness.

Margaret and Colin's relationship is, as Dorothy McMillan notes, 'lived out in fragments during journeys between England and Scotland' (95), and this displacement is also the figure for Margaret's relation to familial and national belonging. Born in Glasgow, our protagonist must recover from her Scottish education which, while declaring that 'the chosen and male shall go forth unto professions while the chosen and female shall be homely, fecund, docile and slightly artistic', also defines Scottishness thus: 'Nothing in a country which is nothing, we are only defined by what we are not. Our elders and betters are also nothing: we must remember this makes them bitter and dangerous' (15–16). 'A place unbounded by history', in a sense, but explosively so for a young woman seeking her way in a land alive with inexpressible resentments.

Margaret meets Colin, a fellow Scot, at the English university where she studies English Literature but he eventually leaves her and she returns to Scotland. When they meet again, she is working in a community centre from which she is eventually fired after rejecting the director's sexual advances. For his part Colin achieves a worse punishment: he is crucified to a floor by a man called Webster, a loan shark in whose activities Colin has sought to intervene. Intriguingly, the resolution to Margaret's story comes about as the men in her life succumb to illness or wounding, her father nearing death, Colin's horrific injuries making him dependent on others' care, and in the middle part of the book, an encounter on a train with a disabled man named James, whose machine enabling speech is disconnected and with whom Margaret communicates by writing.

Writing takes on an increasingly central role in Kennedy's novels and, while it is the dance which, as a child, Margaret enjoyed with her father that, in this first novel, images tentative belonging, writing is also explored as an agent of healing or, alternatively, doom. As she and James part, Margaret writes down her address on a piece of paper and as he struggles to wave goodbye to her it blows along the station platform out of sight. Margaret returns to her carriage with a tightness in her throat and finds 'she cannot settle to read' (170). The sinister Webster (meaning weaver, in this case, of stories or words) talks first to Margaret in a dentist's waiting room, confessing to a murder, well before he muti-lates Colin and before Colin and Margaret have reunited. But at the same time Margaret has in her pocket a letter from Colin that says he wants her back. Margaret wonders if either man has been telling her the truth (46–50).

If dance is a fitting image for a young woman growing up and away from a pleasure-annihilating Calvinism, the relation of writing to pre-destination and self-determination becomes more significant in *So I Am Glad*. In this novel a radio announcer named Jennifer who reads aloud the words of others, has a relationship with a man only objectively verifiable through writings, the seventeenth-century Savinien Cyrano de Bergerac. As Douglas Gifford notes, this tale is in a long Scottish tradition from Stevenson and Hogg to Muriel Spark and Alasdair Gray maintaining an ' "either/or" tension between the supernatural and the psychological', or, alternatively, concerning 'a traumatised mind using displacement and fantastic imagination to simultaneously avoid and redeem the damage from which it hides' (Gifford 620).

In telling her story, Jennifer repeatedly foregrounds its narrativity (Dunnigan 148, 153). She has trouble telling readers about Savinien in the same way she has trouble believing in him when he first appears in her Glasgow flat, and as he has with regard to his own uncomfortable temporal and geographical transition:

Forgive me for the delay. I should be able to tell you who he was without any trouble at all. I don't know why it makes me so uneasy to think of giving his secret away to you. Perhaps, because we had a certain privacy together, I am a little jealous with him now. (47)

It is the secret of intimacy, eventually love, that Jennifer comes to share with Savinien and which changes her relation to the world, and the words through which the world's happenings are conveyed, a process she initially resists but cannot continue to. Savinien is in effect the foreign element that eventually anchors Jennifer, for the first time, to her own era and place, provoking what might be read as an instance of angry Scottishness that colours her reading of the news:

> 'You seem to be developing a tone, Jennifer.'
> A tone.
> The way they said it, a tone was something midway between slight catarrh and a Polish accent. An unnecessary colour in the voice, an air of negative comment.
> Negative comment. I don't know where I could have got that from.
> . . .
> Our prime minister wishes to fine the penniless and homeless for being homeless – not to mention shabby and down at heel. Unforthcoming fines will be used to build prisons in which to store those homeless persons unable to pay fines.
> Can't see a thing wrong in that. (218)

But this tone, or anger, also arises because Jennifer has discovered that what goes on in the world of politics or the nation affects her own private chance of happiness, as, indeed, circumstances set in train centuries ago affect the outcome of Savinien and Jennifer's relationship, bringing home the inextricable proximity of love (*l'amour*) and death (*la mort*), presaged in a letter Savinien writes to her in his native tongue (235):

> Sorry to go on, but I found that I cared about these things. Someone I loved was living here and I cared about them. People who cared about each other were out there, beyond the studio, up to their necks in crap. I had to say.
> I couldn't help it. (220)

If *So I Am Glad* connects the writing of Jennifer and Savinien's story with the question of the value of a life – 'If I was you, that whole *writing a book* thing might make me wonder just what kind of person I could be' (129) – *Everything You Need*'s angle on the value and relation of writing to living and of privacy to community is darker and more brutal. The central character of the novel, Nathan Staples, likewise has a truth he feels compelled to speak, but is unable to. This concerns his daughter Mary, from whom he has been estranged since his wife Maura walked out on him fifteen years ago. Nathan is a writer of thrillers, formerly of more 'literary' fiction to which he aspires to return, and who has arranged for Mary, now a teenager, to spend a period of time as part of the writers' community he inhabits on Foal Island, under his direction. While Nathan longs to tell Mary he is her father, his complicated love for his former wife and fear of rejection prevent this. Like *So I Am Glad*, this novel presents love as bound up with self-abnegation, and Nathan's love for his daughter, like that of Margaret for her father in Kennedy's first novel, is troubled by self-consciousness inseparable from familial duty. The novel is structured in seven parts relating to the term of Mary's fellowship on the island, and by a set of seven stories Nathan is writing, which largely concern Maura, his former wife. The penultimate story recounts Nathan's visiting Maura in London and finding he is the laughable third party in her new relationship, while the final story is very short and is addressed directly to Mary.

Everything You Need is, as commentators have noted, Kennedy's novel about the art of fiction. It includes blackly comic episodes depicting the London publishing scene, largely explored through the relationship of Nathan and his literary agent, the hard-drinking, hard-living Jack Grace, who dies during the narrative and bequeaths to Nathan a horrifying legacy. Nathan must visit the hospital where Jack's body has been donated to medical research and seek out his friend's mutilated limbs. This is Jack's final joke, a test of Nathan's writerly detachment and a jest on the writer's willingness to suffer horror for art. In the end, Nathan recognises Jack by encountering one of his hands:

> It was his, it could only be his. The slightly large knuckles and nicotine staining were irreversibly eloquent, both part of the small identity of the perfect instrument for jabbing out faulty typing, miming gunfire, raising glasses, red-inking corrections, pointing out cretins, building joints, producing a signature of surprising elegance and drumming bar tops, turning pages, patting shoulders, shaking hands, shaking Nathan's hand, shaking Nathan's hand.
>
> *Just fucking like you, leaving me here with all of this.*
>
> Nathan let his fingers close hard around nothing.
>
> *Just fucking like you, Jack.* (473)

The novel is full of instances of similarly flesh-creeping revelation, and the isolation and emotional overheatedness, combined with impotence, sexual and artistic, of the island community, could almost be figured by the ghost of lost connections that is Jack's severed hand. Members of the community are traditionally bound to try and kill themselves, and the narrative opens and closes with two such attempts by Nathan, which plumb the affective proximity of death and infantilism and death and responsibility respectively. The first attempt is dizzying as the reader discovers that what appears to be a last resort is in fact a ritual Nathan needs in order to go on living, an extreme physical theatre that momentarily suspends the outside world as well as the void that has become his life and work: 'The thought of his own care for his own self pushed him in to a tighter curl: a slippery, well-meant hug for the engineer of his salvation. This was always a pleasant stage in recovery' (26).

As the rest of the novel will explore, this deathly circle cannot sustain itself once Mary enters the scene, and it is the receiving of Mary's finished novel and the passing into Mary's hands of Nathan's own narrative that is the instance in which father and daughter declare their love for and trust of each other, although Nathan ultimately refrains from telling Mary who he is. As in Kennedy's other longer fictions, writing is strongly eroticised, and just as sex, here as in *So I Am Glad*, can be violent and unredeeming, so writing is akin to love: physically and emotionally costly, a risk with no guaranteed return. In the final pages of his manuscript for Mary, Nathan imparts to her the writer's final rule:

> *do it for love.*
>   And.
> If you can, forgive me. (567)

Writing first in longhand – 'I'd like my hand to be on it. Old-fashioned of me' (566) – and then typing, Nathan makes of his daughter a last request: that she have need of him. In this respect the novel is legible as a version of the Grail myth, in which the meaning of the sacred object for which knights go on quests is not revealed until they find it, and in the search for which they are required, if necessary, to give their lives. The Grail itself, which, according to myth, originally held the blood of Christ, is the emblem of the redemptive sacrifice that it demands, and is the nobler or more rigorous version of mortal, human love.

Cairns Craig describes Frazer, the Scottish intellectual whose *The Golden Bough*, first published in 1890, was so influential for twentieth-century literary and anthropological enquiry into the function of myth and religion, as a thinker for whom 'the whole history of humanity is the history of its fundamental fearfulness, and its refusal to move beyond the boundaries of that fear-ruled world' (42). This makes every journey into the human imagination 'a journey back into the terrors' of its past, a past that Cairns sees as peculiarly rich, but also peculiarly challenging, for the Scottish literature that is motivated by it (42). Fear and risk is indeed the sense we get at the end of the novel, for which its horrors have perhaps been preparation: Nathan gives Mary, in writing, his lack, his need to be needed, which the writer also needs in the form of his or her readers, and which the writers in this community tend not to have. In giving Mary the end of his writing Nathan arguably puts her needs before his own or follows her lead in giving him her novel. The fact that he is her father fractures his love between familial connection and the shared bond that is the sometime void and sometime creativity that is writing.

Everything You Need is almost Kennedy's exploration of writing as religion, certainly of writing as a kind of all-or-nothing Calvinism, a mode of suffering and joy that can flip between extremes. Nathan feels that Mary is a born writer, but she must nonetheless obey the rules, which include 'there are no rules' (449), and the final rule regarding writing for, or in and out of, love – 'do it for love' (567). Like Adam Mars-Jones and Philip Tew, I do not think *Everything You Need* is a successful novel, if by that we mean pertaining to some kind of holding structure animated by characters about whom we come, in some respect, to care. A violent, if lively, negativity is its paramount tone and theme and by this means it risks alienating the reader. Yet at the same time it does seem to be a logical development in Kennedy's œuvre which explores the void at the heart of love, human finitude, Scottish culture and the work of writing, the performativity of all of which depends on acts of courage, leaps taken as it were across the void but which, paradoxically, do not escape habitation by it. If Nathan is a figure for the Grail myth's Fisher King whose unhealed wound is doubled by his wasted country, then the future of Scottish literature looks bleak indeed. However, if we read this novel in the context of Kennedy's other books and their intransigent exploration of the languages of feminine desire, their sometimes crippling sense of an inter-imbricated history, national and private, and the sense that the writing act, whatever else it is, is performatively important, we may find that her ethics of intimate exploration is upheld and extended, after all.

In this novel it is as though Kennedy has set herself the hardest test of all, and does not much care whether she has passed or failed it. What interests me about the book, though, is its play with states of bordered isolation and borderless excess which can turn into a living death – as life is bordered by its end, which is eternal – or an endless sentence, and the way the writer's dedication to imagined or bordered worlds involves him or her in a loss of boundaries equivalent to love and sexual desire. Although the central figure in *Everything You Need* is Nathan Staples, I agree with Sarah Dunnigan that Kennedy's bravest ventures are those made into the unwritten territory of feminine desire, routinely characterised, in cultural terms, as a region without borders.[6] It is Kennedy's attempt to bring into conversation writing, love, (feminine) sexual desire and Scottishness, all of which have suffered from our inadequacy at describing active voids and states with multiple borders,[7] that is continually compelling, as though our author is cutting away, one by one, the reading habits and conceptions of the world that sustain the life of writing, an experiment with what it is that makes a book, and what it takes to keep the words alive and troubling.

Here Joan Copjec's comment on an ethics she derives from the teachings of Jacques Lacan, whose account of love I have already presented, is relevant since, like Kennedy's fictions, conflict is its mode of operation. That the assuaging of conflict has often been the task required of women, as part of the fantasy of a harmony between the sexes, as Copjec notes, has not protected women from conflict or injustice or 'the worst ethical misconduct' as a result (17). In light of this, Copjec suggests that an ethics based on a good that is impossible . . .

. . . lost, irretrievably lost, because it is only *as* lost, as gone, that it is good, *as* rejected that it is desired – will be radically different from an ethics based on a good that defines an ideal future. Unlike the latter

---

[6] See Sarah Dunnigan, 'A. L. Kennedy's Longer Fiction: Articulate Grace' in *Contemporary Scottish Women Writers* (1997).

[7] In describing feminine sexuality as an active void I have in mind the activity of desire as described by Lacan: active in precise relation to absence, since desire's field of operation is the not yet present, the not yet received. Feminine sexuality suffers historically from a lack of representation, which some see as being redeemable through its increased visibility in language, while others (amongst whom I include myself) regard sexuality as a halt on language, a specific indication of where language meets the limit of its purchase on each body. This does not mean that feminine sexuality cannot be expressed in language, but it does mean that its expression in language will be inexhaustible by language, as all representation of sexuality is. It should be clear from this that to describe (feminine) sexuality as an 'active void' is not to contain or otherwise limit its meaning or expression, but to attest to its complex relation to language. For a helpful discussion of 'the void' and feminine sexuality in Kleinian rather than Lacanian terms, see Jacqueline Rose, *Why War: Psychoanalysis, Politics and the Return to Melanie Klein* (1993), pp.137–90.

this other ethics does not crusade for the cause of harmony; it stakes itself neither on the hope that there will be a time when values will be universal, nor on the pluralist conviction that the space that contains contradictory values is itself neutral, devoid of conflict. In brief, this other ethics is not founded on the belief that an ultimate resolution of conflict is possible, but rather on the insistence that the subject's essential conflict with itself cannot be reduced by any social arrangement. (17)

In a recent essay, Liam McIlvanney suggests that Edwin Muir's gloomy diagnosis of Scotland as the land of the missing centre 'has in part been vindicated, with the novel itself becoming a centre of sorts, taking up the political slack, filling the space where Scottish politics ought to have been', as if in answer to Alasdair Gray's well-known motto: 'Work as if you live in the early days of a better nation' (185). This novel's future success may depend less on what kind of centre it creates as on what avenues for future imagining it augurs, a task inseparable from the conflict that defines not only Scottishness and femininity, as agents of a larger power's – Britain's or humanity's – forward motion, but the very possibility of ethical writing.

Works Cited

Bell, Eleanor Stewart. 'Scotland and Ethics in the Work of A. L. Kennedy', *Scotlands: The International, Interdisciplinary Journal of Scottish Culture*, vol. 5:1 (1998): 105–13

Bozvic, Miran. 'The Bond of Love: Lacan and Spinoza', *New Formations*, 23 (Summer 1994): 69–80

Colley, Linda. *Britons: Forging the Nation 1707–1837*. 1992. (London: Pimlico, 2003).

Copjec, Joan. '*m/f*, or Not Reconciled' in *The Woman in Question: m/f.*, ed. Parveen Adams and Elizabeth Cowie (Cambridge, MA: MIT Press, 1990). 10–18

Craig, Cairns. *The Modern Scottish Novel: Narrative and the National Imagination* (Edinburgh: Edinburgh University Press, 1999).

Dunnigan, Sarah M. 'A. L. Kennedy's Longer Fiction: Articulate Grace' in *Contemporary Scottish Women Writers*, ed. Aileen Christianson and Alison Lumsden (Edinburgh: Edinburgh University Press, 2000). 144–55

Gifford, Douglas. 1997. 'Contemporary Fiction II: Seven Writers in Scotland' in *A History of Scottish Women's Writing*, ed. Douglas Gifford and Dorothy McMillan (Edinburgh: Edinburgh University Press, 1997). 604–29

Kennedy, A. L. *Everything You Need* (London: Jonathan Cape, 1999).

——. *Indelible Acts* (London: Jonathan Cape, 2002).

——. *Looking for the Possible Dance* (London: Secker and Warburg, 1993).

——. 'Not Changing the World' in *Peripheral Visions: Images of Nationhood in Contemporary British Fiction*, ed. Ian A. Bell (Cardiff: University of Wales Press, 1995). 100–2

——. *Original Bliss* (London: Vintage, 1997).

——. *So I Am Glad* (London: Vintage, 1995).

Lacan, Jacques. *Séminaire VIII, Le Transfert* (Paris: Seuil, 1991).

MacCaig, Norman. 'A Note on the Author' in Hugh McDiarmid, *Scottish Eccentrics*, ed. Alan Riach (Manchester: Manchester University Press, 1993). vii–xii

March, Cristie Leigh. Interview with A.L. Kennedy, *Edinburgh Review*, 101 (March 1999): 99–119

Mars-Jones, Adam. 'The Martyrdom of Writing' (review of A. L. Kennedy's *Everything You Need*), *The Observer* 23 May 1999: 576

McIlvanney, Liam. 'The Politics of Narrative in the Post-war Scottish Novel' in *On Modern British Fiction*, ed. Zachary Leader (Oxford: Oxford University Press, 2002). 181–208

McMillan, Dorothy. 'Constructed Out of Bewilderment: Stories of Scotland' in *Peripheral Visions: Images of Nationhood in Contemporary British Fiction*, ed. Ian A. Bell (Cardiff: University of Wales Press, 1995). 80–99

Nairn, Tom. *The Break-Up of Britain: Crisis and Neo-Nationalism* (London: New Left Books, 1977).

Punter, David. 'Contemporary Scottish Gothic: Reconstructing an Absent Nation' in *Postcolonial Cultures and Literatures: Modernity and the (Un)Commonwealth*, ed. Andrew Benjamin, Tony Davies and Robbie B. H. Goh (New York: Peter Lang, 2002). 107–27

Rabaté, Jean Michel. *Jacques Lacan: Psychoanalysis and the Subject of Literature* (Basingstoke: Palgrave, 2001).

Rose, Jacqeline. *Why War: Psychoanalysis, Politics and the Return to Melanie Klein* (Oxford: Blackwell, 1993).

Spark, Muriel. *The Ballad of Peckham Rye* (Harmondsworth: Penguin, 1960).

Tew, Philip. 'The Fiction of A. L. Kennedy: The Baffled, the Void and the (In)visible' in *Contemporary British Fiction*, ed. Richard J. Lane, Rod Mengham and Philip Tew (Cambridge: Polity, 2003). 120–39

Walker, Marshall. *Scottish Literature Since 1707* (London: Longman, 1996).

Lesbian Transformations of Gothic and Fairy Tale[1]

PAULINA PALMER

Genre, Gothic, Fairy Tale

Describing the literary preferences of Rainbow Rosenbloom, the lesbian Jewish heroine of *The Dyke and the Dybbuk* (1993), Ellen Galford humorously refers to her predilection for what she terms the '*mind candy*' of 'dyke-detective thrillers, biographies of self-destructing rock stars, science fiction tales of intergalactic space wars, and one very racy lavender bedtime story from an obscure transatlantic press' (40). Galford's itemising of the different forms of lesbian genre fiction that Rainbow enjoys makes an appropriate opening for this essay since it is the recasting of popular genres – a trend that started to achieve prominence in lesbian literary production around the mid-1980s, supplanting in popularity realist forms of narrative such as the 'coming out' novel – that furnishes the context for her fiction. Galford, it is interesting to note, omits from her list the one particular genre which she herself generally utilises as the frame for her novels. This is lesbian Gothic and the reworking of fairy-tale conventions and motifs which it frequently involves.[2] The reason she decides not to include it is perhaps that, as *The Dyke and the Dybbuk* is itself a striking example of the genre, reference to it would be redundant.

The growth of lesbian Gothic, as well as having its origin in the development of lesbian genre fiction, reflects the influence of certain mainstream writers, Angela Carter in particular, who created 'feminist' versions of Gothic. Carter's well-known collection of fairy tales *The Bloody Chamber* (1979), though certainly not inscribing a lesbian viewpoint and transmitting in certain episodes, as Patricia Dunker argues, an ideology that is heterosexist, has nonetheless furnished a stylistic model for writers who are interested in experimenting with the genre (6–7). The development of lesbian Gothic also reflects certain shifts of perspective which have recently occurred in cultural theory and lesbian-gay politics. Just as in post-structuralist and queer theory,

---

[1] This essay is dedicated to Cambridge Lesbian Line.
[2] See Paulina Palmer, *Lesbian Gothic: Transgressive Fictions* (1999).

the lesbian is regarded as an 'eccentric' disruptive subject who transgresses sexual and social conventions, so the narratives that portray her and inscribe her sexuality are also expected to disrupt traditional patterns and forms.[3] Gothic, in its propensity to question conventional versions of reality, foregrounds the abject and the grotesque, and creates narratives that are fractured and convoluted, clearly suits these criteria.

It was, in fact, Galford herself who, with other writers such as Jeanette Winterson,[4] helped to initiate the vogue for lesbian Gothic in the 1980s and early 1990s with the publication of her novels *The Fires of Bride* (1986), a recasting of the figure of the witch and her radical feminist associations, and *The Dyke and the Dybbuk*. The latter, as well as creating an innovative slant on the theme of spectral visitation, reworks fairy-tale motifs of magical transformation and romantic quest.

In addition to utilising Gothic and fairy-tale conventions and motifs to represent and discuss lesbian identification and desire, Galford also employs them to explore marginalised national-ethnic identities and culture. Galford's personal history and the different identities that she herself boasts make her admirably suited to this. Though Jewish American by birth, she now lives in Edinburgh and, as her witty analysis of Scottish culture and politics illustrates, is Scottish by adoption. While a focus on lesbian-feminist culture and perspectives underpins all her work, her treatment of her national and ethnic identities varies from text to text. Teasing out the resonances of the term 'queer', Eve Sedgwick draws attention to the fact that 'A lot of the most exciting recent work around "queer" spins the term outwards along dimensions that can't be subsumed under gender and sexuality at all.' She comments on 'the ways that race, ethnicity and postcolonial nationality crisscross with these and other identity-constituting, identity-fracturing discourses' (8–9). Galford's investigation of the tension and interaction existing between a lesbian-feminist identification, on the one hand, and national and ethnic identifications, on the other, vividly illustrates Sedgwick's observation in fictional form. The approach Galford adopts to these issues is post-structuralist in emphasis, indicating her belief that the identifications we adopt tend to be constructed rather than innate. They are made, not given by nature.

---

[3] See Teresa de Lauretis, 'Eccentric Subjects: Feminist Theory and Historical Consciousness' (1990), 145; Marilyn Farwell, *Heterosexual Plots and Lesbian Narratives* (1990), pp.12–13.

[4] See the discussion of Winterson's *The Passion* (1987) and *Sexing the Cherry* (1989) in Palmer, *Lesbian Gothic*, pp.49–51 and pp.78–85.

Indicative of the vitality of the tradition of fiction that Galford has helped to initiate is the influence it has exerted on other authors of lesbian fiction. One of the most inventive of these is the Irish writer Emma Donoghue. Donoghue, commencing her literary career a little later than Galford, develops its key features. Her novel *Stirfry* (1994), a recasting of the lesbian 'coming out' novel set in Dublin, employs Gothic imagery of mermaids and monsters to depict the heroine's discovery of her lesbian orientation and to evoke the tension she experiences between her *Irish-lesbian identifications*, while her set of stories *Kissing the Witch* (1997) creates a lesbian recasting of certain well-known fairy tales. Although Donoghue's Irish identity debars her from occupying a central place in this collection, reference to her fiction is certainly relevant to the discussion of Galford. Her imaginative development of the narrative strategies that Galford initiated illustrates the value they hold for later writers, while at the same time providing a foil to her work.

Before embarking on a discussion of the fiction of the two writers, it is necessary to comment in general terms on the lesbian recasting of fairy-tale structures and motifs in which they engage. Like the reworking of other forms of genre fiction such as the thriller, it confronts the writer of lesbian fiction with intriguing contradictions. From a negative point of view, the fairy tale, as exemplified by the literary versions produced by Charles Perrault and the brothers Grimm, tends to encode a reactionary gender ideology of male assertiveness and enjoyment of adventure, and female subordination and passivity, which is at odds with lesbian-feminist values. Traditionally employed to acculturate young girls into accepting codes of conventional femininity, the fairy tale frequently relegates the heroine to the conventional hetero-patriarchal role of trophy and object of exchange, portraying her moving from the protection of her father to that of the male hero.[5] In addition, as Sandra Gilbert and Susan Gubar argue in their analysis of *Snow White*, the female characters portrayed in the genre are generally depicted not as allies and friends but as rivals and enemies competing for male attention (37–44).

However, the problematic aspects of the fairy tale as a candidate for lesbian-feminist revision are offset by certain positive features. As Jack Zipes argues in his discussion of *Little Red Riding Hood*, the oral versions of the genre which pre-dated present-day literary adaptations are often

---

[5] See Karen E. Rowe, 'Feminism and Fairy Tales', *Women's Studies*, 6:3 (1979), pp.237–57.

considerably less chauvinistic in viewpoint than the versions of Perrault and the brothers Grimm with which the present-day readers are familiar, frequently foregrounding attributes of female independence and initiative (227–60). This is the case, in fact, not only with Nordic tales but also with those from the Arab world. Discussing the famous collection *The Book of the Thousand and One Nights*, Adriana Cavarero draws attention to the celebration of female ingenuity and knowledge, as well as narrative skill, embodied in the portrayal of Queen Sheherazade, the heroine of the frame narrative, who each night succeeds in postponing her execution and performs the feat of 'keeping death outside the circle of life' by delighting the sultan Shahriyar with her storytelling (123). Another female-friendly feature of the collection, one which Western readers tend to ignore, is that Sheherazade recounts the initial story not to the sultan himself but to her younger sister who, in fact, invites her to tell it. The narration of the tales thus originates in an intimate relationship between two women. The sultan is not, as readers generally assume, 'the explicit addressee of a tale that is requested by him but rather only a listener knowingly seduced by Sheherazade's narrative art and her strategy of *suspension*' (123). *The Thousand and One Nights* exemplifies, according to Cavarero, the tradition of the female storyteller, such as 'old witches and wise wet-nurses' (122), bearing witness to the fact that 'There is always a woman at the origin of the *enchanting* power of every story' (122).

Moreover, as is the case with other subsections of Gothic such as the vampire narrative,[6] even those aspects of the fairy tale that appear least amenable to lesbian revision such as the reactionary ideology that the present-day literary versions frequently inscribe, do not deter writers from attempting to revise them but have the reverse effect. They act as a spur to their skills of recasting. The strategies of parodic reworking which Galford and Donoghue utilise in transforming the genre reveal connections, in this respect, with Luce Irigaray's concept of mimesis and Judith Butler's theory of gender as performance. Both theories hinge on the concept of the subversive effect of the parodic re-enactment of oppressive roles and images. Irigaray proposes that the female subject, instead of attempting to reject outright the roles and scripts which masculinist culture assigns to her, a task that she regards as futile, should challenge them surreptitiously by re-enacting them in a parodic manner (76). Butler

---

[6] See Richard Dyer, 'Children of the Night: Vampirism as Homosexuality, Homosexuality as Vampirism' (1988), pp.47–72.

argues that lesbian and gay roles, such as butch/femme and drag, rather than imitating heterosexual gender roles, as has been generally assumed to be the case, enact a transgressive commentary on them, thus exposing their inauthenticity. She regards the abject, the realm to which society has traditionally relegated the homosexual, not as a position of impotence but as the site from which the gay community can challenge hetero-patriarchal power and the regulatory discourses that serve to enforce it. She describes parodic mimicry, in fact, as one of the strategies available to lesbians and gay men to resignify the boundaries of the abject ('Imitation' 13–31). Galford and Donoghue adopt a similar strategy. By parodically reworking in their novels and stories the grotesquely misogynistic representations of femininity such as the witch, the mermaid and the giantess that fairy tales inscribe, they likewise engage in an attempt to renegotiate and resignify the boundaries of the abject, thus helping to redeem the lesbian from the image of 'the monstrous feminine' which homophobic culture projects upon her.[7]

Witches and Wise Women: Changing the Story

The witch is, of course, a key figure in Nordic fairy tale, playing a malevolent role in a number of well-known stories including *Hansel and Gretel* and *The Sleeping Beauty*. She also features prominently, in a very different guise, in the radical feminist theory of the 1970s and early 1980s. Deliberately inverting the image of the witch as a source of evil, Mary Daly in *Gyn/Ecology: The Metaethics of Radical Feminism* (1978) portrays her as a signifier of female independence and commitment to lesbian-feminist sisterhood which patriarchy, by recruiting women into heterosexual relations and encouraging them to conform to a model of docile femininity, seeks to suppress. Daly dedicates her study to her sister 'Hags, Harpies and Crones' (xii). Creating her own inimitable blend of theory and myth, she invites the reader to liberate 'the Wild Witch within her' by accompanying her on a journey intended to inspire 'the Lesbian imagination in All Women' (xiii).

Galford, writing in the later period of the 1980s and 1990s, while influenced by the radical feminist re-evaluation of the witch achieved by

---

[7] See Barbara Creed, *The Monstrous Feminine: Film, Feminism and Psychoanalysis* (1993), pp.67–72; Creed, 'Lesbian Bodies: Tribades, Tomboys and Tarts' in Elizabeth Grosz and Elspeth Probyn, ed. *Sexy Bodies: The Strange Carnalities of Feminism* (1995), pp.86–103.

Daly and Robin Morgan, adopts an approach which, in its postmodern emphasis on role and performativity, creates images that are very different. The witch emerges from her text not only as a signifier of female independence and marriage resistance but also as a cultural construct that patriarchal culture seeks to project upon women who refuse to conform to its conventions, and that the latter, by means of a strategy of parodic reworking, seek simultaneously to resist and exploit. Galford's portrayal of the witch, as well as advertising the fictionality of the motif by means of intertextual allusions, responds fruitfully to a reading in terms of Irigaray's theory of masquerade and mimesis. Basing her analysis on the discussion of femininity by the 1930s analyst Joan Riviere, Irigaray describes the masquerade as the acting out by the female subject of a series of male-defined roles and scripts 'at the price of renouncing their own desire' (133). She also proposes a strategy that the female subject can employ to challenge and exploit male-defined roles and identities. She terms this 'playing with mimesis' (76). Woman, she argues, by parodically mimicking conventional images of femininity and introducing into her performance an element of excess, can expose their artifice and inauthenticity. In this way, she can resist male control and hopefully achieve a degree of agency. The female characters whom Galford portrays, in subjecting the role of witch to parodic re-enactment, perform an inventive version of this strategy.

The action of *The Fires of Bride* takes place on Cailleach, an imaginary island off the coast of Scotland contemptuously described by an unappreciative Lowlander as a 'miserable hole, the outermost island of the Utter Utter Hebrides' (5). In Gaelic Cailleach means 'the Crone', a word recalling the radical feminist terminology of Daly. The island, as its name signals, represents a woman-identified space where women, in accord with radical feminist values, can create their own community relatively free from male control. Galford opens the novel by sketching three different cultural scenarios for which it might furnish the setting: 'gothic thriller', 'late Victorian romance' and 'wicked caper movie' (31). This self-conscious gambit has the effect of foregrounding the fictionality of the island and situating the narrative in the context of the lesbian-feminist transformation of popular genres.

The female characters depicted as inhabiting Cailleach or visiting it, whose intertwining stories comprise Galford's narrative, are all writers, artists or mystics. Maria who, visiting the island as a tourist, ends up making her life there, is a painter and sculptor who, unbeknown to herself, has psychic powers. In achieving access to the island's turbulent past, she discovers that she has a double in an earlier period of history.

This is the eleventh-century nun Mhairi who entered the local convent in order to avoid being coerced into an oppressive marriage. Finding scope for her artistic talents in illuminating religious manuscripts, she devoted her brief life to making copies of the Book of Bride, an apocryphal gospel recounting the life of the female twin of Jesus Christ which the orthodox Catholic Church seeks to suppress as heretical. The figure who mediates between the two women, persuading Maria to visit the island and herself unearthing a copy of Mhairi's Book of Bride, is Catriona, clan chieftain and, as becomes apparent from her high-handed behaviour, resident witch. Catriona owns the castle that dominates the island and, exploiting her reputation for witchcraft, inveigles Maria into a love affair and introduces her to the lesbian-feminist community of Cailleach.

The sufferings experienced by the eleventh-century Mhairi and her sister nuns exemplify the persecutory uses which male-supremacist society makes of the construct of the witch. On learning that the women are engaged in producing copies of the Book of Bride, the Vatican sends an emissary to put an end to the project and destroy the heretical document. Mhairi meets her death imprisoned in an underground chamber, while the future generations of women who share her devotion to the cult of St Bride and tend the sacred flame which forms its centre are condemned to execution as witches. As Galford, commenting on the activities of the witch-finders in 'the Burning Times' (131), observes, 'The men of the place grew ever more vigilant, and zealously dispatched any suspected woman to the boot, the rope and the stake at Inverness' (132).

In contrast to Mhairi and the other devotees of St Bride who, on account of their resistance to male control, are typecast as witches by the medieval Church and, as a result, suffer brutal persecution, Catriona, the female figure who rules the island's social life in the twentieth century, adopts the role voluntarily, exploiting it to the advantage of herself and the female community. She invites Maria to the island and, by dint of a mixture of bribery and bullying, persuades her to return to the career of artist which, due to financial insecurity and lack of recognition, she has temporarily renounced. As is typical of the complexity of Galford's postmodern narrative, ambiguity exists in certain episodes as to whether Catriona merely enacts the role of witch or really enjoys magic powers.

As well as playing a significant role in the action of the novel, Catriona is a vehicle for Galford's playfully satiric treatment of motifs relating to witchcraft, both traditional and radical feminist. The witch as representative of the abject who lives in a dirty house full of 'filthy secrets' is humorously parodied in the description of Catriona's turret room where she sleeps surrounded by bookcases crowned with stuffed herring-gulls, cases of Little Arctic butterflies and boxes overflowing with ancient manuscripts (Creed 77). Intertextual references to classic myth and fairy tale foreground the power that she wields. On first experiencing her hospitality, Maria confesses to regarding her as a cross between Circe and the witch of Nordic fairy tale. She is scared that her uncanny hostess will transform her 'in classical vein into a squealing pig, penned up in a sty with other bewildered ex-dinner guests' (41) or serve her up, in a manner reminiscent of the witch in *Hansel and Gretel*, as 'a tid bit on a baking tray on the scrubbed wooden table in the castle kitchen' (41).

The portrayal of Catriona and her witch-like persona also gives Galford the opportunity to comment humorously on radical feminist constructs of womanhood. She simultaneously celebrates and gently ridicules the idealised image of the radical feminist hags and crones whom Daly delineates. In addition, it enables her to explore the interaction between lesbian and Scottish identifications experienced by the female characters in the novel and to investigate the ongoing struggle they wage with the country's misogynistic institutions and chauvinistic attitudes. While utilising episodes from Scottish history as the frame for her narrative, she also introduces a wittily satiric depiction of the Scottish tourist industry, exposing its commercialised packaging of native culture.

In contrast to Galford who makes the lesbian recasting of the witch central to her account of life on an imaginary Hebridean island, Donoghue reworks a collection of traditional fairy tales in which she plays a key role. 'The Tale of the Shoe', portraying the witch in her benevolent guise of wise woman, creates a lesbian version of *Cinderella*, a famous example of the genre. Subverting both the ideology of heterosexual romance and the focus on female rivalry which the tale traditionally inscribes, Donoghue foregrounds instead the positive aspect of female relationships and explores the connections existing between mother–daughter relations and lesbian love.

'The Tale of the Shoe' opens in a conventional manner with Cinderella lamenting her entrapment in a routine of domestic drudgery. She despondently describes how 'I raked out the hearth with my fingernails, and scoured the floor until my knees bled' (3). In this case, however, she performs these wearisome tasks not because anyone forces her to do so but from a masochistic impulse of self-punishment. The death of her mother has deprived her of female identification and nurture, plunging her into an abyss of *déréliction*, the condition of alienation and despair to which, according to Irigaray, women are reduced in a phallocentric society which refuses to acknowledge the importance of a female genealogy (Whitford 91, 107).

However, her depression is suddenly lifted by the unexpected appearance of a mysterious woman, a substitute for the conventional fairy godmother. The transformation that the woman achieves in Cinderella's outlook is brought about not by means of magic but by the simple fact that she knew her mother and is thus able to empathise with her grief. As Cinderella comments, employing imagery of magical transformation, 'My old dusty self was spun new. This woman sheathed my limbs in blue velvet. I was dancing on points of clear glass' (5). In her mood of euphoria she asks her new friend to take her to the ball at the palace. Here, as romantic convention dictates, she encounters the figure of the prince and becomes involved in a typical scenario of heterosexual romance: 'Out on the steps he led me under the half moon, all very fairy tale' (7). However, with a perception alien to the heroine of the traditional fairy tale, she self-critically watches herself perform a version of the feminine masquerade, confessing that 'I danced like a clockwork ballerina and smiled till my face twisted' (7). The prince, moreover, rather than appearing the ideal lover, strikes her, on the contrary, as 'an actor on a creaking stage' (6). To avoid his marriage proposal, Cinderella escapes from the ball, dismissing the heterosexual future he offers her as bland and suffocating, 'white and soft, comfortable as fog' (7). On finding her woman friend awaiting her return, she regards her with new eyes. Recognising her attributes of intelligence and emotional warmth, she admits, in a phrase which alerts the reader to Donoghue's deliberately subversive aims, that she 'had got the story all wrong' (8). It is the woman, not the prince, whom she loves. She is unconcerned about the shoe which she dropped on leaving the ball, recognising that, as the majority of women are content with an orthodox heterosexual future, the prince will quickly find another girl to fit it.

Urban Fairy Tales

Discussing the part which an urban environment plays in the formation of lesbian identity and culture, Elizabeth Wilson describes the lesbian as 'the inhabitant of the great cities', a figure defined by her sexuality and by the fact that she 'stands outside the family' (169). The lesbian's relationship with the city, foregrounded by Wilson in 1986, has subsequently been examined by other theorists and critics. Whereas Gill

Valentine explores the lesbian's '(Re)negotiating the "heterosexual street"', Sally Munt, elaborating from a queer perspective the ideas of Walter Benjamin, discusses the concept of 'the lesbian *flaneur*' who, by appropriating the male prerogative of the gaze, reclaims the urban space for women. These ideas form the context of Galford's *The Dyke and the Dybbuk* and are further developed in Donoghue's *Stirfry*. The two novels, in combining a focus on an urban location with motifs of magical transformation, the lesbian heroine's quest for romance and her encounter with a monstrous Other, merit the designation 'urban fairy tales'.

Obvious differences are apparent between the two novels, stylistically and in terms of content. Galford's *The Dyke and the Dybbuk* utilises a London setting and is a work of fantasy creating a humorous lesbian variation on that antiquated cliché of Gothic fiction and film, the family curse. This particular curse, as the female dybbuk Kokos who is dispatched by Mephistico Industries to execute it explains, originated in the Middle Ages in a humble Eastern European dorf when an orphan girl of mixed Jewish–Gentile parentage sought to take revenge on her Jewish lover Gittel for betraying the vow of sisterhood they had sworn by agreeing to marry. Directing the curse not only at this particular Gittel but at all subsequent ones until the thirty-third generation, she expresses the wish that they will disappoint their misogynistic husbands by giving birth only to daughters and, an even more scary fate, be possessed by a dybbuk, a Jewish demon whose mission is to possess the human subject with the aim of driving her mad. The action of Galford's novel hinges on the complex relationship that develops between the infernal Kokos and the lesbian Rainbow, the present-day recipient of the curse, who, in an attempt to reject her Jewish upbringing and liberate herself from her family, has moved into a shabby flat in the Portobello Road and taken a job as a taxi-driver.

Donoghue's *Stirfry*, on the contrary, is a predominantly realist text charting the adventures of the seventeen-year-old student Maria in the city of Dublin and exploring the relationship she forms with her two flatmates Ruth and Jael. Maria initially occupies the role of naive ingénue. Raised in a Roman Catholic family in the provinces, she has little knowledge of homosexuality and at first fails to recognise the signs of her flatmates' lesbian orientation. These include the phrase 'No bigots' in the advert for the flat-share (3), the Cretan labrys which Ruth has painted on the kitchen window, and frequent indirect allusions to lesbian sex. Her accidental discovery of Ruth and Jael's sexuality disturbs and disorientates her, and the latter stages of the narrative centre on her ambivalent response of repulsion/attraction to it. The novel concludes with her not only coming to terms with her flatmates' lesbian orientation but also discovering her own and when, as eventually occurs, the two decide to separate, forming a relationship with Ruth.

Nonetheless, despite their differences in content and style, Galford's and Donoghue's novels display significant common features. Both, in depicting the lesbian protagonist's exploration of city life, imaginatively recast motifs appropriated from Gothic and fairy tale. Returning culture to a state of nature, they transform the city into a fantasy landscape evoking the dark forest which furnishes the setting for numerous Nordic fairy tales such as *Little Red Riding Hood* and *Hansel and Gretel*. The demon Kokos in *The Dyke and the Dybbuk*, with a supernatural perception denied the human Rainbow, glimpses at night 'a large black bear, broken loose from someone's dream of a Lithuanian forest, stumbling through the gardens of South Tottenham' (64). She describes how 'a headless rooster, white feathers bloodied, lands on a roof after a long passage over oceans, delivering a tropical curse to terminate a lovers' quarrel' (64–5). In addition, she magically transforms the plunge pool at the public baths into a fathomless well in which the hapless Rainbow finds herself 'entangled', in typical horror-movie fashion, by 'something slipping across her body like ribbons of seaweed' (69).

The Dublin location of *Stirfry* is represented undergoing a similarly sylvan shift. Sitting on the top deck of the bus home, the heroine Maria settles down to enjoy 'twenty minutes of dream time, now, as the floodlit city corners flared into black suburban avenues. The knobbled branches of overhanging horse chestnut trees cracked against the windows, on and off, pulling her back to consciousness' (22). Magical transformations take place in both her external environment and her internal psyche. The attic flat she shares with Ruth and Jael appears at night to be 'floating in a pool of light on top of the city' (84), while, in a dream-cum-nightmare, she finds herself unexpectedly metamorphosed into a bird 'hurtling through a canyon, her wings flaring out behind her' (97).

The encounter with a mysterious-monstrous Other that the protagonists of both novels experience in their quest for identity and romance is likewise described in Gothic and fairy-tale imagery. In Galford's *The Dyke and the Dybbuk* it is Kokos who, as suits her identity as demon, is initially assigned the role of monster. Personae which she adopts in an attempt to terrify Rainbow and drive her mad include Brocken Spectre and underwater squid. In addition she frequently speaks in phrases with fairy-tale associations. Parading her demonic credentials, she proudly tells her colleagues at Mephistico Industries that her CV includes 'three successful joint ventures with Islamic djins and affrits, in medieval Spain, where Jewish and Arabic magicians explored forbidden ground together' (48). She also describes Rainbow's romantic quest to win the beautiful Riva, the respectable wife of a Jewish scholar with whom Rainbow inappropriately falls in love, in fairy-tale terms, comparing her to the hero facing the 'deadly dragons' of her beloved's contempt (129).

In Donoghue's *Stirfry* the role of monstrous Other is initially assigned to the lesbians Ruth and Jael. This homophobic image is projected upon the couple by the youthful Maria. Living in 1980s Ireland where homosexuals are regarded at worst as 'mortal sinners' and at best as 'pitiable case histories' (77), Maria initially finds her flamates' sexuality disconcerting and scary. The role of monster which she unconsciously projects upon them is represented in imagery of grotesque femininity appropriated from fairy tale. In the bathroom of the flat she shares with them she comes across a ceramic toothbrush mug in the form of a mermaid (18), while the portrait of the couple she sketches accidentally takes on the appearance of 'the two headed monster in a fairy-tale, the kind of thing the hero had to fight' (126). It alternatively reminds her of 'a gargoyle with two tongues for waterspouts' (126).

However, as suits the lesbian-feminist interrogation of reactionary values which is their aim, both Galford and Donoghue, far from endorsing the concept of the lesbian as monstrous, seek, on the contrary, to challenge it by deconstructing the binary opposition normal/abnormal. As a result, the roles they assign to their characters in this respect are by no means fixed. Galford cleverly engineers a role reversal between the demon Kokos and the lesbian Rainbow, the object of her haunting, thus prompting the reader to question which, if either character, represents the monstrous Other and which the norm. Kokos's task as a dybbuk, as she has learnt from the infernal mentor with whom she studied, is to possess the human subject whom she is appointed to haunt in order to 'transform her into something Other than what she was before' (39). Here, however, she encounters difficulties since, as she sarcastically remarks on first meeting Rainbow, 'By any conventional standards this rather eccentric individual is pretty Other to begin with' (39). The fashionably queer image which Rainbow cultivates, with her 'grating of spikes' haircut and 'faded purple T-shirt bearing a clenched fist' (40), makes her appear, in Kokos's opinion, decidedly grotesque. And, instead of utilising her domestic skills to attract a Jewish husband, as a nice

Jewish girl should, Rainbow lives in a chaos of unwashed clothes and forms intimate relationships with women.

Donoghue, while emulating Galford in deconstructing the binary opposition normal/abnormal, adopts different tactics to achieve this end. Instead of engineering a role reversal between her characters as Galford does, she portrays her heroine Maria, motivated by the promptings of lesbian desire, recognise the inauthenticity of the binary. Although, on first discovering her flatmates' lesbian orientation, Maria positions herself as 'normal' in opposition to their 'abnormal', on subsequently recognising her feelings of attraction toward Ruth she is forced to admit that her own sexuality is by no means as orthodox as she had assumed. The novel concludes, in fact, with her mentally redeeming Jael and Ruth from, to cite Butler, 'the domain of abject beings, those who are not yet subjects' and acknowledging their full subjecthood (*Bodies* 3). The transformation which her flatmates undergo in her eyes, in casting off their monstrous associations and emerging as fully human, resembles the transformation which concludes the fairy tale *Beauty and the Beast*. Donoghue, in fact, explicitly advertises the link with the tale by portraying Maria in an earlier episode playfully addressing Jael by the nickname 'beast' (95).

In order to emphasise Maria's readiness to accept and even enjoy manifestations of sexual difference, her own included, Donoghue parodically recasts imagery inscribing 'the monstrous feminine' in positive terms. The fantasy image that Maria conjures up of flying over the city of Dublin at night, 'black air between her legs, the office windows glinting as she skimmed by' (28), relates her to the figure of the witch, while, lying in bed, fingering the folds of bedspread, she pictures herself as a 'giantess, fondling a landscape of motorways' (30). She even catches herself admiring the statue of Anna Livia, described as a 'reclining giantess in bronze' and a 'monster, out of all proportion' (87), which adorns the Dublin city centre. Her feelings of affection for the statue mirror her growing affection for Ruth, the example of 'the monstrous feminine' with whom she shares her home (87).

As the above discussion illustrates, the form of fiction that Galford helped to initiate, and the narrative strategies she employs, as well as furnishing the ground for her own novels, have had an impact on contemporary writers, providing them with ideas and material for development. The transformation of Gothic and fairy-tale conventions, in which she, and subsequently Donoghue, engage creates an effective vehicle for representing the transgressive effects of lesbian desire and interrogating the image of the lesbian as a signifier of 'the monstrous feminine'. They also furnish a means to investigate the tensions and interaction between the female characters' lesbian identification, on the one hand, and their national and ethnic affiliations on the other. Galford's *The Dyke and the Dybbuk* concludes with the dybbuk Kokos congratulating herself on her brilliant powers of storytelling and depicting herself and her fellow demons as positively 'bursting with ideas for plots and engineering special effects' (248). Kokos's description is humorously self-reflexive, giving an apt comment on Galford's skilful recasting of Gothic and fairy-tale conventions and the radical uses to which she puts it.

Works Cited

Butler, Judith. *Bodies That Matter: On the Discursive Limits of 'Sex'* (London: Routledge, 1993).

——. 'Imitation and Gender Insubordination' in *Inside/Out: Lesbian Theories, Gay Theories*, ed. Diana Fuss (London: Routledge, 1991). 13–31

Cavarero, Adriana. *Relating Narratives: Storytelling and Selfhood*, trans. Paul A. Kottman (London: Routledge, 2000).

Creed, Barbara. 'Lesbian Bodies: Tribades, Tomboys and Tarts' in *Sexy Bodies: The Strange Carnalities of Feminism*, ed. Elizabeth Grosz and Elspeth Probyn (London: Routledge, 1995). 86–103

——. *The Monstrous Feminine: Film, Feminism and Psychoanalysis* (London: Routledge, 1993).

Daly, Mary. *Gyn/Ecology: The Metaethics of Radical Feminism* (London: Women's Press, 1979).

Donoghue, Emma. *Kissing the Witch* (Harmondsworth: Penguin, 1999).

——. *Stirfry* (London: Hamish Hamilton, 1994).

Duncker, Patricia. 'Re-Imagining the Fairy Tales: Angela Carter's Bloody Chambers', *Literature and History*, 10:1 (Spring 1984): 3–14

Dyer, Richard. 'Children of the Night: Vampirism as Homosexuality, Homosexuality as Vampirism' in *Sweet Dreams: Sexuality, Gender and Popular Fiction*, ed. Susannah Radstone (London: Lawrence & Wishart, 1988). 47–72

Farwell, Marilyn. *Heterosexual Plots and Lesbian Narratives* (New York: New York University Press, 1990).

Galford, Ellen. *The Dyke and the Dybbuk* (London: Virago, 1993).

——. *The Fires of Bride* (London: Women's Press, 1986).

Gilbert, Sandra and Susan Gubar. *The Mad Woman in the Attic: The Woman Writer and the Nineteenth-Century Literary Imagination* (New Haven: Yale University Press, 1979).

Irigaray, Luce. *This Sex Which Is Not One*, trans. Catherine Porter with Carolyn Burke (Ithaca: Cornell University Press, 1985).

Lauretis, Teresa de. 'Eccentric Subjects: Feminist Theory and Historical Consciousness', *Feminist Studies*, 16:1 (Spring 1990): 115–50

Morgan, Robin, ed. *Sisterhood is Powerful: An Anthology of Writings from the Women's Liberation Movement* (New York: Random House, 1970).

Munt, Sally. 'The Lesbian Flaneur' in *Mapping Desire*, ed. David Bell and Gill Valentine (London: Routledge, 1995). 114–25

Palmer, Paulina. *Lesbian Gothic: Transgressive Fictions* (London: Cassell-Continuum, 1999).

Rowe, Karen E. 'Feminism and Fairy Tales', *Women's Studies*, 6:3 (1979): 237–57

Sedgwick, Eve Kosofsky. *Tendencies* (London: Routledge, 1994).

Valentine, Gill. '(Re)negotiating the "Heterosexual Street": Lesbian Productions of Space' in *Body Space: Destabilizing Geographies of Gender and Sexuality*, ed. Nancy Duncan (London: Routledge, 1996). 146–55

Whitford, Margaret, ed. *The Irigaray Reader* (Oxford: Blackwell, 1991).

Wilson, Elizabeth. *Hidden Agendas: Theory, Politics and Experience in the Women's Movement* (London: Tavistock, 1986).

Zipes, Jack. *Don't Bet on the Prince: Contemporary Feminist Fairy Tales in North America and England* (Aldershot: Ashgate, 2001).

Demisting the Mirror: Contemporary British Women's Horror

GINA WISKER

Contemporary British women horror writers critically engage with and develop a range of settings and concerns familiar in more conventional, male-authored horror. Yet they are scripting roles for women and the more radical amongst them frequently refuse the disempowerment resulting from conventional horror that consistently configures women as victims, femmes fatales, hags and whores. They investigate the spaces, settings, representations, roles and myths that restrict and abject women. They revive the ghost story, favourite of male and female writers alike, and emphasise its gendered significances, and they revitalise mythic figures – Medusa, witches, female vampires. They often re-script the abject scripts usually allotted to such conventional figures, undercutting the cultural assumptions that construct and constrain them. Even more radically, they refuse the 'horror turn': that neat closure which shuts down the subversive energies and restores order at the end of a horror fiction. In this, they not only disturb familiar figures, but also, by troubling conventional narrative structure, question the values that use it as a vehicle. Irony, the oxymoron, and the combining of genres enable subversive moves, destabilising the complacency of conventional horror which only terrifies and disgusts in order to eventually overpower, and restore a status quo predicated upon largely masculine values, and a social imbalance of power between the sexes. As Mark Jancovitch comments:

> Throughout its history, horror has been concerned with forces that threaten individuals, groups, or even 'life as we know it'. It has been concerned with the workings of power and repression in relationship to the body, the personality, or to social life in general. (118)

Power, oppression, silencing and repression are the stuff of horror, deriving from our essential fears of being forced, denied, controlled, displaced out of ourselves, into constraining roles and constricting places, unable to resist or refuse.

Horror often threatens or enacts violence, and exposes our secret fears. What is hidden and suppressed in the familiar is frequently spatialised in horror, literally emerging from beneath the surface, through cracks, up through the floorboards, or trapped up in the attic, in the corners. American Virginia Andrews incarcerates children in an attic in *Flowers in the Attic* (1979), Caitlyn Kiernan has spiders creeping up from hell in the cellar in *Silk* (1998), invading the body and transmuting or entwining it. Something lurking, monstrous, repressed, bodied forth in a demon spirit, ghost or monster, bursts or creeps out: 'qualities, feelings, wishes and objects which the subject refuses to recognise or rejects in himself . . . expelled from the self and located in another person or thing' (Laplanche and Pontalis 349). Alternative selves emerge, the animal beneath the skin, the werewolf, or vampire, the lurking death in us all, the mummy or zombie.

We might be terrified of that which emerges from the cracks and fissures, from beneath the skin, but equally, what is subversive questions cultural conventions and can offer alternatives. In this liminal position, horror works its contradictory magic: it exposes and undercuts other readings, other possibilities. Much contemporary women's horror seizes these radical opportunities and erodes cultural boundaries and differences. It repositions female horror figures, likely to be marginalised or destroyed in conventional horror, and redefines that which is clean/unclean, good/bad, black/white. Radical horror acts politically, restoring the excluded, questioning the complacently established:

> Far from constructing this attempt at erosion as a mere embrace of barbarism or chaos, it is possible to discern it as a desire for something excluded from cultural order – more specifically, for all that is in opposition to the capitalist and patriarchal order which has been dominant in Western society over the last two centuries. (Jackson 176)

The abject Other is recognised as a projection of and from the self. Confronting that which horrifies and disgusts, and recognising ourselves in it, is a way of overcoming our fears and owning up to them, admitting them to be parts of ourselves. Much women's horror insists on this recognition of our selves in the construction of that which has conventionally been seen as Other, as disgusting, as abject. By refusing closure and punishment, the restoration of order of conventional horror, it leaves a space for new visions and relations, new insights and practices.

History of British Women's Horror

British women's horror has a long history. It was, after all, a British woman writer – Mary Shelley – who, it can be argued, began the whole genre of horror when she published *Frankenstein* (1818). British women writers often included horror elements, most frequently in Gothic romances. It can also be found lurking beneath melodrama or sensation novels. Another favourite mode is that of the ghost story. Women have always written ghost stories it seems, not least because of their familiar domestic setting. Haunted houses, returned rivals and domestic tyrants from beyond the grave echo the kinds of threatened and constrained lives many women live in domestic contexts. Some ghosts represent the repressed violence and desire for retribution that women feel. Others merely reinforce a constrained status quo from beyond the grave.

Subversive figures are also recuperated. Sylvia Townsend Warner's *Lolly Willowes* (1926) provides a model for the revaluation of the witch. Avoided because an outsider, unconventional, skilled with herbs and midwifery – women's skills – witches were rejected and feared, on the margins of conformist society. Lolly, in refusing her role as spinster aunt, a dependent (her money taken over by her brother) and a carer, an adjunct to the family, seizes her independence and sets up home alone with a cat in a country village. Lolly recognises herself as a witch, her alternative powers nurtured by her environment and her new positive sense of identity. Warner has Satan as the gardener – a role traditionally assumed by Christ – and Lolly, the follower, chooses her own route happily. Djuna Barnes's Gothic *Nightwood* (1936) also uses elements of horror. The nightmare world that Robin cruises defamiliarises familiar places and activities, destabilises identity. Later in the century, Daphne du Maurier explores the return of the repressed in *Rebecca* (1938), horror undercutting the lies of romantic love, the force of male power. In recognising that evil is part of ourselves, du Maurier too sees that we construct an Other, a feared enemy, a figure of horror, when we need instead to confront ourselves, face up to contradictions:

> The evil in us comes to the surface. Unless we recognise it in time, accept it, understand it, we are all destroyed, just as the people in 'The Birds' were destroyed.[1]

Her short stories 'The Birds' and 'Don't Look Now' debunk the myth of the strong father figure's ability to cope with all forces. One man cannot protect his family from the birds' invasion of the home. Another, seeking his dead daughter, is murdered by a masquerading

[1] Daphne du Maurier, letter to Maureen Baker-Minton, 4 July 1957.

dwarf – he too fails in this male role of solver of mysteries, bringer of order.

These are some of the quite recent British roots of contemporary women's writing in the horror genre. Horror is a transgressive outlet for the examination of fears and desires; it touches us all and offers pleasures and terrors through discoveries of secret, confined, threatening places and selves. Despite Shelley, du Maurier and others, horror has been considered an unusual genre for women writers. As Lisa Tuttle points out, 'Women writers tend to be seen either as rare exceptions, or redefined as something else – not horror but gothic; not horror but suspense; not horror but romance, or fantasy, or something unclassifiable but different' (2–3). Women horror writers often transgress the boundaries of genre, intermixing crime, romance, sci-fi and horror. Subversive troubling of neat genres destabilises the form, as horror destabilises our complacency. Much conventional horror is predicated upon a need to disturb then reinforce a status quo that privileges the everyday manifestations of patriarchy. Most terrifying is an event that threatens or breaches the boundaries of the home, the body or property. This last includes the partner whose controlled loyalty, sexuality and dependability must be taken as given for our own sense of safety. Of ultimate terror in conventional horror is the figure of the transgressive sexually voracious woman who cannot be contained, the castratrix, a devouring embodiment of the 'vagina dentata' myth. In this myth, male fears of female power, sexual and otherwise, are transferred and transmuted into an image of a lovely but ultimately fatal female figure, Medusa–Eve, a snake-haired sensual monster of man's own creation. Once she has attracted and overpowered the helpless male, drawn in by the ungovernable lusts incited in him, she destroys and devours him. What these characters-caricatures have in common is their sexuality, and the male fears they represent. Their fate is abjection, defined by Kristeva as those substances which the body needs to reject, make Other, in order for the subject to be able to recognise itself, to literally have space for itself.[2] According to Kristeva, the first object of abjection is the mother, prefiguring the extradition of women from predominantly male social territory, to the borders of the imagination, either idealised or demonised, but definitely Other, and thus to be restrained or destroyed. The mother and sexually aware woman are terrifying; and women's bodies are a focus of fear and loathing.

[2] See *Powers of Horror: An Essay on Abjection* (1982).

However, this recognition of the Other, the impulse to abject, can also be turned to positive effect in contemporary women's horror. Recognising that the Other is our other half, that we offload fears of death onto this Other, this monstrous female construction, can be a liberating insight. Celebrating our Other is empowering. It undercuts binary oppositions by showing that self and Other are twin sides of the same. For some writers this yoking of opposites is actually enacted through language, as in Angela Carter and the American Poppy Z. Brite. In their confrontational, oppositional and carnivalesque work, horror provides an entertaining and provocative vehicle for interrogating gender representations and assumptions, as well as other configurations of power.

Women horror writers often explore specifically gendered configurations of horror, investing different *spaces*, *places* and *relations* with its power. Daphne du Maurier utilises many of the techniques and narrative trajectories of conventional horror but transgression and unease trouble the ostensible closure of her narratives. In 'The Birds' the people will be destroyed, not rescued. In *Rebecca* the dead wife only *seems* to have been burned and routed in the conflagration that devoured Manderley: she lives on in her effects on the second marriage and the second Mrs de Winter. Rebecca's legacy permeates contemporary horror writing; the unease she leaves us with is developed into fully fledged refusals of closure, and celebratory transgressions. Contemporary women horror writers, American and British, such as Angela Carter, Suzy McKee Charnas, Anne Rice, Melanie Tem and others also concentrate on rewriting horror's representations of women's bodies, and on recognising and reinvesting the domestic setting and the lie of romance with horrific overtones. They critique configurations of gender and power, reclaiming horror's impetus as a vehicle for insight, imaginative illumination and social critique.

What is Different about Contemporary British Women's Horror?

British women's horror is in many respects not that dissimilar from US or Australian horror. However, much British women's horror is located in the history, the solid structures and the settings of the UK and its relationships abroad. Mists and fogs are used in Susan Hill's London and the North in *The Woman in Black* (1983) and *The Mist in the Mirror* (1992). Fay Weldon's three girls in the Fens in *Growing Rich* (1993) are particularly constricted by the lack of job opportunities

and anything but a dull future in domestic service, or a factory, pluck-
ing and gutting chickens or selling them in a shop. The endless, flat,
wet, dullness of the Fens and its sea coast, exploited by developers, is
a perfect setting for murder. It is also perfect for the cruising pimp of
the devil. Some characters in British horror return from abroad, as in
Emma Tennant's *Faustine* (1991) and Hill's *The Mist in the Mirror*.
Several British horror characters have travelled and lived in the
Far East, seeking roots, capitalising on legacies, a colonial heritage.
Historically, removal to the colonies could be a way of getting a char-
acter off stage for a while (Sir Thomas Bertram in Austen's *Mansfield
Park*). In Hill's *The Mist in the Mirror* the colonial legacy is one of
wealth, evil secrecies, oppression, a blighting of future generations.
Colonial powers are indicted.

   Both location and economic situation inflect British women's horror.
Period settings range from Dickensian London, updated or not – Hill's
The Mist in the Mirror, Carter's *The Magic Toyshop* (1967) – to memories
of the swinging '60s: Tennant's *Faustine*. Property, title, name, inheritance are as popular as in the nineteenth century in some texts, for
example, Tennant's *Women Beware Women* (1983). The particularly
British interpretation of constraining roles and locations for women's
lives are also a feature. The single, jobless mother in Tennant's *Two
Women of London* (1989) has less chance of a successful life than the
still rather socially beleaguered, professional woman (Jekyll to her
Hyde). A young girl in the nineteenth century can only really be a
governess or companion unless she marries well, as in Carter's version
of 'Bluebeard' in *The Bloody Chamber* (1979). Marriage, a semi and a
clutter of kids or a dead-end job await Fenland A-level failures – as in
Weldon's *Growing Rich* – when stories are set in the UK (although,
of course, not all are).

   More often than not horror is *but one element* in narration, which
also depends upon other genres. Romantic fiction is most frequently
troubled by elements or cross-overs, intrusions from horror, undercutting its illusions. Destabilising elements, defamiliarisation, the monstrous, or violence erupt from the ostensibly safe family home or intrude
upon family sagas (*Wild Nights, Women Beware Women, Faustine*), rites
of passage, growing-up tales (*Growing Rich, The Life and Loves of a She-
Devil, The Magic Toyshop*, 'The Bloody Chamber', and 'Company of
Wolves'). These tales do not usually set out to shock but to ironise,
undermine and fundamentally question what is taken as given in British
women's lives, settings, roles, opportunities and the myths and formulae
which condition and repress.

Of horror works by contemporary British women writers, Susan Hill's ghost stories are the most conventional. They do not challenge the format of the ghost story and they feature male protagonists, but they do concentrate on domestic tragedy (for example, *The Woman in Black*) highlighting the lingering deadly control of those who influence the young, blighting their lives. Hill's work has all the accoutrements of horror – mysterious doppelgangers, strange characters hiding or leading to secrets, documents revealing tantalising and ultimately dangerous, threatening information and nuances, revengeful ghosts.

Angela Carter, Emma Tennant and Fay Weldon favour comedy, parody, the grotesque and the carnivalesque to expose the social and cultural myths that horror peddles about women. They rewrite familiar horror tales ('Dr Jekyll', 'Bluebeard'), deconstructing either the roles women play in these, or the gendered subtexts which silence, victimise and demonise women. Carter's vampire ('Lady in the House of Love') dramatises the deadly qualities of buying into myths of romantic love. Tennant's *Two Women of London* and *Faustine* explore the destructive hypocrisy of materialistic consumer roles for women, which encourage them to sell their souls for youth. But in each tale women go unpunished. Most frequently the horror enacted by women is seen as a response to the contradictions and violence they suffer in contemporary society (in which many collude). Why punish what society has itself constructed as abject? Like contemporary feminist crime writing, women's horror is unlikely to destroy the carnivalesque or devilish powers it unleashes. Figures of horror are our other selves, we need to recognise them, embrace them, not drive them to the village edge, burn or drown them. Pacts with the devil are common, as in *Faustine*, *Growing Rich*, *The Life and Loves of a She-Devil* (1983). Sometimes this is a folly – if it offers only another male master, a blinkered buying into consumerist, socially constraining lies. Sometimes the bargain, as with Sylvia Townsend Warner's earlier *Lolly Willowes*, is a recognition and celebration of one's own other self, the very role the devil plays in myth, a genuine alternative to the constraints of domesticity, dependency and a secondary role. Witches figure in several of Tennant's tales (for example, *Wild Nights*), representing freedom and imagination, flight from constraint, or a real ability to punish injustice.

Fay Weldon's *The Cloning of Joanna May* (1990) technologically develops the horror of body doubles as a betrayed husband seeks to control his freed wife by cloning her, only to find several free-spirited identical looking women instead of the one. In *The Life and Loves of a She-Devil*, Weldon empowers her incarcerated domestic housewife,

Ruth, to cast off the stifling role of long-suffering wife. In taking revenge on her silly, unfaithful husband, Bobbo, she totally transforms her own life and body, deconstructing the lies of romantic fictions in the process. In *Growing Rich* the boredoms of women's constrained lives in an average nowhere – the Fens – are temporarily countered. Weldon is quite likely to have her characters nonetheless colluding to some extent with social constraints and available gender roles; Carmen marries Sir Bernard in *Growing Rich*. Much worse, Ruth has her freedom in *The Life and Loves of a She-Devil* but chooses to attract back her empty-headed husband. Was this all for love in the end? Are the myths of romantic fiction being ultimately reinforced? Weldon offers carnival and fun but points out the widespread cultural limitations of myths peddled through romantic fiction. All her women, however critical or in league with the devil, are stuck with romantic love. Society and its myths seem unchangeable.

Of all the women writers discussed here, Angela Carter is the most deconstructive, challenging and celebrated. Her use of the oxymoron dramatises contradictions, exposes destructive fictions and sloughs them off. She uses oppositional Gothic structures and Gothic language, the twinning of opposites, and troubles myths and constraints to critique sexualised power relations. Carter transforms fairy tales, rereading myths of monsters and beautiful heroines, and refuses their often implicit conservative meanings, their subtexts of social and sexual power relations. I have explored elsewhere (1993, 1998) how Carter deals with the iconisation of woman, her critique of the ways in which women are reified, which she rightly recognises as a horror scenario. Carter's living dolls fight back, refuse to be puppets (Melanie in *The Magic Toyshop*) or destroy their puppet masters ('The Loves of Lady Purple'). She rewrites horror scenarios: that of 'Bluebeard' in the Duke's attempts to refuse his newest wife–victim knowledge and power in 'The Bloody Chamber'. She writes of the romantic fiction of eternal undying love in the reversed vampire myth of 'Lady in the House of Love'; and she empowers a new Little Red Riding Hood to recognise, come to terms with and celebrate the beast in herself and the lover in the beast when she embraces the werewolf in 'The Company of Wolves'. Carter's tales confront the gender imbalances in traditional fairy tales. She exposes the beliefs on which they are based and foregrounds their constructions of horror as false and negative, fabrications which set out from very conservative values to render woman as hag, victim, whore, her virginity a talisman, her innocence a jewel to own and preserve. Carter rewrites, rewarding rather than punishing those who recognise the beast and the Other in themselves. Technically and linguistically, her work operates at the level of paradox, irony and the oxymoron. It utilises forms that enable expression of dualism, contradictions held in balance. Carter uncovers the horror latent in the familiar. It exists, she shows us, in domestic servitude (Aunt Margaret in *The Magic Toyshop*, silenced by her necklace choker); in pornographic reification and fetishisation of women (Fevvers and her friends in alcoves at Madame Schreck's dungeon brothel in *Nights at the Circus*); in myths which stake women vampires for their sexuality, and refuse to allow women to value sensuality (always killing off the beast in werewolf tales).

Carter overturns what is normally considered terrifying, writes from a perspective more likely to be that of women (and other marginalised groups), and exposes and subverts what for horror is a new target: the seamy and sadistic side of patriarchal controls. In so doing, she reclaims the subversive powers of horror, reinstating it as form and forum for the acting out of disturbing critical fantasies to articulate what Western culture tends to disavow and avoid. In her hands the ostensibly adored but ultimately incarcerated, disempowered and sexually victimised 'living doll' breaks out of the domestic trap and celebrates her own identity and sexual power. Its celebratory excess moves beyond even carnival, creating what James Donald calls 'the noise of negotiation and dialogue' (17). There is no need to put the circus away at the end of the show – everything changes.

Susan Hill – Ghost Stories

Family claustrophobia, denials, losses, contained futures and living death are familiar scenarios in Hill's contemporary ghost stories, *The Woman in Black* and *The Mist in the Mirror*. The return of the repressed not only haunts but also fatally disrupts the lives of those unlucky enough to encounter the revengeful dead. Hill's tales of the dead impinging on the living depict the confusions of relationships. She creates social microcosms with delicacy, emphasising vulnerability.

The Woman in Black, her most famous novel, utilises ghost-story formulae, first-person narration and a traditional family fireside, Christmas Eve storytelling session. Located at a wet, isolated northern marshland house recalling Dickens's Miss Havisham's home in *Great Expectations*, the novel features a gaunt, bereaved, ghostly mother whose child died in a marshland tragedy when his carriage overturned.

The narrator's family is destroyed in a similar accident, cursed by the ghostly presence. The novel is a new version of the family ghost story with a spectral femme fatale, her curse a domestic tragedy. Like du Maurier's male characters, the father figure is helpless to prevent the deaths of his family.

The novels have typically English Gothic horror settings of isolated houses, misty marshes and cobbles (*The Woman in Black*), labyrinthine London streets and distant, haunted northern villages and a school (*The Mist in the Mirror*). *The Mist in the Mirror* also adopts the traditional ghost-tale formulae and an archaic nineteenth-century tone with words such as 'dreech' and 'mizzle' framing, with a rather bleak Dickensian air, the tale told to the narrator by Sir Jamie Monmouth after an evening in a very upper-class, British men's club. Monmouth has been living abroad in Malaysia and *his* colonial legacy is a trunk containing, among other things, information on an evil, influential man, Conrad Vane, who has preyed on and bullied male children. Monmouth's tale involves tracing Vane's history and influences, visiting a typical British public school, a traditional location of oppression, bullying and secrecy. Vane's main victim was a relation of Monmouth's and his curse could pass to his *own* sons. Monmouth avoids marriage and fatherhood as a result. Hill's story is a critique both of elements of masculinity and of the British colonial heritage. While Britain developed and ruled in colonies (Malaysia–Malaya in this instance), generations of an evil, colonially financed power blighted future generations.

Emma Tennant – Devils, Magic, Witches and Rewriting Established Horror

Several contemporary women horror writers concentrate on the lie women are sold about the importance of beauty and material goods. Cosmeticised cover-ups and commodity fetishism exploit their heroines, causing their downfall. This is both moral warning and a mixture of horror and the comic or satirical. Emma Tennant's *Faustine*, a potent, magical, haunted-house story, features the devil himself as one of the three narrators, taking the last revelatory part. This outrageously fantastic novel works by revitalising memory, exploring the evil magical power of a selfish, consumer-oriented desire for eternal youth and beauty, eternal sexual, financial and social power. In so doing, it provides an interesting critique of the values of the 1960s and 1970s as translated into the more sober, capitalist Thatcherite 1980s and 1990s. As a

Thatcherite-period piece, it warns against materialism and commodity fetishism. Magic and humour predominate; its social critique is clear.

The protagonist, Ella, returns from Australia seeking her roots and her fondly remembered grandmother, finding the house harbouring links to her past, and finding her grandmother magically altered. Her gradual discoveries resemble those of a dreamer who tries matching image and dream to a rapidly disappearing reality. These are stock horror techniques, seducing the reader with a sense of déjà vu. Ella's return to this house of her past catches us out with its familiarity: 'I have been here before' (27). The present tense, first-person narrative creates an overpowering personal immediacy. Ella starts discovering things about her past that do not add up. Hidden secrets concerning her absent grandmother seem increasingly related to a powerful, glamorous, materialistic 1960s media success, the beautiful Lisa Crane, whose past glories are replayed in film and text around the house. Lisa mixed with Warhol, Lisa mixed with the Rolling Stones; she controlled and succeeded in a world devoted to hype, consumerism, sex and drugs and rock and roll.

Lisa and Grandmother Muriel turn out to be one and the same, but at a price. Grandmother Muriel, drudge and nurturer, sold her soul to the devil, disguised (topically) as a television salesman. She believed the media hype of miracle changes. The scenario is soap opera, but it exposes the oscillations between constraint in poverty and the glitter of consumerism's deceits which fuel women's socially constructed, socially regulated and similarly constraining desires. In a Faustian scenario, the television salesman promised her eternal youth, and got her to sign what she thought initially was a kind of hire purchase agreement, in exchange for what the devil himself acknowledged has no place in a consumer society: her soul. Harry, the rather flash devil, points out it was the decade when 'Sympathy for the Devil' was a hit, and the world could be seen as 'a gigantic recording studio, where the movie of life, printed on an indestructible tape, would play and play' (34). However, the legacy is poisoned, the message a con. Muriel wished to escape her oppressive female life cycle of ageing and loss of consumer worth, and in doing so she chose a design for eternity, as did the bewitched youth culture, sold on her own hype. The devil points out, 'Everyone had forgotten that unendingness was Satanic chaos' (48). Like her society, she has sold her soul. Magic here is a devilish activity, literally leading women down the garden path to the everlasting bonfire, though its formal use in the novel is to expose such cons and consumer hype which bedazzle and enslave women. Muriel–Ella walks off with her eternal partner at the book's close. Ella is a sacrifice to Muriel–Lisa's youth, cannibalistic tendencies of house and family claustrophobia:

> Borne along by the wind, the young woman can be seen walking up the drive of Woodfords Manor, her arm in the arm of the visitor, who wears black boots built up at the heel and a dark suit. It can only be the effect of light and shade from the moon – the swirling party colours from the windows of the house – that gives the impression of an old woman, huge in the faint glow from the fires in the woods, running up the drive after them. (125)

The funny, shock revelation renders farcical and deadly the lure of a consumer image, of unrealistic, unlikely sexual power, and materialistic success for women condemned to invisibility. When the soul is sold and eternal youth culture embraced, there *is* nothing else. Women so conned happily connive in the sacrifice of their families. Muriel's offspring, Ella, pays the price. Tennant's novel critiques the different deceits of different decades in Britain and their effects on women.

Fay Weldon – Cruising Mephistopheles

Romantic fictions perpetuate some of the powerful controlling versions of women's roles and constrain versions of women's sexuality. They peddle dangerous myths about women, which contemporary feminist writers deliberately highlight and deconstruct. Performing constrained gendered roles, unaware of their constructedness, is bound to lead to tears and destruction.

Weldon explores issues of women's conformity to stereotypes and cosmeticised images in *The Fat Woman's Joke* (1967) and again in the revenge taken by the monstrous Ruth in *The Life and Loves of a She-Devil*. Self-designed surgery leaves Ruth transformed into a doll-like beauty, a romantic fiction icon. However, she has made a pact with the devil on the way. Ruth, a captive housewife living in a suburban housing-estate hell (Eden Grove), has been entirely valued in relation to her domestic abilities (liable to accident) and her role as a hostess and mother (ill fitting and rarely successful). This is *all* 1960s and 1970s society offers women, American or British, suggests Weldon. But Ruth's cosmetic surgery is like the pact made by Muriel–Lisa in Tennant's *Faustine*, an unsatisfying sell-out to media versions of the ideal woman. Feminists have found this denouement irritating but its ironies and limitations are also illustrations of how our cultural context limits us as women. In *Growing Rich* magic and horror are intertwined. The demonic critiques restrictive roles open to ordinary women – three Fenland girls. The magical triad of girls, as in *The Cloning of Joanna May*, ultimately gives them power over the machinations of the male Mephistopheles, Driver. He insists that they are in his control, their happiness his gift, their suffering his punishment. All of this is gauged in relation to obedience in all matters personal and sexual by Carmen, the woman chosen for his current bought soul, Sir Bernard.

Weldon uses comedy and plays along with romantic fiction. An offer of opulence, glamour and perfect beauty for the woman who hitches a permanent lift with Driver, Mephistopheles at the wheel of a Fenland BMW, gives way to domestic bliss with Sir Bernard as Carmen's husband. Weldon shows she is acquainted with witchcraft, magic and sorcery in the three novels *The Life and Loves of a She-Devil*, *The Cloning of Joanna May* and *Growing Rich*, which have found their way to the television screen (and, in the case of the first, the US movie screen too). Their swift popularity, especially that of *Growing Rich*, also testifies to our fascination with the supernatural, with magic, and with Weldon's own brand of ironic, comic analyses of contemporary interactions between power, wealth, identity and sex. In terms of horror, the setting is constrained, oppressive; a mixture of tasteless, small-town sprawl, and the threatening, soggy vacancy of miles of Fenland. The lives of the girls are similarly dully constrained. If this is parochial fiction, then Weldon intends it as such. Britain is composed of the urban, the suburban and the rurally isolated. The girls have nowhere to go.

Horribly familiar, Fenedge incarcerates Annie, Carmen and Laura, their A-level results unable to provide any traditional escape through scholarship, condemning them to dull marriages (Laura to Woody, who makes sheds), or jobs such as chambermaid (Annie) or chicken-gutter (Carmen). Carmen's slobbish parents win loads of money, embarking on a round-the-world cruise, and Annie meets a rich sheep-farmer while tacking down carpet in Bellamy's hotel. She is whisked away to thousands of head of sheep and the alternative small-minded community of New Zealand (where Weldon grew up). Landscapes change but small minds are legion.

Slices of everyday life are packed together with a desperately dull familiarity like supermarket sliced bread. And if one breathes a word of criticism, as one must if one has any imagination, temptation is close at hand. We are warned, 'Now it is dangerous to speak these thoughts aloud in case the devil, in one of the many forms he takes, is flying by: and he often is, especially in such places, for it is here he locates his safe houses' (1). This version of horror derives from the familiar and from the claustrophobia of the girls' existence. Driver has much to offer in such circumstances. And there are genuinely, as Carmen says, only three ways out of a small-minded small town in the middle of nowhere: 'You can work your way out, you can sleep your way out, you can sell your soul to the Devil' (8). As their English teacher, who introduced them to both *Dr Faustus* and *The Witch of Endor*, would point out, each girl seems to be choosing one of these traditional routes or having it thrust upon her.

Local legend, cursed plague graves, myth, superstition, and the magic prevalent in English literature combine in the heads of the girls, in the atmosphere around them, and in the tones of the book's television series. In the novel, additional generic 'magic' resides in the form of the claimed omniscience of the narrator figure. Wheelchair-bound, s/he sees all and might even cause some of it. Told through a narrator, the tale has both the legitimacy of a ghost tale and the dubious status of what could be a lie – always a way to debunk and deny the irrational, the horrifying and the supernatural.

Dashing and dangerous, Driver ominously glides the BMW into view each time Carmen is tempted, and offers to stop time, provide her with riches, reward for going along with his plans and marrying the middle-aged Sir Bernard, whose material desires and wishes Driver constantly fulfils in the hope of gaining his soul. Using video images, Driver offers: 'If I can stop the moon, I can make a moment last for all eternity. Indeed, I can fast-forward and rewind the world, not just put it on pause. Think what that does for sex' (89). 'But that's how it is with demon lovers,' comments Fay Weldon (89).

Carmen's refusal of Driver's pimping brings bad luck. She loses her boyfriend to Poison Poppy and develops spots. When she agrees she transforms into a bimbo, the consumer-packaged ideal woman, product of the fickleness and bad taste of men's versions of the dream woman. The results are predictable, and hilarious. Carmen's legs lengthen, her bust expands, her nails, feet, expression, all turn into the model cover-girl ideal, and she squirms awkwardly while men gawp and offer her jobs, lifts, meals, the future:

> Something's wrong with me. It must be hormonal. I reckon I've gone from an A cup to a C overnight. It's disgusting. I flop when I walk. And my waist's got small, so my hips poke out in a ridiculous way. And I swear my legs are longer, or somehow my skirt has got shorter. (46)

Weldon combines fun with horror and laces it with 'girl power'. What Ruth (*She-Devil*) and Lisa-Muriel (*Faustine*) might seek, a cosmeticised, enhanced, culturally stereotypical 'woman', Carmen finds alienating and disgusting. She feels ridiculous. Her mouth cannot utter criticism. She is silenced, doll-like. Her friends compare her to the Incredible Hulk. However, her discomfort is short-lived. Refusing the offer of a job as an air hostess, she reverts to normal size.

It is a very British, very socially and geographically located piece of ironic fiction in which the horror elements are both threatening and amusing. They also provide a cutting social critique for a British society hooked on *Brookside, EastEnders, Coronation Street, Emmerdale, The Archers*, soaps which hype up the everyday monotony of urban, sub-urban and rural dullness by accelerating the little that happens.

As horror text, *Growing Rich* mixes the genres of soap and horror. Horror is in the familiar. Carmen, by routing the devil with the aid of her friends, saves the soul of her husband. Radical feminist critics might balk yet again at Weldon's ultimately collusive ending after so much liberating magic. However, as all three girls are married and live relatively happily ever after, Weldon has it both ways, as does her protagonist, Carmen. After all those horror films of the devil and his minions among us, *The Omen* (1976), *The Exorcist* (1973), *Friday the 13th* (1980), this everyday Fenland version which mixes ordinary school leavers, feminism and romantic fiction with 'old-wives'-tale' maxims about the proximity of the devil to the disaffected is a welcome, ironic addition both to our current fascination with magic and horror and to our constant concern over relationships, and sexual, personal and worldly power. Its solutions are amusingly questionable, its resolutions are only temporary: the problems and the temptations are, like the devil's minions, legion:

> But then nothing exciting ever happens in Fenedge these days. A tradition has grown up that you must never insult the town aloud, or hope too vehemently to escape it, in case the devil happens to be flying by, and overhears, and all hell breaks loose. (250)

Conclusion

Contemporary British women's horror challenges conventional, constrained horror roles for women, and the 'horror turn' which returns all subversive devices to order. Instead, it celebrates Otherness, reinvestigates the magical, finds the devil in the everyday, the witch in ourselves, debunks the myths, revalues the roles seen as threatening. Some writers accept a limited challenge; society is only gradually going to change, girls must marry, romantic fictions still provide a model. Others, particularly Carter, challenge and overturn everything. It is horror used to subvert and then to create a new status quo. This work is socially, politically and sexually subversive, entertaining and disquieting: magic realism with a healthy dose of sexual politics.

Contemporary British women's horror, like horror writing in general, is sometimes quite conventional, its main feature being a setting often in the UK, or a critique of British ways of life (suburban, urban, focusing on inheritance, and so on). However, the work of Tennant, Weldon and Carter in particular invests horror with a missing dimension of gender. It focuses on exposing the social contradictions, domestic incarcerations, sexualised cruelties and dangerous spaces that are absent from conventional (male dominated) horror but are everyday fears and nightmares for women. More radically, it undercuts the neat reinforcement of the status quo which conventional horror embraces in its closure, its packing away and staking of that which is terrifying because Other, abject, threatening to that status quo. It refuses and exposes the demonising of our animal nature, our other selves, into the figures of witches, werewolves, vampires, hags, femmes fatales. And it reclaims these creatures as ourselves, using the comic and the ironic as well as the terrible to explore their potential to reveal and celebrate what we are.

The mirror of the title of this essay and Susan Hill's *The Mist in the Mirror* is one that reflects versions of ourselves, as does all good horror. Demisting this self-reflection, a housewifely task, allows us to see more clearly how the figures of horror – the monstrous Other – *are* our own reflections, ourselves, and products of the flaws and fears engendered in our own culture. Demisting is a demystifying activity.

Works Cited

Andrews, Virginia. *Flowers in the Attic* (London: HarperCollins, 1993).

Baldick, Chris. *The Oxford Book of Gothic Tales* (Oxford: Oxford University Press, 1993).

Barnes, Djuna. *Nightwood* (London: Faber & Faber, 1963).

Carter, Angela. 'The Bloody Chamber' in *The Bloody Chamber* (London: Penguin, 1981). 7–41

——. 'The Company of Wolves' in *The Bloody Chamber* (London: Penguin, 1981). 110–118

——. 'The Lady in the House of Love' in *The Bloody Chamber* (London: Penguin, 1981). 93–108

——. *The Magic Toyshop* (London: Virago, 1967).

——. *Nights at the Circus* (London: Chatto & Windus, 1987).

Donald, James. *Sentimental Education: Schooling, Popular Culture and the Regulation of Liberty* (London: Verso, 1992).

du Maurier, Daphne. 'The Birds' in *The Birds and other Stories* (Harmondsworth: Penguin, 1952). 17–43

——. *Rebecca* (Harmondsworth: Penguin, 1938).

Hill, Susan. *The Mist in the Mirror* (London: Sinclair Stevenson, 1992).

——. *The Woman in Black* (London: Mandarin, 1983).

Jackson, Rosemary. *Fantasy: The Literature of Subversion* (London: Methuen, 1981).

Jancovitch, Mark. *Horror* (London: Batsford Cultural Studies, 1992).

Kiernan, Caitlyn. *Silk* (New York: ROC, 1998).

Kristeva, Julia. *Powers of Horror: An Essay on Abjection*, trans. Leon S. Roudiez (New York: Columbia University Press, 1982).

——. *Strangers to Ourselves*, trans. Leon S. Roudiez (New York: Columbia University Press, 1991).

Laplanche, J. and J. B. Pontalis. *The Language of Psychoanalysis*, trans. Donald Nicholson-Smith (London: Hogarth, 1985).

Tennant, Emma. *Faustine* (London: Faber & Faber, 1991).

——. *Two Women of London* (London: Faber & Faber, 1989).

——. *Wild Nights* (London: Faber & Faber, 1979).

——. *Women Beware Women* (London: Faber & Faber, 1983).

Townsend Warner, Sylvia. *Lolly Willowes* (London: Virago, 1993).

Tuttle, Lisa. *Skin of the Soul* (London: Women's Press, 1990).

Weldon, Fay. *The Cloning of Joanna May* (London: HarperCollins, 1990).

——. *The Fat Woman's Joke* (London: Coronet, 1987).

——. *Growing Rich* (London: HarperCollins, 1992).

——. *The Life and Loves of a She-Devil* (London: HarperCollins, 1983).

Wisker, Gina. 'Angela Carter and Horror' in *Gothic Horror: A Reader's Guide From Poe to King and Beyond*, ed. Clive Bloom (Basingstoke: Macmillan, 1998). 233–49

——. 'At Home all was Blood and Feathers: The Werewolf in the Kitchen' in *Creepers: British Horror and Fantasy in the Twentieth Century*, ed. Clive Bloom (London: Pluto, 1993). 161–76

Index